Business Ethics and Leadership from an Eastern European, Transdisciplinary Context

Sebastian Vaduva • Ioan S. Fotea
Andrew R. Thomas
Editors

Business Ethics and Leadership from an Eastern European, Transdisciplinary Context

The 2014 Griffiths School of Management Annual Conference on Business, Entrepreneurship and Ethics

Springer

Editors
Sebastian Vaduva
Griffiths School of Management
Emanuel University of Oradea
Oradea, Romania

Ioan S. Fotea
Griffiths School of Management
Emanuel University of Oradea
Oradea, Romania

Andrew R. Thomas
College of Business Administration
The University of Akron
Akron, OH, USA

ISBN 978-3-319-45185-5 ISBN 978-3-319-45186-2 (eBook)
DOI 10.1007/978-3-319-45186-2

Library of Congress Control Number: 2016955436

Printed on acid-free paper

This Springer imprint is published by Springer Nature
The registered company is Springer International Publishing AG
The registered company address is: Gewerbestrasse 11, 6330 Cham, Switzerland

Preface

Since the financial crisis crippled the world economy in 2008, the debate on business ethics and leadership has dominated the public sphere at all levels of interest, from common people to the elites in educational institutions, governments, businesses, and NGOs. Naturally, constructive and transdisciplinary discussions need to take place that take into consideration the specific context of each situation, so that propositions upon which to build the future can be formulated. These discussions unfold in an ever more intricate world of business, powered by ever more pervasive and intelligent technology and brought together by globalization. In this world, organizations are faced with new and more complex ethical issues in their pursuit to serve clients, gain profits, motivate employees, collaborate with partners, and act responsibly towards the environment and society.

A wise approach of changing the future is to understand the mistakes of the past, because one must learn how to overcome the past mistakes in order to develop a better future. But a necessary approach to building a better future is by looking at the world through a transdisciplinary mindset. This allows us to see the world as a complex whole, fosters creative interaction between fields of knowledge, opens doors for knowledge and innovation flow across disciplines, and allows the tackling of complex problems and situations. Given the current context of our world this is an approach that we ought to pursue.

This book brings together the academic views of scholars and the energy of young researchers to provide insights into a wide range of aspects pertaining to the field of business and leadership within the overarching debate on ethics and transdisciplinarity.

The papers in this book were discussed and disseminated at the 5th Annual Griffiths School of Management International Conference, organized by Emanuel University of Oradea during May 2014. The Conference provided a platform for academics and practitioners in the field of business and leadership to interact and debate on the different dimensions of ethics in business and leadership in the context of transdisciplinarity and knowledge-based society.

The purposes of Chap. 1 are to clearly define the term lean operations, provide a normative definition of business purposes, and then discuss in what manner and how well lean operations foster and support these business purposes. The original principles that undergirded lean operations supported both business purposes, but the most recent common lean practices focus on achieving the first purpose through higher efficiencies and lower costs at the expense of providing meaningful work. The trending predominant use of the shareholder model for defining business purposes is suggested as the major contributor for this finding.

Leadership is a research field that is growing in Romania but still necessitates more input of knowledge and experience in order to shape and validate a Romanian leadership model. Chapter 2 explores the main practical implications for decision-making and managerial action in organizations that adopted spiritual leadership or are willing to follow such an approach.

The private healthcare sector is experiencing an unparalleled growth in Romania. In Chap. 3 authors share an industry-based perspective on the Romanian healthcare system with the objective of diagnosing the capacity, structure, and trends facing this sector. Based on the bivalent feature of public-private sector, this study follows the distribution of customers between the two sectors and motivational factors behind this approach.

Chapter 4 studies the consumer perception of Yield Management (YM) with an example in the hotel sector by exploring four YM practices that might be suitable in hotel context. This analysis is undertaken through an empirical study of the behavior of 505 customers. The empirical analysis reveals that the assumption according to which YM induces dissatisfaction in all circumstances is rejected. But when a practice of YM is perceived as unfair, it causes a loss of customers.

The author of Chap. 5 aims to identify the conditions of globalization that have led to suppose that transnational corporations are economic agents that negatively impact business ethics from the perspective of corporate governance. The method of study is based on a thorough theoretical and literature review and the results obtained confirm the negative impact, considering that the use of corporate social responsibility programs are strategies to increase profits and global power rather than to achieve social impact.

The chaos and uncertainty that manifest in the marketplace of the current global economy create a tremendous pressure on any company's board of directors. In addition to the pressure coming from the marketplace many other aggravating factors are manifesting, such as the stakeholders attitude, the growing demand for workers with specialized skills, and the increasing involuntary losses of high-performing workers or managers. Chapter 6 starts from revealing the main steps of effective human resource planning, among which succession planning plays an important role and continues with advancing a new knowledge-based leadership model that will increase the likelihood of obtaining sustainable business effects in the actual economy. The discussion leads to several case studies that are relevant for the importance of succession planning, namely Aldis, Edy Spedition, Banca Transilvania, or Tarom.

Chapter 7 is researching the problem of ecological economy and sustainability in the countries of Eastern Europe as a complex phenomenon that requires a transdisciplinary approach. Starting with the analysis of the evolution of this desiderates and the current situation in this field, this study stresses the role and importance of having a society that strives for a sustainable economy.

Chapter 8 reviews the issues of the debate on Artificial Intelligence and argues in favor of the view that the human mind is a far too complex and elusive entity for the claim of "complete reproduction" to be valid.

In Chap. 9, the authors argue that the true power behind social media lies in its ability to provide new, more genuine, more efficient, and readily available data for business decisions. The paper includes a proposed framework and mapping process for extracting data from social media into the various marketing functions.

The pervasive phenomenon of institutional decoupling in the modern society is analyzed in the context of organizational ethics by the author of Chap. 10. Using an exploratory approach, the author investigates seven cases of decoupling in seven medium-sized firms. The results outline the contextual elements leading to decoupling situations, the rationalization of top managers and the strategies employed to control and exploit the decoupling situation.

The authors of Chap. 11 stand to maintain the highest level of productivity by better understanding exactly how workforce motivation is currently evolving rather than relying on potentially dated assumptions. This conceptual paper, and corresponding exploratory study, was initiated to specifically examine perceptions of workplace motivation in Romania between employees and managers. The exploratory examination was accomplished by means of a survey of Romanian workers in the Romanian cities of Oradea, and Bucharest, the capital of Romania. The survey, and consequent interviews of employees and managers from six companies, demonstrates that both Romanian managers and employees give the impression to have an acceptable understanding of what motivates the employee.

Outdoor Management Development (OMD) has been a feature of British management learning since the mid-1970s and has been adopted across the globe since then. Early proponents of OMD such as Creswick and Williams (1979) emphasized the imaginative use of the outdoors as a means to challenge entrenched managerial attitudes, enabling managers to become more than they were, and to steer businesses through an unforeseeable future. In Chap. 12, the author examines four challenges to the early Williams/Creswick approach to the outdoors, with certain focus on the ethical implications of those challenges.

Small and medium size enterprises represent the engine of any economy and a considerable source of jobs. Yet, their Achilles' heel is represented by the financial management of such entities. Chapter 13 reviews and advises on the financing methods that are available for this category of business in the context of Romania's legislation and taxation.

The main challenge the economy of Eastern Europe is facing nowadays is how to put the economic development and sustainability on a dynamic equilibrium track, enabling its social system to provide a functional well-being. Chapter 14 is a study of the ecologic policy process in the last four decades, showing the system inputs at the international, regional, and national levels. An important conclusion of this article is the idea that the economic policies of the Eastern European countries must take into consideration all legal and strategic policies achievements and try to continue to develop this process towards a transdisciplinary approach in all decisions and actions by transition to new levels of sustainable development.

Finally, Chap. 15 deals with the looming threat of corruption in Eastern European administrative and business settings. Transparency International Romania recommends collective integrity commitments as the optimal trans-institutional instrument for fighting corruption and developing businesses of good reputation and enhancing society at large; to that end, TI has already facilitated the signing of five Integrity Pacts connecting businesses, academia, healthcare, and civil society. In so doing, they have gathered multiple lessons and tips for the Romanian business environment, including its stakeholders, which emphasize the socio-economic benefits of integrity and accountability in developing societies.

We trust that you will find this volume useful.

Oradea, Romania — Sebastian Vaduva
Oradea, Romania — Ioan S. Fotea
Akron, OH, USA — Andrew R. Thomas

Contents

Chapter 1
Lean Operations and Business Purposes: Ethical Considerations

Thomas M. Smith

Abstract *Lean* is a popular term that has been applied to many current business strategies and practices. Unfortunately, the term has come to mean many different things and has thus caused much confusion in both the academic and the practitioner world. In addition, lean has come to be seen as a positive influence in mostly every business situation. Therefore, the purposes of this chapter are to define clearly the term *lean operations*, provide a normative definition of business purposes, and then discuss in what manner and how well lean operations foster and support these business purposes.

Lean operations are shown to strongly support the normative business purpose of providing goods and services so that communities can thrive, but has a very mixed outcome when it comes to supporting the second normative business purpose of providing opportunities for meaningful work. The original principles that undergirded lean operations supported both business purposes, but the most recent common lean practices focus on achieving the first purpose through higher efficiencies and lower costs at the expense of providing meaningful work. The trending predominant use of the shareholder model for defining business purposes is suggested as the major contributor for this finding.

Keywords Operations management • Lean thinking • Lean operations • Lean practices • Business purposes • Meaningful work

Operations Management (OM) has been defined as the creation of customer value through the effective and efficient management of processes (Johnston et al. 2003). Another way to understand the function of OM is in terms of the classic microeconomic concepts of supply and demand. Within this framework, the primary objective of OM can be seen as trying to match the production and delivery of products and services (supply) to the given demand for these products and services. Recent strategies that were used to accomplish this objective focused on the necessity to control, reduce, manage, and understand variation (Stratton 2008; Poiger 2010). This has given rise to a

T.M. Smith, Ph.D. (✉)
Hope College, Holland, MI, USA
e-mail: tsmith@hope.edu

S. Vaduva et al. (eds.), *Business Ethics and Leadership from an Eastern European, Transdisciplinary Context*, DOI 10.1007/978-3-319-45186-2_1

confusing and jumbled mix of several interrelated concepts, theories, constructs, principles, and practices, usually falling under the label of a three-letter acronym. Almost all of these interrelated concepts, theories, constructs, etc. can be grouped under the common umbrella heading of ***lean operations*** (Shah and Ward 2003).

The objective of this chapter is to analyze lean operations, both at their theoretical underpinnings and the implemented practices, through the lens of two specific and different perspectives. The first one deals with a nuanced understanding of the primary purposes of business. The second perspective stems from the first and examines lean operations in light of the literature on the meaning of work. In essence, the purposes of this chapter are to examine how well the principles and practices of lean operations (a) support the primary purposes of business and (b) foster a sense of meaningful work.

The chapter will be structured in the following manner. First, a normative discussion on the primary purposes of business will set the context for the remainder of the chapter. Following this will be a detailed discussion and definition of lean operations and its associated practices. Once the purposes of business have been established and lean operations have been defined, a model will be developed in order to discuss the role of lean operations in fulfilling these purposes. A discussion and review of the literature on meaningful work will be necessary in order to assess this role. Finally, the ethical implications of both the concepts and practices of lean operations will be examined.

1.1 Primary Purposes of Business

Beginning in the early 1970s, the predominant answer to the question of the primary purpose of business gradually changed from a more generic objective of providing for social needs and making a social contribution to a more focused approach of profit maximization (Friedman 1970). This approach has since become more tightly defined as the maximization of shareholder wealth (Lazonick and O'Sullivan 2000). Although not as widely accepted as the shareholder model, a broader based concept known as the stakeholder model (Freeman 1984) was introduced in the mid-1980s. A fundamental thesis of stakeholder-based argument is that organizations should be managed in the interest of all their constituents, not only in the interest of shareholders (Laplume et al. 2008).

Uneasiness over the inadequacies of these models, in terms of the negative unintended consequences of the shareholder model and the cumbersome practicality of the stakeholder model, has led to a rethinking and revisiting of the primary purposes of the business organization. Perhaps the most vocal critic, at least on management's fixation on profits, has been Peter Drucker. When discussing the requirements of management and of learning about the behavior of individuals, he speaks quite clearly when he states, "The profit motive and its offspring maximization of profits are … irrelevant to the function of a business, the purpose of a business, and the job of managing a business" (Drucker 2001: 39). In a similar vein, Khurana (2007) argues that management education needs to return to the ideals of professionalism and professional leadership that guided it in the past. The first step of this reformation process needs to be a close examination into the multitude of purposes for business, with a special emphasis upon identifying the ***primary*** purpose(s).

1.2 Biblical Foundations

Many have suggested that the Bible is the proper place to begin when trying to determine the appropriate purposes for business (Alford and Naughton 2001; Van Duzer 2010). The legitimization of business is often justified in the Cultural Mandate found in Genesis 1:26–28. Business is seen as one of several institutions that are uniquely established to carry out the tasks listed in the mandate. Within this context, the institution of business appears best suited to "work the fields" and "give order to creation" (Van Duzer 2010).

Two models of business have recently emerged utilizing this perspective as the basis and the starting point—the Common Good Model (Alford and Naughton 2001) and the Genesis-Stewardship Model (Van Duzer 2010). Both models incorporate the notion and necessity of profit and profitability. However, profit and wealth maximization play a subservient role to a greater good. Alford and Naughton (2001) make a distinction between *foundational* and *excellent* goods. They characterize profitability as a foundational good. Van Duzer (2010) makes a similar distinction, but he draws a line between *instrumental* and *intrinsic* purposes. He characterizes profitability as an instrumental purpose, one that is required in order to accomplish higher, intrinsic purposes.

DePree (1989) and Pollard (1996), both business leaders of Fortune 500 companies, have also suggested that business purposes require a more nuanced understanding than simply the maximization of shareholder wealth. Although they do not develop a robust business model, they do suggest that some purposes serve as *means* while others serve as *ends*. DePree utilizes breathing to illustrate his point. Breathing, he states, is like profitability. It is a means to an end. It is not the end. In other words, we breathe in order to live, but our primary purpose in life is not to breathe.

1.3 Other Foundations

Christian authors and managers are not the only group that has called for a rethinking of business purposes. In addition, this is not simply a recent phenomenon. In his seminal book on management, Drucker (1954) asserts that the role of managers, and thus the role of the business, is to make the strengths of its members productive and to promote the growth and development of the individuals while they work. These themes are highlighted and further expanded upon in work done by Maciariello and Linkletter (2011). Later in his career, Drucker (2001) made a powerful argument that the primary purpose for all business organizations was to create a customer.

Deming (1986), responsible for laying the foundation for the total quality management (TQM) movement, was adamant that the primary purposes were to satisfy customers and provide jobs and more jobs. All improvements and gains made by the company through their TQM efforts were ultimately done to achieve these ends. Finally, in a very volatile and unprofitable industry, Southwest Airlines has been one of the most successful, and profitable, companies by stressing employee satisfaction as their top priority (Gittell 2003).

Two distinct, yet related conclusions can be drawn from the previous discussion. First, a proper and clear understanding of the purposes of a business organization needs to involve a classification of these purposes into some sort of a categorization scheme. The categories of instrumental/intrinsic, foundational/excellent, and means/ends have been suggested in the literature. This classification allows one to see the priority, the cause/effect, and/or the relationships among the various purposes. Second, when defining the primary purposes of business organizations, profitability and the maximization of shareholder wealth is not a foregone conclusion. Nor is it necessarily the proper one. It certainly isn't the only viable one.

For the purposes of this chapter, and in keeping with the above discussion, business purposes will be classified using the Genesis-Stewardship Model proposed by Van Duzer (2010) that utilizes the distinctions of instrumental and intrinsic purposes. The primary first-order intrinsic purposes suggested by Van Duzer also seem to incorporate in the best way the multitude of perspectives discussed in the literature. Therefore, as stated in his model, the primary intrinsic business purposes will be defined as the following: (a) to provide the community with goods and services that enable it to flourish and (b) to provide opportunities for meaningful work that will allow employees to express their God-given creativity. Profitability and wealth maximization remain an important purpose of the business, yet it is relegated to an instrumental role.

1.4 Lean Operations

We need to have a clear understanding of lean operations principles and practices in order to investigate how they support the primary purposes of a business organization. Unfortunately, there is much confusion surrounding this term, both in terms of incorrect usage and in an overlapping of several popular lean concepts and programs.

1.5 Concepts and Definition

One possible way to understand lean operations is to identify the complementary subsystems that that have been placed under the umbrella term. These subsystems include the Toyota Production System (TPS), of which Just-in-Time (JIT) is a subset, TQM, Total Preventative Maintenance (TPM), Continuous Improvement

Subsystem \ Underlying Concept	Supplier-related	Internally related	Customer-related
TPS/JIT	✓✓	✓✓	✓
TQM	✓	✓✓	✓✓
TPM		✓✓	
Kaizen	✓	✓✓	
DFMA	✓	✓✓	✓
Supplier Management programs	✓✓		

✓✓ = heavy emphasis
✓ = moderate emphasis

Fig. 1.1 Matrix of the subsystems and underlying concepts for lean operations

(Kaizen), Design for Manufacture and Assembly (DFMA), and Supplier Management programs (de Treville and Antonakis 2006; Stratton 2008). Another structuring scheme that has been used is to identify the underlying and operational constructs undergirding lean operations (Shah and Ward 2007). The underlying constructs break down as (a) supplier-related, (b) internally related, and (c) customer-related. One can further delineate these constructs into operational constructs. For example, the operational constructs that are internally related would include a pull mentality, a focus on flow, short setup times, controlled processes, productive maintenance, and involved employees. A matrix that combines these two schemes is found in Fig. 1.1.

Although a few of the subsystems consider all three concepts, none of the subsystems fully captures the essence of the three underlying concepts. There are also certain axiomatic mathematical laws that have been associated with lean operations that are not captured within the matrix. The most common of these laws states that all variability within a system must be buffered by some combination of capacity, inventory, and time (Hopp and Spearman 1996). Thus, by combining the concepts, subsystems, and laws, one can arrive at a very comprehensive, yet concise, definition of lean operations. The definition utilized in this chapter will use the structure suggested by de Treville and Antonakis (2006), Shah and Ward (2007), and Poiger (2010). Given this approach, the definition used in the remainder of the chapter, and one that is suggested for future work in this field, is specified in the following lines. ***Lean operations*** is an integrated management system that is intended to maximize the capacity utilization and minimize the inventory and time buffers of a given operation through minimizing system variability (related to supplier, internal, and customer processes and requirements).

1.6 Practices

There has been a myriad of practices that have been used by companies to implement lean concepts into their operations (Schonberger 1982; Womack et al. 1990; Forza 1996; Shah and Ward 2003). Terms such as Kanban, SPC, and Jidoka have been used to categorize some of these practices. Unfortunately, the practices themselves are often identified as the essence of lean operations and thus add to the existing confusion for practitioners (and for academicians) and limit the effectiveness and pervasiveness of lean thinking.

In keeping with the definition of lean operations, and adapted from de Treville and Antonakis (2006), Fig. 1.2 provides a list of common lean practices associated with their primary objective.

1.7 Meaningful Work

Now that we have a clear definition of lean operations—its concepts and resulting practices—it is time to take a preliminary look at how well this prevalent OM strategy fosters the primary intrinsic business purposes of providing goods and services that allow a community to flourish and of providing opportunities for meaningful work.

1.8 Provision of Goods and Services

When one recalls the objective of operations management, it should not be surprising that any strategy used to accomplish this objective would focus on providing goods and services. The question to ask is how well (measures of efficiency) the strategy provides these goods and services and if these goods and services allow the community to flourish (measures of effectiveness). In terms of social and material gains, a strong argument can be made regarding the efficiency and effectiveness in which the implementation of lean concepts and lean thinking have helped to foster increased life expectancies, standards of living, and the overall quality of life. Although an interesting argument to consider, pursuing the connection between lean operations and the flourishing of the community is not one of the objectives of this chapter.

The connection that is of more interest to this researcher, and one of the primary objectives of this chapter, is the one between the concepts and practices embedded in the definition of lean operations and the primary business purpose of providing opportunities for meaningful and creative work. In order to understand this connection, it is imperative that a clear understanding of what is meant by the term "meaningful work" needs to be developed.

Practice \ Objective	Inventory/Time reduction	Capacity utilization	Variability reduction
Flow-control mechanisms (Kanban)	✓✓		✓
Set-up time reduction (SMED)	✓✓	✓	✓
Flow-based layout (assembly line or cells)	✓✓		✓
Line balancing (signaling)		✓✓	✓
Increase line speed (no additional resources)		✓✓	✓
Standardization of Processes			✓✓
Documentation of Processes			✓✓
Control of processes (SPC)			✓✓
"Fool proof" mechanisms (Jidoka, Poka-Yoke)		✓	✓✓
Visual displays of quality-related data			✓✓
Supplier management tools(↓ suppliers, info sharing)			✓✓
Demand-Smoothing	✓		✓✓
Short cycle Times	✓		✓✓
Cross-training	✓	✓	✓✓
Manufacturability of parts			✓✓
Clean and tidy environment			✓✓

✓✓ = direct emphasis

✓ = indirect emphasis

Fig. 1.2 Matrix of the practices and objectives for lean operations

1.9 Provision of Opportunities for Meaningful Work

Any discussion in the area of meaningful work must begin with the Job Characteristics Model (JCM) proposed by Hackman and Oldham (1976). The JCM is based on the idea that the job task itself is the key to employee motivation and satisfaction. It states five core job characteristics that influence three critical psychological states. In turn, these psychological states influence work outcomes. Figure 1.3 provides a diagram of these proposed relationships. The meaningfulness of one's work is one of the critical psychological states and is postulated as being determined by the design (characteristics) of the job task.

Parker (2003) modified the JCM model and applied it specifically to lean practices. She looked at three specific lean practices and tried to model their effect on employee outcomes. She proposed that work characteristics mediated the link between the practices and the outcomes. Figure 1.4 provides a diagram of her modified model. Hasle (2014) utilized a similar model, but modified it on the front end to include such variables as the lean context, implementation, and thinking that informed the lean practices in the first place.

Both of these works are useful in that they attempt to look at the job design characteristics that are specific to lean operations. Yet within each of these two models, the construct of meaningful work has been dropped from the model. Even within the JCM model, although meaningful work is an important variable, it is viewed as a means to a higher end—higher job and organizational performance.

Turning to the literature on meaningful work helps to alleviate this problem. Rosso et al. (2010) have nicely summarized recent findings in this field. In their review, the authors proposed a model that defined meaningful work from both the sources and the underlying mechanisms. The sources include self, others, the work context, and spiritual life. The mechanisms include authenticity, self-efficacy, self-esteem, purpose, belongingness, transcendence, and cultural and interpersonal sense making. Combining

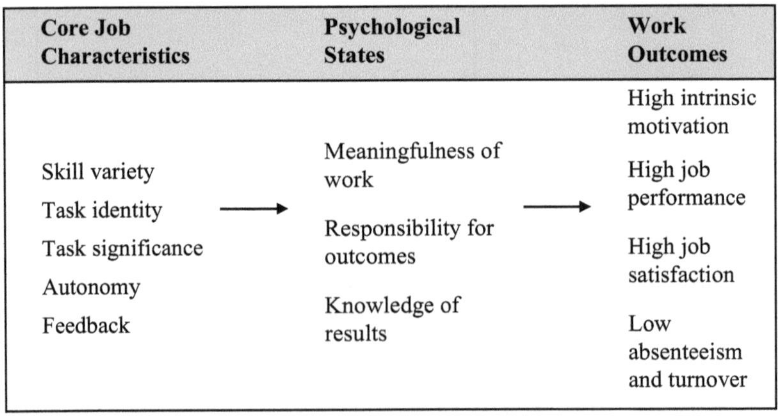

Fig. 1.3 The relationships among the variables within the JCM model

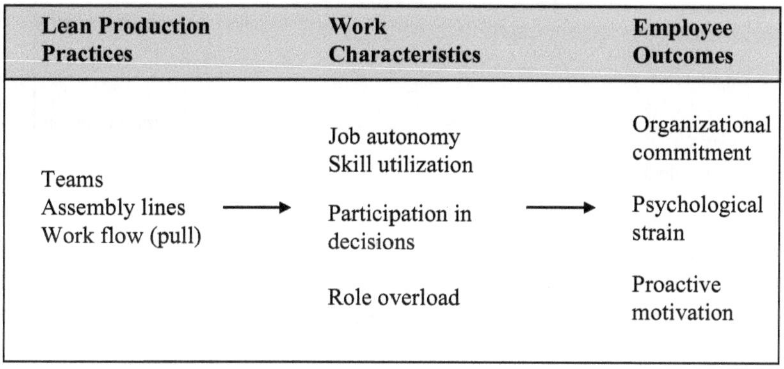

Fig. 1.4 The relationships among the variables within Parker's model

Direction / Motive	SELF	OTHERS
AGENCY	Individuation	Contribution
COMMUNION	Self-Connection	Unification

Fig. 1.5 The four major pathways to meaningful work

these thoughts led the authors to develop a 2×2 theoretical framework for understanding the pathways to meaningful work. This framework is presented in Fig. 1.5.

Thus, in utilizing the terms of Rosso et al. (2010), of particular interest for this chapter is gaining an understanding of how one of these specific sources of meaning (work context) influences the various mechanisms that lead to meaningfulness. In other words, by utilizing the framework, the research question can be further clarified as to how well the concepts and practices of lean operations foster the individuation, contribution, self-connection, and unification pathways to meaningful work.

One final modification to Parker's model is necessary. Job characteristics are not simply the result of manager-led top-down job design, but are also shaped by employee-led bottom-up job crafting (Berg et al. 2013). This process can shape job characteristics through changing tasks, changing relationships, or changing perceptions.

By incorporating these ideas and insights into Parker's original model, a clearer picture emerges into how lean operations affect meaningful work. The modified model is shown in Fig. 1.6. This model will be used to structure the critique of lean principles and practices. So, the research questions can be clarified and restated in terms of the model: (a) how well do lean principles support

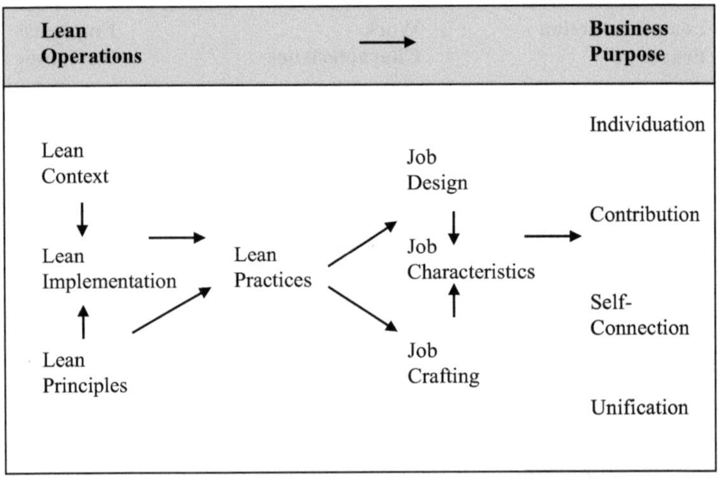

Fig. 1.6 The modified mediated model

meaningful work through their influence on job design and job crafting and (b) how well do lean practices support meaningful work through their influence on job design and job crafting?

1.10 Critique of Lean Operations

In order to perform this critique, the notion of lean operations will be divided into two parts: the principles that form the foundations of lean operations, and the practices that are implemented in order to support these principles.

1.11 Lean Principles

Lean subsystems and concepts were introduced in a previous section. Further discussion is necessary in order to perform an adequate critique. Shah and Ward's (2007) identification of lean operational constructs is a good place to begin. Their list includes ten constructs that include supplier feedback, JIT delivery, developing suppliers, involving customers, pull mentality, continuous flow, low setup times, controlled processes, productive maintenance, and involved employees. Almost all of these constructs directly influence job design and to a lesser extent, job crafting. Only one construct, involved employees, has a positive and proactive influence on meaningful work. This can be seen through the pathways of individuation and contribution. The other nine constructs, as observed, have a neutral or even negative effect on meaningful work through their influence on the type of tasks required to fulfill these principles. It is interesting to note that nine out of the ten constructs seem to be focused on one of primary intrinsic purpose of business set forth in the Genesis-Stewardship Model—providing goods and services for the community to thrive, to the almost total exclusion of the other.

The critique becomes a bit more favorable when we examine the writings and thoughts of the originators of lean thinking (Sugimori et al. 1977; Monden 1983; Deming 1986; Ohno 1988). For example, the two foundational concepts of TPS are (a) cost cutting through the removal of waste and (b) making full use of worker's capabilities—treating workers as human beings with consideration and dignity. One of the key concepts undergirding TQM is that of process management, both in technical (continuous improvement) and in human (employee fulfillment) terms. Although not antagonistic to the goal of meaningful work, these principles support meaningful work primarily when they are supporting a higher purpose. So, the principles of making full use of worker's capabilities and having involved employees can be seen as *instrumental* objectives serving a higher objective of increased efficiencies and production.

1.12 Lean Practices

When looking at the list of common lean practices in Fig. 1.2, one can see that the objectives of these practices are geared directly or indirectly toward the reduction of variability. Therefore, the design of the jobs and the tasks necessary for variability reduction may or may not have anything to do with moving down one of the pathways to meaningful work. In fact, we once again see the notion of instrumentality come into play. In other words, if a practice does in fact lead to more meaningful work, it is simply because it is a means to a greater end. For example, the practice of cross-training can easily be seen as leading to individuation and self-connection, but the primary objective of this practice is the reduction of cost through the full utilization of employees.

In addition, some of the lean practices could have a destructive effect on meaningful work. For example, the standardization of processes calls for the same task to be repeated in the same way every time. This will have a negative impact on individuation and self-connection, while greatly limiting the amount of job crafting available to the employee. In addition, the job design of increasing line speeds without adding additional resources will have a negative impact on the pathways of contribution and unification, and once again limit the amount of job creating available to the employee.

1.13 Conclusions

Prior to analyzing lean operations, one needs to determine the appropriate criteria in which to make the critique. In doing so, an argument was made that the primary intrinsic purposes of business, and thus the ultimate purposes of lean operations, is (a) to provide the community with goods and services that enable it to flourish and (b) to provide opportunities for meaningful work that will allow employees to express their God-given creativity. A model was then proposed that one of the major ways in which lean operations influences these business purposes was through their direct effect on job design and the amount of job crafting that was possible within this design. Lean operations have clearly made significant positive contributions toward achieving the first of these two business purposes. Of greater interest for this researcher was the influence that lean operations had through the mediating effect of job design on the second purpose of business—providing opportunities for meaningful work.

The original concepts and principles that undergird lean operations seem to share the same dual purposes as those defined in this chapter. Upon closer investigation, it becomes clear that the principles of utilizing the full capabilities of workers and employee involvement, those principles that support providing opportunities for meaningful work, are in fact *instrumental* objectives for the purposes of higher efficiencies and lower costs. Therefore, it is not surprising that the design of jobs to meet these principles it is often times overlooked when weighed against designs that meet directly the efficiency and cost purposes.

Current lean practices line up with the current definition of lean operations as given in this chapter. The current literature on lean operations almost exclusively defines this term in the language of variability reduction. Therefore, once again, it should not be surprising that the primary objective of lean practices focus on the reduction of variability. One unfortunate result of this trend is that some practices are actually in conflict with providing meaningful work.

The overall influence of lean principles and lean practices on fostering meaningful work, as defined by the Four Pathways model, is quite disappointing. However, if a business is guided by the shareholder model, then lean operations represents a very effective hiring strategy. This strongly implies that defining the primary intrinsic purposes of a business are of primary importance because it is these purposes that guide and inform not only the principles and practices that one implements, but also how these principles and practices will be measured and evaluated. So, one cannot answer how well lean operations foster business purposes until the business purposes are clearly defined.

References

Alford, Helen J., and Michael J. Naughton. 2001. *Managing As If Faith Mattered: Christian Social Principles in the Modern Organization*. Notre Dame, IN: University of Notre Dame.

Berg, Justin M., Jane E. Dutton, and Amy Wrzesniewski. 2013. Job Crafting and Meaningful Work. In *Purpose and Meaning in the Workplace*, ed. B.J. Dik, Z.S. Byrne, and M.F. Steger, 81–104. Washington, DC: American Psychological Association.

de Treville, Suzanne, and John Antonakis. 2006. Could Lean Production Job Design Be Intrinsically Motivating: Contextual, Configurational, and Levels-of-Analysis Issues. *Journal of Operations Management* 24: 99–123.

Deming, W. Edwards. 1986. *Out of the Crisis*. Cambridge, MA: MIT, Center for Advanced Educational Services.

DePree, Max. 1989. *Leadership is an Art*. New York: Bantam Doubleday Dell Publishing.
Drucker, Peter F. 1954. *The Practice of Management*. New York, NY: Harper and Row.
———. 2001. *The Essential Drucker*. New York, NY: HarperCollins.
Forza, Cipriano. 1996. Work Organization in Lean Production and Traditional Plants: What are the Differences? *International Journal of Operations and Production Management* 16(2): 42–62.
Freeman, R. Edward. 1984. *Strategic Management: A Stakeholder Approach*. Boston: Pitman.
Friedman, Milton. 1970. The Social Responsibility of Business is to Increase Its Profits. *The New York Times Magazine*, September 13.
Gittell, Jody Hoffer. 2003. *The Southwest Airlines Way: Using the Power of Relationships to Achieve High Performance*. New York, NY: McGraw-Hill.
Hackman, J. Richard, and Greg R. Oldham. 1976. Motivation through the Design of Work: Test of a Theory. *Organizational Behavior and Human Performance* 16: 250–279.
Hasle, Peter. 2014. Lean Production—An Evaluation of the Possibilities for an Employee Supportive Lean Practice. *Human Factors and Ergonomics in Manufacturing and Service Industries* 24(1): 40–53.
Hopp, Wallace J., and Mark C. Spearman. 1996. *Factory Physics*. Long Grove, IL: Waveland Press.
Johnston, Robert, et al. 2003. *Cases in Operations Management*. Essex, UK: Pearson Education Limited.
Khurana, Rakesh. 2007. *From Higher Aims to Hired Hands*. New Jersey, NJ: Princeton University Press.
Laplume, Andre O., Karen Sonpar, and Reginald A. Litz. 2008. Stakeholder Theory: Reviewing a Theory That Moves Us. *Journal of Management* 34: 1152–1189.
Lazonick, William, and Mary O'Sullivan. 2000. Maximizing Shareholder Value: A New Ideology for Corporate Governance. *Economy and Society* 29(1): 13–35.
Maciariello, Joseph A., and Karen E. Linkletter. 2011. *Drucker's Lost Art of Management: Peter Drucker's Timeless Vision for Building Effective Organizations*. New York, NY: McGraw-Hill.
Monden, Yasuhiro. 1983. *Toyota Production System: Practical Approach to Production Management*. Norcross, GA: Industrial Engineering and Management Press, IIE.
Ohno, Taichi. 1988. *Toyota Production System: Beyond Large-Scale Production*. Portland, OR: Productivity, Inc.
Parker, Sharon K. 2003. Longitudinal Effects of Lean Production on Employee Outcomes and the Mediating Role of Work Characteristics. *Journal of Applied Psychology* 88(4): 620–634.
Poiger, Martin. 2010. Improving Performance of Supply Chain Processes by Reducing Variability. Doctoral dissertation, Vienna University of Economics and Business.
Pollard, William C. 1996. *The Soul of the Firm*. New York, NY: HarperCollins.
Rosso, Brent J., Kathryn H. Dekas, and Amy Wrzesniewski. 2010. On the Meaning of Work: A Theoretical Integration and Review. *Research in Organizational Behavior* 30: 91–127.
Schonberger, Richard J. 1982. *Japanese Manufacturing Techniques: Nine Hidden Lessons in Simplicity*. New York, NY: The Free Press.
Shah, Rachna, and Peter T. Ward. 2003. Lean Manufacturing: Context, Practice Bundles, and Performance. *Journal of Operations Management* 21: 129–149.
———. 2007. Defining and Developing Measures of Lean Production. *Journal of Operations Management* 25: 785–805.
Stratton, Roy. 2008. Theory Building: Relating Variation, Uncertainty, Buffering Mechanisms and Trade-offs. Paper presented at the World Conference on Production and Operations Management, Tokyo, Japan, August.
Sugimori, Y., K. Kusunoki, F. Cho, and S. Uchikawa. 1977. Toyota Production System and Kanban System Materialization of Just-in-Time and Respect-for-Human System. *International Journal of Production Research* 15(6): 553–564.
Van Duzer, J. 2010. *Why Business Matters to God (And What Still Needs to Be Fixed)*. Downer's Grove, IL: InterVarsity Press.
Womack, James P., Daniel T. Jones, and Daniel Roos. 1990. *The Machine that Changed the World*. New York, NY: Harper Collins.

Chapter 2
Spiritual Leadership: Implications for Managerial Action

Mariana Nicolae, Irina Ion, and Elena Nicolae

Abstract The study explores the main practical implications for decision-making and managerial action in organizations that adopted spiritual leadership or that are willing to follow such an approach. Spiritual leadership is a relatively innovative concept, defined as that type of leadership that aims to "create vision and value congruence across the individual, empowered team, and organization levels and, ultimately, foster higher levels of both organizational commitment and productivity" (The Leadership Quarterly 16:835–863). Our study will first review the theoretical contributions to the spiritual leadership research agenda and then will assess its development and limitations. The critical evaluation of the specialized literature will contribute to the underlining of the main implications in terms of managerial behavior; will highlight the criteria spiritual leaders use for decision-making; and, more generally, will explore how the adoption of a spiritual leadership approach influences managerial action in organizations.

Keywords Spiritual leadership • Managerial behavior • Decision-making

2.1 Introduction

The present study explores the main practical implications for decision-making and managerial action in organizations that adopted spiritual leadership or are willing to have such an approach. It will first review the theoretical contributions to the spiritual leadership research agenda and then will assess its development and limitations. The emergence of spirituality in the organizational context challenges the traditional approaches to science formed in the twentieth century.

The critical evaluation of the specialized literature will contribute to the underlining of the main implications in terms of managerial behavior, will highlight the criteria spiritual leaders use for decision-making, and, more generally, will explore how the adoption of a spiritual leadership approach influences managerial action in organizations.

M. Nicolae, Ph.D. (✉) • I. Ion, Ph.D. • E. Nicolae
Bucharest University of Economic Studies, Bucharest, Romania
e-mail: mariana.nicolae@rei.ase.ro; irinazgreaban@yahoo.com; elena.nicolae@rei.ase.ro

S. Vaduva et al. (eds.), *Business Ethics and Leadership from an Eastern European, Transdisciplinary Context*, DOI 10.1007/978-3-319-45186-2_2

The practical value of studying spirituality for twenty-first-century managers is related to their increased need to better understand the behavior of the human resources in a broader, spiritual, and moral context, in order to further increase business competitiveness.

2.2 Literature Review

The rapid development of the spiritual leadership research agenda shows that the topic "has the potential to emerge as a powerful and courageous innovative management paradigm for the twenty-first century" (Crossman 2010: 604). Spirituality at work means, according to some researchers, an alternative to religion, particularly in the USA, where there is a relatively strong discussion on the topic (Kent Rhodes 2006). For other researchers, however, it is a means of harmonization. For example, for Hicks (2003: 115), workplace spirituality is about accepting and committing to a particular way of thinking about oneself, about the meaning of work, and about the workplace or the organization and finding a balance.

The topic is relatively new in the arena of organizational behavior and it is related to the inclusion in this field of the broader concept of spirituality. The inclusion of spirituality in the organizational behavior, leadership, and management is explained by various factors in literature, such as an ever-growing and generalized dissatisfaction with increasing materialism (Hoppe 2005) or growing wage inequality, the reengineering processes, downsizing, and workers' demoralization (Ashmos and Duchon 2000: 134–135). Ciulla (2000) points out that one of the most terrifying and depressing stories in the news for the majority of Americans in the mid-1990s was about the "best companies." These decided to downsize and were paying off a great number of employees not because of an economic depression but because they decided to "do more with less" in order to be competitive in a globalized marketplace. Another factor that is usually considered important is the growing need of companies to use their workers' creativity more, in the conditions of an increased competition. In this context, starting with the 1980s, organizations started to attach more importance to the role that emotions, moral, ethical values, and subjectivity play in making business and managerial decisions. Since the 1980s, spirituality issues attracted researchers to the field of organizational behavior, especially due to its novelty and to its challenging nature.

One important article in the field of spiritual leadership was the article of Mitroff and Denton (1999): *A Study of Spirituality in the Workplace*.

Fry (2003) defines spiritual leadership (2003: 694) as "comprising the values, attitudes, and behaviors that are necessary to motivate intrinsically one's self and others so that they have a sense of spiritual survival through calling and membership." Fry proposes a model based on intrinsic motivation, religious and ethical values, building it around three concepts: hope/faith, vision/mission, and altruistic love. Later on, Fry et al. (2005) refined his definition, considering that spiritual leadership has the objective to "create vision and value congruence across individuals, empowered teams, and organization levels and, ultimately, foster higher levels of both organizational commitment and productivity" (Fry et al. 2005: 183). Sanders et al. (2003: 40–41) define spiritual leadership as the extent to which organizations encourage and engage a sense of meaning and interconnectedness among their employees in both peer and hierarchical arrangements. Moore and Casper (2006: 110) see it as an internal value, belief, attitude, or emotion, attaching to it a strong humanistic dimension. Frye et al. (2007: 247) define it as a relational process aiming at constructing, coordinating, and transforming self, others, and the organization. Hackett and Wang (2012: 880) describe spiritual leadership through attributes such as honesty, integrity, caring, compassion, humility, sensitivity, fortitude, temperance, love, and faith. Nicolae et al. (2013) engage in a review of the literature of spiritual leadership and define it as that line of leadership based on moral, ethical, and religious values, embodied in the organizational culture and aimed at accomplishing both social and business ends, such as improving working conditions, decision-making processes, and motivation.

Empirical tests and objective measures of spiritual leadership were also developed. We use the literature review of Nicolae et al. (2013) to underline some of these, as follows. According to MacDonald (2011: 195), there are well over 100 tests of spirituality and related constructs, like spiritual well-being, spiritual transcendence, or self-transcendence. Moore and Casper (2006: 110) propose three theoretical constructs measuring workplace spirituality: perceived organizational support, affective organizational commitment, and instinct job satisfaction. Another example of a measurement instrument is Beazley's Spirituality Assessment Scale (Beazley 1998: 157). Other examples include Sanders et al. (2005) that use the "Organizational Spirituality Assessment scale" and the "Organizational Leadership Assessment" developed by Laub in 1999. Kass et al. (1991) developed a measurement instrument, called "INSPIRIT." It was designed to assess personal conviction of God's existence and the perception of a highly internalized relationship between God and the person. Ashmos and Duchon (2000) created the "Inner Life Scale," using a 7-point Likert-type scale, including statements about spirituality. Another measurement instrument is the "Virtuous Leadership Scale," developed by Sarros and Barker in 2003. It incorporates the seven attributes of humility, courage, humor, passion, and wisdom, integrity and compassion, manifested in servant leadership and forming the base of moral leadership.

2.3 Implications for Managerial Decision-Making and Action

If the research agenda in the field is refining the paradigm of spiritual leadership, the implications for managerial decision-making and action are also important. Spiritual leaders act on different premises and follow different criteria when establishing the policies of their companies. Spiritual organizations are different also in the drivers of their vision, missions, motivations, practices of stimulating effort or operational management, but also in the perception of the individual and the group.

First, spiritual managers act on *different premises*. One difference in the premises of managerial decision-making is the critical evaluation of rationality as the pillar of human action. The traditional leadership models were mainly based on the

Cartesian–Newtonian principles and the rationalist philosophies of Descartes. Those approaches to leadership have followed a rationalist perspective in order to discover universal "leadership" characteristics (Ford and Lawler 2007). In consequence, the main purpose was to demystify successful practices of leadership and to replicate them in companies or academic programs. Unfortunately, those endeavors are more consistent with early approaches to management, in their search for rationality, certainty, and predictability (Ford and Lawler 2007: 409). However, those directions have many times proven to be unsuccessful in front of the uncertainty and turbulence in which the twenty-first-century organization develops its activity. Spiritual leaders replace full rationality with bounded rationality and spirituality, as important explicative factors of organizational behavior. Thus, uncertainty and the acceptance of nonrationality are two important working premises that spiritual leaders base their decisions on.

Other distinctive feature of spiritual leaders is that they are willing to motivate human resources by *intrinsic rewards*. Thus, human resource policies aim to create inspiration, intrinsic motivation, and spiritual values. Decisions on human-resource motivational policies are based on discovering the employees' calling and on identifying the meaning of the actions to be run by the leader and the followers. In what concerns stimulating the effort, spiritual leaders aim to foster efforts by underlining the conviction, trust, and the importance of a task for business performance, while traditional motivation policies rely more on the stimulation of intelligence, rationality, and problem-solving (Boorom 2009).

Another difference in the spiritual managerial and business actions is that *the spiritual leader will try to balance social and business ends*, profit raising, and altruistic love. Spiritual leadership is differentiated by its aim of accomplishing both social and business ends, together with altruistic love, membership, and calling. Especially membership, altruistic love, and calling are concepts exclusively characteristic of spiritual leadership. They represent more than the sum of moral, ethical, and religious values embodied in the organizational culture. These values justify the simultaneous application of rational determinants and of moral, ethical, and religious beliefs in business decision-making, transforming spiritual leadership into a unique managing style.

If it is common for organizations to emphasize the importance of individualized consideration, to foster personal attention and to treat employees as individuals, spiritual leaders have a different approach to the issue of the individual versus group membership. They consider the group to be the nucleus of the organization, fostering membership; despite this, there is also emphasis put on the appreciation of individual employees (Boorom 2009).

Spirituality at work is a double way concept, in which values, personal characteristics, and interests are manageable simultaneously with the endeavor for profit raising. Spiritual leaders are also focused on *improving workers' creativity*, which has become an imperative in today's crowded business arena with its discourse of the knowledge and creative economy. In fact, due to the strong emphasis on boosting creativity, spiritual leaders respond to an important human need: for work to be meaningful.

The values of spiritual leaders, or at least those to which these leaders theoretically adhere, are compassion and caring, courage, generosity, questioning, service, stillness, peace, and thankfulness (Crossman 2010). The emphasis on moral values

Table 2.1 Differences between transactional, transformational, servant, and spiritual leadership attributes

Transactional leadership attributes	Transformational leadership attributes	Servant leadership attributes	Spiritual leadership attributes
Leader–follower exchanges	Inspiration	Service to others	Social ends
Contingent reward	Intellectual stimulation	Principled	Business ends
Management by exception	Influence	Stewardship	Altruistic love
	Intrinsic motivation	Spiritual values and beliefs	Membership
	Consideration		Calling

Source: After Northouse (1997: 134–135), *apud* Beazley and Gemmill (2006: 259) and the authors' contribution

is extremely important in spiritual leadership, as compared to traditional leadership approaches, in which moral values do not constitute, by any means, guiding criteria for business action. The most salient characteristic of this type of leadership is that managerial behavior is justified by the simultaneous application of rational determinants and moral, ethical, and religious beliefs. This view challenges traditional theories of organizational behavior and managerial decision-making, by proposing a spiritual, nonrational dimension in organizational processes. In addition, this approach to values allows spiritual leaders to follow not only business ends, but also social ones, enabling leaders to have wider aims in their actions.

In order to better understand the distinctiveness of spiritual leaders, we draw a comparison between different types of leadership, based on Northouse (1997: 134–135, cited in Beazley and Gemmill 2006: 259). Northouse (1997) conducts a comparison between the transactional, transformational, and servant leadership attributes. To this comparison, we added the most prominent spiritual leadership characteristics, in order to elaborate a better picture of the characteristics of the attributes of spiritual leadership. The results are presented in Table 2.1.

Table 2.1 positions spiritual leadership as an evolutionary leadership style which aims at balancing the social and business ends, profit raising, and altruistic love, in quest of a spiritual significance to the complex problems today's organizations face in society. In this quest, the leader himself or herself is spiritually dedicated and involved in organization's management.

In Romania, as in the other ex-communist countries, leadership and managerial culture is still recovering from more than 50 years of communism. During the transition period, new businesses have emerged in Romania in spite of the "formal" political and economic institutional limitations. The general perception, however, of both practitioners and researchers is that theory and practice are still underdeveloped as far as leadership is concerned. The field of general research in leadership in Romania is still trying to catch up with the international literature; unfortunately, it does so mainly only with the Anglo-Saxon one. Another aim of research is creating a bridge between the newest international conversations on the topic and the generally mainstream, classical theories of the field. This explains why discussions and research on spiritual leadership in business organizations are, to the best knowledge of the authors, almost nonexistent in the Romanian public sphere (Nicolae 2011).

2.4 Conclusions

Based on the issues formulated above, we could draw the profile of the spiritual leader by stating that the coordinates of his/her behavior should be related to social ends and the importance of calling, extrinsic motivation, and group membership. This profile clearly has to be improved by further research that should also extend and detail the implications of spiritual leadership on managerial action. However, this profile represents only a starting point for further research and discussion.

Nicolae et al. (2013) were the first authors investigating issues on spiritual leadership and the promoters of a Romanian research agenda. In practice, only a few companies seem to be aware of the impact leadership has, in general, on the organizational efficiency. In this context, spiritual leadership is probably a misunderstood concept for the Romanian companies or even a taboo since it is not discussed and clarified in the business contexts. Romanian business organizations are still in the era of the professionalization of their management and leadership.

On the other hand, new adequate paradigmatic approaches for the conceptualization and measurement of spiritual leaders should be developed, in order to prevent research from reaching trivial results (Fornaciari and Dean 2001) and to improve business practice and decision-making. In any case, practitioners should prevent a negative application of spiritual leadership, as for example derived from the approach to spirituality as a managerial tool for manipulating public perception or employees' behavior for achieving profits (Crossman 2010; Fornaciari and Dean 2001). There are no studies in the literature that analyze the potential negative side effects of workplace spirituality, such as "divisiveness, discrimination, misuse, and superficiality," also possible sources of organizational conflicts (Crossman 2010; Fornaciari and Dean 2001); this should also be a possible line of research in spiritual leadership.

References

Ashmos, B.J., and D. Duchon. 2000. Spirituality at Work: A Conceptualization and Measure. *Journal of Management Inquiry* 9(2): 134–145.

Beazley, H. 1998. *Meaning and Measurement of Spirituality in Organizational Settings: Development of a Spirituality Assessment Scale*. Doctoral dissertation, George Washington University. Dissertation Abstracts International, 9820619.

Beazley, D., & Gemmill, G. 2006. Spirituality and Servant Leader Behavior. Journal of Management, Spirituality & Religion, 3(3), 258–270.

Boorom, R. 2009. *Spiritual Leadership: A Study of the Relationship between Spiritual, Leadership Theory and Transformational Leadership*. PhD thesis, Regent University, School of Global Leadership and Entrepreneurship.

Ciulla, B.J. 2000. *The Working Life—The Promise and Betrayal of Modern Work*, 151–157. New York, NY: Three Rivers Press.

Crossman, J. 2010. Conceptualizing Spiritual Leadership in Secular Organizational Contexts and Its Relation to Transformational, Servant and Environmental Leadership. *Leadership and Organization Development Journal* 31(7): 596–608.

Ford, J., and J. Lawler. 2007. Blending Existentialist and Constructionist Approaches to Leadership Studies: An Exploratory Account. *Leadership and Organisational Development Journal* 28(5): 409–425.

Fornaciari, C.J., and K.L. Dean. 2001. Making the Quantum Leap: Lessons from Physics on Studying Spirituality and Religion in Organizations. *Journal of Organizational Change Management* 14(4): 335–351.

Fry, L. 2003. Toward a Theory of Spiritual Leadership. *The Leadership Quarterly* 14: 693–727.

Fry, L.W., S. Vitucci, and M. Cedillo. 2005. Spiritual Leadership and Army Transformation; Theory Measurement and Establishing a Baseline. *The Leadership Quarterly* 16: 835–863.

Frye, J., L.G. Kisselburgh, and D. Butts. 2007. Embracing Spiritual Followership. *Communication Studies* 58(3): 243–260.

Hackett, R.D., and G. Wang. 2012. Virtues and Leadership: An Integrating Conceptual Framework Founded in Aristotelian and Confucian Perspectives on Virtues. *Management Decision* 50(5): 868–899.

Hicks, D. 2003. *Religion and the Workplace: Pluralism, Spirituality, Leadership*. Cambridge: Cambridge University Press.

Hoppe, S. 2005. Spirituality and Leadership. *New Directions for Teaching and Learning* 2005(104):83–92, Winter 2005.

Kass, J.D., et al. 1991. Health Outcomes and a New Index of Spiritual Experience. *Journal of Scientific Study of Religion* 30: 203–211.

Kent Rhodes, E.D.D. 2006. Six Components of a Model for Workplace Spirituality. *Graziadio Business Review* 9(2). http://gbr.pepperdine.edu/2010/08/six-components-of-a-model-for-workplace-spirituality/.

MacDonald, D.A. 2011. Studying Spirituality Scientifically: Reflections, Considerations, Recommendations. *Journal of Management, Spirituality and Religion* 8(3): 195–210.

Mitroff, I.I., Denton, E.A. 1999. A Study of Spirituality in the Workplace. Sloan Management Review, available at http://strandtheory.org/images/Spirituality_in_the_workplace-Mitroff_Denton.pdf.

Moore, T.W., and W.J. Casper. 2006. An Examination of Proxy Measures of Workplace Spirituality: A Profile Model of Multidimensional Constructs. *Journal of Leadership and Organizational Studies* 12(4):109–118. ProQuest Central.

Nicolae, M. 2011. *The dynamics of leadership theory and practice in the context of Romania's integration in the European Union*. Unpublished Ph.D. thesis, publicly defended in 2011 at the Bucharest University of Economic Studies.

Nicolae, M., I. Ion, and E. Nicolae. 2013. The Spiritual Leadership Agenda. *Review of International Comparative Management* 14(4): 551, October 2013.

Northhouse, P. 1997. Leadership. Theory and Practice. SAGE Publications, Inc. 2nd edition.

Sanders, J.E., W.E. Hopkins, and G.D. Geroy. 2003.From Transactional to Transcendental: Toward an Integrated Theory of Leadership. *Journal of Leadership and Organizational Studies* Spring, 9(4).

Sarros, J.C., and C. Barker. 2003. *Virtuous Leadership Scale. Australian Management Character Survey*. Australian Institute of Management/Monash University study. http://www.ai.com.au/research/amcs.html.

Chapter 3
Current Trends on the Private Medical Market in Romania

Nicolae Al Pop and Beniamin Grozea

Abstract This chapter focuses on the confrontation between the public and private sectors of Romanian healthcare services of the last decade. Its objectives concern a "diagnostic analysis" of the capacity, structure, and trends of this market. Based on the bivalent feature of the public–private sector, this study will follow the distribution of customers between the two sectors and motivational factors of this approach. The structure of the Romanian medical system became focused on the Bismarck-type medical services, taken from the functional systems of countries like Germany, Austria, Belgium, Switzerland, France, and other Nordic countries. This approach, however, has shown itself ineffective due to the corrupt system in Romania that generated big losses. The unbalanced ratio between the employed population and the inactive population contributes to the main premise of underfunding the public sector. Apparently, this element would greatly favor the private system for the solvent. The major difficulties in the legislative system, the disloyal elements of interference in this competition, and the public disorientation and misinformation when opting for the private health system are all subject to an in-depth analysis of this research based mainly on secondary data. This chapter aims to open the premises of a multitude of studies together with field and desk research in order to reposition the private healthcare in the place it should hold within the Romanian healthcare economy, considering the fact that Romania is a European Community country.

Keywords Healthcare • Medical system • Private medicine • Romanian healthcare

3.1 Introduction

The structure of the Romanian medical system is focused on the Bismarck framework for social services, taken from the functional systems of Germany, Austria, Belgium, Switzerland, France, and the Nordic countries, and its aim was to reach the same success in Romania. The social health insurance system type of "Bismarck"

N.A. Pop, Ph.D. (✉) • B. Grozea
Bucharest University of Economic studies, Bucharest, Romania
e-mail: nicolae_al_pop@yahoo.com; beniamin@grozea.net

S. Vaduva et al. (eds.), *Business Ethics and Leadership from an Eastern European, Transdisciplinary Context*, DOI 10.1007/978-3-319-45186-2_3

took the name of Otto von Bismarck (1815–1898), the first Chancellor of the German Empire. He created a system of social solidarity and thus in 1881 introduced a system of state social insurance; in 1883 introduced the system of social health insurance; and in 1889 introduced a system of retirement and disability pensions.

When this system was created, the premises were established for the success of such a project: a high birth rate, a sustained increase of the population, and a small number of retired people who not only fit into the inactive population. These categories of persons also require social services (pensions) and healthcare services to a greater extent than the active, usually younger population. The sources of funding of this system consisted of compulsory contributions from wages, mandatory contributions payable by employers for employees, and state grants.

3.2 Trends in the Romanian Medical System

This approach, however, was ineffective in Romania due to a corrupt system, riddled with losses, which has ignored the premises initially stated by Otto von Bismarck, namely a society of mostly the young, able to pay for a social system that would benefit just a minor part of the population.

In addition to not fulfilling these premises, the Romanian medical system registered precisely the opposite of sustainable high performance due to a corrupt environment responsible for many losses, a system that is currently considered "underfunded" and which does not have the ability to provide quality health services or adequate facilities. Currently, the financing of the healthcare system in Romania is provided in proportion of 80 % from contributions to the National Health Insurance House (CNAS) and 20 % of the funding is granted from the Romanian state.

Taking into consideration the disproportion between the total population of Romania—of 21.26 million—and the active population, of 9.45 million, corresponding to a 44.4 % of contributors to the CNAS, together with the increasing development of the underground economy (INS 2013). This facilitates the payment of the minimum wage accepted by Romanian state (with the difference given by informal payments), the payments to CNAS are at a minimal level, creating an overworked and underfunded system.

On the other hand, the same medical system also works in the Netherlands, for example, but in that country, the medical insurance system based on the Bismarck model has obtained successful results. Experts say that the great results of this system are linked directly to the careful choice of the most professional managerial teams and the best medical specialists for the management of the medical facilities. Moreover, another factor that has to be taken into consideration is the fact that, in the Netherlands, political interference with the healthcare system is extremely limited, almost nonexistent.

Several insurance companies operate in the Netherlands, and medical providers seek to offer the best medical systems in order to attract more patients, which, of course, will generate incomes proportional to the volume and the complexity of the treated medical cases.

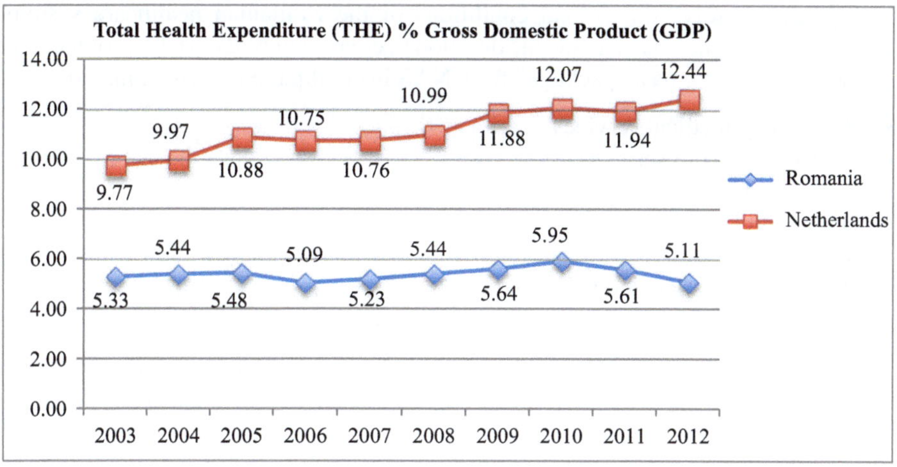

Fig. 3.1 Total health expenditure %

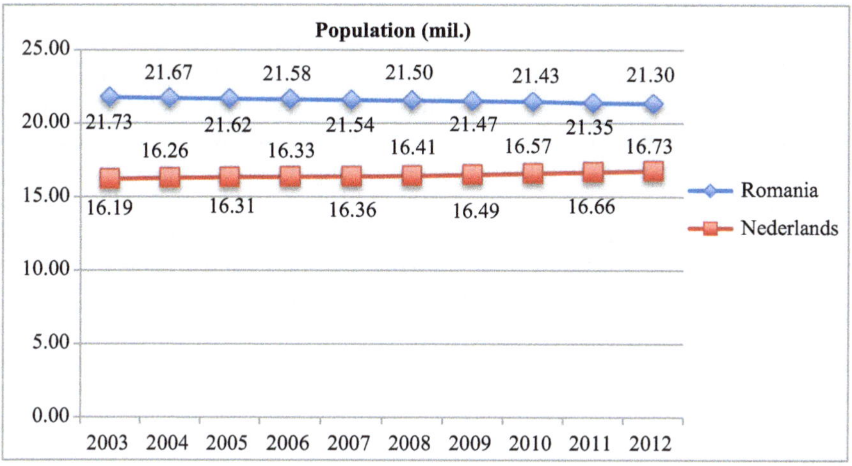

Fig. 3.2 Comparison between the evolution of Romania and Netherland's population

Analysis Fig. 3.1 (WHO, *Global Health Expenditure Database*), on the proportion of GDP allocated for healthcare by the two countries, namely Romania and the Netherlands, shows that the Netherlands allocate double the budget for healthcare compared to Romania.

This context renders possible the correct functioning of a Bismarck medical system, together with the accompanying professional personnel.

The corroboration of Figs. 3.1 and 3.2 illustrates that there are antagonistic trends between the two countries regarding the evolution of population, more exactly, Romania's population is shrinking, and the Netherlands' population is growing, which benefits the healthcare system of the Netherlands.

In order to solve the critical conditions of the Romanian healthcare system, authorities in the field have made the decision to create a minimal package of medical services called "the basic package" for CNAS insured patients, which includes:

- Emergency medical services
- Preventive health services
- Family medicine
- Outpatient services
- Inpatient services
- Healthcare at home and palliative medicine
- Medication with and without personal contribution

This project will definitely bring some relief to this system of inefficient spending, but, on the long run, the population will need complex medical services not included in this basic package.

3.3 Characteristics of the Private Medical System in Romania

The private medical services market in Romania works differently from the classical model of markets in general, due to information asymmetry between providers, consumers, and financers of the healthcare system and because the decisions to acquire health services do not follow the classic supply-demand mechanism.

Doctors are the most informed persons (by the nature of their profession); they can induce the behavior of patients, because patients can't determine whether or not their symptoms are severe, don't know what form of therapy is required, and have very little information about the effectiveness of existing treatments (Drăgoi 2010, p. 82).

Consumers of healthcare services, on the other hand, also have an atypical behavior, caused by their limited capacity of decision-making, their underlying emotional issues, and their lack of information on the characteristics of medical services required.

Healthcare providers in Romania operate in a market characterized by certain features:

- The difficulty of determining accurately the demand for medical services (Rădulescu 2008).
- It is extremely difficult to compare in an objective manner the medical services, which makes the decision of acquiring medical services an emotional one, generally related to the doctor–patient relationship.
- Ethical issues, which concern the doctor–patient relationship (confidentiality), the distance between research and treatment (Cetină 2009, p. 292; Rădulescu 2008, pp. 48–49), and so on.

In 2012, the medical services market in Romania was about €5.3 billion. In the same year, the incomes from private medical services in Romania were worth €500 million, of which 50 % were direct contributions from patients and private companies, and the difference was settled by CNAS (Chilom 2012, p. 12).

3.4 Trends in the Development of Healthcare Insurances in Romania

The authors believe that the only consistent, functional, and long-term sustainable solution is the transition from statutory insurance (CNAS) to the private healthcare insurances. This is a lingering process, similar to the pensions' transition from Pillar I to Pillar II; the aim is that, in a certain period, the insurance system will be taken over entirely by the private insurers.

Of course, the transition will not be easy, having to cross a broad spectrum of threats, but this system will solve the existing problems; will bring benefits such as the patients' experience, the doctors' salaries, the quality of healthcare treatments; and, last but not least, will eradicate the informal payments in public facilities. This system is tested and it works in private facilities. Further still, the authors exposed some proposals based on successful examples from EU countries and based on one of the authors' personal experience in this field.

An important step Romania will have to take would be to eradicate the restriction of tax deductibility for private healthcare insurances. At this point, a company may acquire private health insurances for its employees, but the amount of each insurance is deductible only up to the threshold of €250/year, respectively €20.83/month, given that the premium of a private insurance for a 30-year-old person is of €1000/year, respectively €83.33/month.

Another important step to be taken by the Romanian government is the liberalization of healthcare insurance. It is important that the population be able to choose between the statutory insurance (CNAS) or a private insurance. The authors also propose, in this context, the introduction of mandatory possession of healthcare insurance (private or statutory) of any kind for every Romanian citizen, regardless of age, occupation, or medical history. The transition from statutory insurance to private insurance can be achieved through a process similar to the pensions' shift from the first pillar to the second pillar.

Currently, the healthcare budget consists of contributions (employees and employers) to the CNAS amounting 80 % and another 20 % in state grants. Thus, employees would have to choose whether to remain insured by CNAS or to opt for other private insurance. A percentage of 10.7 % of the gross salary of employees consisting of employee contribution and employer contribution for the employee, which currently is paid to CNAS, would then be transferred wherever the employee decides, and the state should add the 20 % grant, in addition to contributions from the salary, as it happens today.

Students would benefit from only a grant from the state, correlated with age, which would allow them to be eligible for both CNAS and private insurance. Given their low incidence of serious illnesses and the fact that the treatment they require is less expensive, insurance premiums should not be too high for them.

For the retirees, 10.7 % of the pensions should be transferred to CNAS or to a private healthcare insurance, and the state should bring a grant of more than 20 %, due to their higher incidence of sicknesses and chronic illnesses that require expensive and lengthy treatments.

Benefits of the presented model can be summarized as it follows:

- Private insurers will agree to provide insurances to the population for much lower premiums and will understand that the consisted profits of this business reside in volumes.
- The authors are convinced that, compared to the present system of statutory insurance, characterized by fraud and losses, private insurers will ensure that fraud does not happen.
- The quality level of healthcare services will increase with the growing competition from the private and the state sector, because the patients will be able to choose where to be treated: in a private hospital or in a public hospital, depending on the insurance plan and the level of contributions. As a result, the relieving of the public medical system, concomitant with the adequate funding, will exponentially increase the quality of healthcare in public hospitals.
- It will establish the premise of paying the right salaries to medical professionals and will contribute to the return of the medical elite to Romania.
- It will eliminate informal payments in the public medical system because patients will understand that they or someone else (the insurance company) paid for the medical care, a concept not currently understood clearly by the patients; healthcare professionals will not be interested in informal payments due to proper remuneration.
- With the introduction of private healthcare insurance, these companies will be interested in specific prevention programs for their clients because it is cheaper to prevent than to cure. This will establish the priceless concept of prevention in Romania.

Furthermore, in order to ensure the limitation of doctors' exodus, the authors propose the physicians who have received free tuition from the state during their studies be assigned to work an equal period in the service of the Romanian state. Otherwise, if they decide to leave the public facilities, they would have to pay to the state the amount of money consisting in their tuition, for all the years they have studied. In what regards the private healthcare sector in Romania, the latter could experience great development along with the implementation of the previously mentioned system adjustments.

According to a Mednet (2013) study, in September 2013, it was found that both in Bucharest and at the national level (cities of over 100,000 inhabitants) the addressability of private healthcare has increased from 57 % in 2009 to around 80 % in 2013. The main reasons patients are turning to private medical facilities are:

- The continuous expansion of private clinics, medical facilities, laboratories, and private hospitals while increasing their ability to treat patients
- The professionalism and friendliness of the staff and the superior technical equipment of clinics and of private hospitals
- The financial difficulties and the precarious state of public health

The significant mutations outlined above are reflected in Fig. 3.3.

At the same time, the study by Mednet found that, in 2013, about a third of respondents from Bucharest (31.8 %) exclusively accessed the private medical sector.

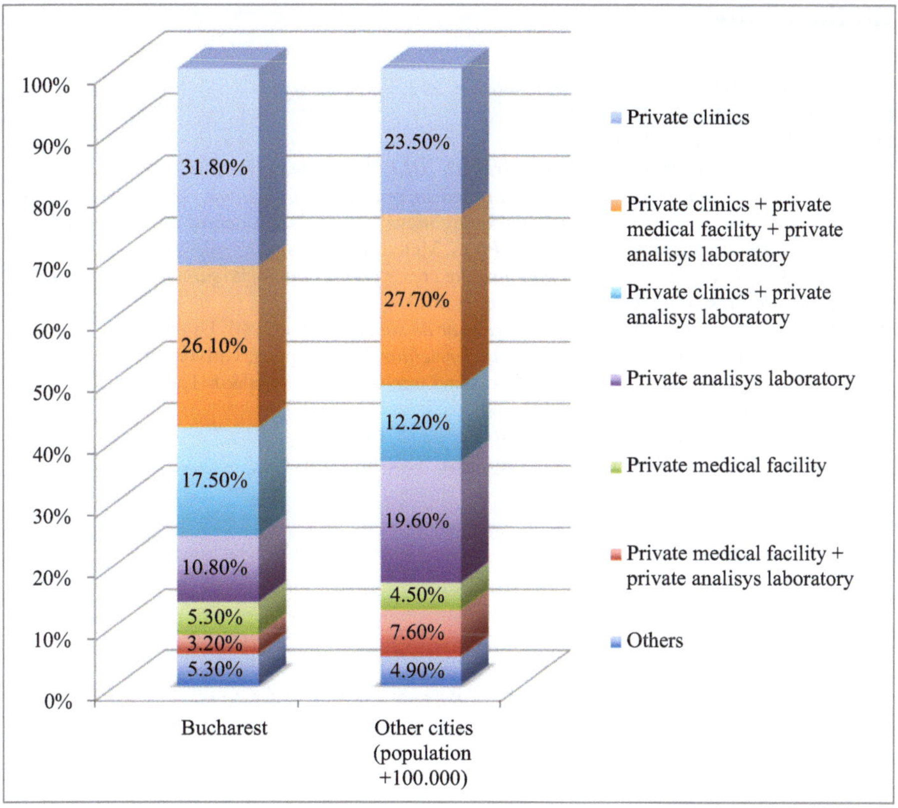

Fig. 3.3 Shifts in patients' healthcare choices

Outside of Bucharest (cities of +100,000), still in the year 2013, 27.7% of respondents went to a medical clinic, a private medical facility or have accessed a private analysis laboratory.

3.5 Conclusions

The authors suggest the involvement of marketing in improving the health system in Romania, a concept also supported by Zaiţ (2002). According to Kotler et al.'s (2009) concept, developed in the early years of the third millennium, the holistic approach finds fertile ground for its application in the healthcare area as well.

A strong effort is required to change the mentalities inherited from the statist economy and deeply rooted in the collective mind, according to which the State is responsible to "restore" or "repair" health. Concern for the individual's health will be felt in the health of the community, because individual health is the basis of the concept of public health (Vorzsák 2004).

Bibliography

Cetină, Iuliana. 2009. *Marketingul serviciilor*, p. 292.

Chilom, Emilian Marius. 2012. p. 12.

Drăgoi, Mihaela Cristina. 2010. p. 82.

INS. 2013. *Ocuparea si şomajul in trimestrul III, 2013*. Press release no. 309.

Kotler, P., Dipak Jain, et al. 2009. *Marketingul în era digitală. O nouă viziune despre profit, creştere şi înnoire. (Original title: Marketing moves. A new approach of profits, growth, and renewal)*. Bucureşti: Harvard Business Press, Meteor Business.

Mednet. 2013. *Piața serviciilor medicale private creste constant datorita numărului tot mai mare de apelanți*. Press release no. 10, September 2013.

Rădulescu, Violeta. 2008. *Marketingul serviciilor de sănătate*. Bucureşti: Uranus.

Vorzsák, Álmos (Coord.). 2004. *Marketingul serviciilor*. Cluj-Napoca: University Press.

World Health Organization. Global health expenditure database. ws=0&d=1.www.cnas.ro/download/1532/Anexa%20Norme%202014.pdf.

www.cnas.ro/download/1532/Anexa%20Norme%202014.pdf.

Zaiţ, Adriana. 2002. *Marketingul Serviciilor*. Iaşi: Sedcom Libris.

Chapter 4
Governance Particularities of Romanian Family Business

Silvia Fotea and Samuel Echevarria

Abstract Family businesses in Romania are not distinctively treated, tracked, or researched neither at legal/administrative level nor in the academic or business-consulting arena, but rather included in the large category of small and medium size enterprises (SMEs). Given the limited knowledge that exists regarding their particular way of functioning in Romania, this chapter aims to shed some light on the corporate governance dimensions of Romanian family businesses and identify the particularities of their decision-making process, succession perspective, and family communication. Who are the actors that play a role in the decision-making process of the family businesses in Romania? What is the prevalent criterion for granting participation to decision-making process? What are the levels of family involvement and how is the information sharing taking place? What are the prospects of succession? These are questions that will be answered during this research study. The chapter is based on primary data collected during a nation-wide study among SMEs in Romania and is exploratory in nature.

Keywords Family business • Corporate governance • Trans-generational perspective • Decision-making process • Succession

S. Fotea, Ph.D. (✉)
Emanuel University of Oradea, Oradea, Romania
e-mail: silvia.fotea@emanuel.ro

S. Echevarria, Ph.D.
Bucharest University of Economic Studies, Bucharest, Romania
e-mail: sam.echevarria@emanuel.ro

S. Vaduva et al. (eds.), *Business Ethics and Leadership from an Eastern European, Transdisciplinary Context*, DOI 10.1007/978-3-319-45186-2_4

4.1 Introduction

Family businesses represent the backbone of most economies in the world. They employ a significant percentage of the total workforce and record significant levels of turnover, investments, and accumulated capital (Allouche et al. 2015; Hoy and Sharma 2010; Howorth et al. 2010).

In the academic arena, the phenomenon of family businesses, both social and economic in nature, is receiving increased attention among economic researchers, both because of its pervasiveness worldwide but also because of its impact on entrepreneurship (Aldrich and Cliff 2003; Kellermanns et al. 2008). Studies in the field consider it to be the "oxygen that sustains the fire of entrepreneurship" (Edward et al. 2003).

Romania's economic landscape is dominated by small and medium size businesses (SMEs). Their role as a major employer and contributor to the gross domestic product define them as an essential influence on the economic well-being of this country. Although not treated distinctively from a legal standpoint (neither tracked, researched, nor included in the official statistics of the country), family businesses represent a major part of the SME category in Romania and consequently play a critical role in the economy of the country (Szabo and Szabo 2014). From an economic and geo-political point of view Romania is a pivotal player in the European Union due to its strategic location as a gateway that connects West and East. Therefore the economy of this country is important for the economic and social well-being of the European continent.

Given the critical role family businesses play and the limited knowledge that exists regarding their particular way of functioning in Romania, this chapter aims to overcome some of these shortcomings by shedding some light on the corporate governance dimensions of Romanian family businesses and by identifying in what ways they are different than nonfamily businesses. This chapter pursues three main directions, namely decision-making process, succession, and communication, and will attempt to answer the following questions pertaining to these directions: (1) Who are the "actors" influencing the decision-making process in Romanian family businesses? (2) On what criteria are they allowed access to decision-making and what role do outside influences play in the decision-making process? (3) To what extent do family businesses in Romania have a trans-generational perspective in their business and are practicing succession planning? (4) To what extent are family-businesses in Romania sharing the information regarding the life of the business with members of the family? and (5) How often and to what degree of formality is the sharing of information taking place?

The reminder of this chapter is organized as follows: First, we consider the theoretical dimensions of family businesses as an organizational form and we describe the role corporate governance plays in the complexity of family business system. Second, we present a short overview of Romania's SMEs and family business landscape. Third, we describe the methodology, data collection, and results resulting from a recent nation-wide study among SMEs in Romania.

4.2 Family Businesses Particularities

Family businesses represent a complex and dynamic system composed of other systems (the institution of the family and the business system being the two major components) that interact with each other and internally in particular ways determined by the pattern of cycles that can be identified in the life span of family business (Vaduva et al. 2011; Ward 2004; Basco and Perez Rodriguez 2009; Litz 2008; Klein 2010). In this complex system, the interactions between family and business give birth to idiosyncratic resources (Brunninge and Melander 2010), and a certain "familliness" (unique, inseparable, and synergistic resources and capabilities arising from family involvement and interactions (Habbershon et al. 2003) that make result in a very heterogenous group of organizations where difficulties exist in creating predictable models of organizational behavior (Miller and Le Breton-Miller 2006; Freiling and Grossman 2014)). The complex and multifaceted nature of family businesses result in a diversity of governance choices which contribute to the variety of forms and shapes takeoff development and to a debated discourse in terms of recorded performance. Consequently, the literature concerning family business is characterized by a strong debate in many of the aspects that set these organizations apart.

Although family businesses are commonly recognized as a prevailing, long-standing phenomenon and important contributors to the economic development and wealth creation around the world (Mazzi 2011; Vaduva et al. 2011), the literature indicates that only 30 % of these type of entities survive over the second generation of a family, and just 15 % survive through the third generation (Bracci and Vagnoni 2011).

Critics of family businesses indicate that this particular organizational form is weakened by practices that spring from its inherent nature such as unhealthy nepotism (Chua et al. 2003), lack of professional management (Chandler 1990; Bloom and Reenen 2007), prevalence of conflicts (Faccio et al. 2001), skepticism regarding financial markets (Claessens et al. 2002), and reluctance to utilize outside advice (Chua et al. 2003) which in turn leads to inadequate access to capital, family moods dominate competence when it comes to succession (De Massis et al. 2008) and the pressures of meeting the ever increasing needs of a growing family (Miller and Le Breton-Miller 2006).

On the other side of the debate there is a growing body of studies which indicate that family businesses outperform nonfamily businesses (Allouche et al. 2015; Miller and Le Breton-Miller 2006; Dyer 2006). Still, the evidence presented by different studies concerning the performance of family businesses are curious given the lack of consensus among researchers regarding the definition of what constitutes a family business (Miller et al. 2007).

In spite of the existing debates, there is general agreement that family businesses are important for economic development and need to be further studied in order to discover more concerning their functions and how they can enhance their performance (Aldrich and Cliff 2003; Zahra et al. 2004).

4.3 The Role of Corporate Governance in Family Businesses Performance

When it comes to firm performance research studies agree upon four typical factors qualified as determinants of performance, namely industry, governance, firm characteristics/structure (e.g., social capital, strategy), and management (the impact of the owner/entrepreneur/manager) (Dyer 2006).

Among the range of factors that have been identified to positively influence business performance, corporate governance has become a focal point in the last 15 years (Taylor 2013). It is considered to positively influence both microeconomic efficiency due to its impact on firm behavior, innovativeness, and entrepreneurial activity (Miladi 2014) and the industrial competitiveness of countries (Maher and Thomas Andersson 1999).

The ethical roots of the financial crisis in 2008 and the pervasiveness of globalization have given enormous practical importance to the concept of corporate governance and has called forth more research studies on what "good" corporate governance means and how it affects performance.

The range and structure of corporate governance configurations are determined by cultural, historical, and institutional contexts worldwide and explain the broad body of research that has been produced on the subject while highlighting the difficulty in isolating a single governance framework that can fit the multifaceted needs of companies (Corbetta and Salvato 2004).

At its core corporate governance deals with the separation of ownership and management and plays the role of safeguarding shareholder's financial interests (La Porta et al. 2000; Shleifer and Vishny 1997). In the pursuit of this goal, corporate governance employs a set of instruments that monitor, incentivize, and control the activity of managers (Taylor 2013).

Much of the research on corporate governance has focused on large corporations (Miller and Le Breton-Miller 2006), on the effects of ownership concentration on performance (Demsetz and Villalonga 2001) and on development of mechanisms that would allow managers to make choices that will in turn lead to performance improvement (Coles et al. 2001), the board being the most commonly investigated mechanism (Brunninge et al. 2007; Corbetta and Salvato 2004; Huse 2000).

Although SMEs play an important role in the economies of most countries, especially those with a transition economy like Romania, the number of corporate governance studies focusing on this category is limited (Miladi 2014; Haalien and Huse 2005), especially in the context of developing countries (Taylor 2013; Ben Hamad and Afef Karoui 2011). Yet, research agrees that "good governance" is critical to SME performance and for positive economic development and growth. Gabrielsson and Huse (2005) argue that the growth challenges faced by SMEs have their roots in governance characteristics (c.f. Gedajlovic et al. 2004).

By pursuing the task of investigating the governance dimensions of family businesses in Romania this chapter is filling an existing knowledge and information gap, thereby making an important contribution to the literature.

More recently, this research stream has attracted more scholarship and on of the most important resulting insights is that the SME governance model is not merely a downsized version of a large publicly held firm (Brunninge et al. 2007). Most small and medium size companies feature unsophisticated and noncomplex governance structures (Cowling 2003). The entrepreneurial logic that guides SMEs, the strong influence of the leader, the transparent line between ownership and management, the concentrated ownership, and the involvement of multiple family members, as is the case of family businesses calls for a special research focus.

In the case of family businesses, the governance issues are even more complex given the multifaceted nature of this category, a category that gives birth to a great variety of governance decisions (Freiling and Grossman 2014). These diverse governance decisions can lead to significant differences in their behaviors, capabilities, and ultimately performance (Miller and Le Breton-Miller 2006; Bennedsen et al. 2010). The family business organizational form presents, on the one hand, the advantage of concentrated ownership as a governance variable. Studies indicate this organizational relationship to be an enhancer of performance due to the fact that it allows for intense monitoring of cost reductions (Jensen and William Meckling 1990) and an increased stewardship attitude (Davis et al. 1997). On the other hand, the inherent characteristics of this category (nepotism, capital restrictions, conflicts, etc.) may also affect performance in a negative way.

Although results of studies confirm the difficulty of attributing superior performance to a particular governance variable (Brunninge et al. 2007, Miller et al. 2007) there are four fundamental dimensions that shape governance forms and mechanisms and have implications on the performance of the organization, on resource-allocation decisions and capability development (Miller and Le Breton-Miller 2006):

- Level and mode of family ownership
- Family leadership
- The broader involvement of multiple family members
- The planned or actual participation of later generations

In this respect, family firms represent an attractive laboratory for researchers to address governance questions that are of general interest, especially in territories and cultures where little is known about them, as is the case of Romania.

4.4 Study Methodology

Our study is based on a nation-wide survey among existing SMEs in Romania and was administered from March 26 to April 9, 2014 using an online questionnaire consisting of 34 questions disseminated through the Qualtrics platform.

The study invited the entire population of SMEs in Romania to participate and the analysis is based on responses of 517 SMEs who answered the questionnaire. Out of the 517 responding SMEs, 231 self-identified as family businesses (answered "Yes" to the question "Are you a family business" and meet the criteria of family ownership and family involvement in the business according to family business definition).

Because of the exploratory nature of the study no attempt was made to make any inferences or discuss generalizations. The main objective of the study was to produce baseline information that would help develop further analysis. We are well aware of the lack of probability testing but for this pioneering research effort in Romania we wanted to focus on the general trends.

The objective of this research endeavor is threefold. First, to identify the dimensions and the centrality of decision-making processes in Romanian family businesses. Questions under investigation include: (1) Who are the "actors" influencing the decision-making process in Romanian family businesses? and (2) What role does family membership play in participation within the business decision-making.

The second objective of this research is to evaluate whether family businesses in Romania possess a trans-generational perspective on the business and to what extent they practice succession planning.

Third, we want to establish to what extent family-businesses in Romania share information regarding the life of the business with members of the family, how often and to what degree of formality is the sharing of information implemented?

4.5 General Overview of SME Sector and Its Role in National Economy

The entrepreneurial tradition is still in its youth in Romania as given the transition to a free market economy began only in 1990 and after 40 years of a centralized economy. The Romanian economy still experiences the consequences of that period, a period which reduced the entrepreneurial capacity of an entire generation to almost zero. Given this reality, an entire generation of Romanian society is absent from the role of experienced, role-model entrepreneurs in the marketplace (Szabo and Szabo 2014).

The integration into the European Union in 2007 introduced Romania's SME sector to a unifying legislative framework aimed at fostering a healthy growth of the sector. Registering a total number of 718.519 entities, Romania's SME sector is dominated by small and medium-sized enterprises, with fewer microenterprises, the majority of SMEs being incorporated in wholesale and retail trade, manufacturing and services. These three sectors together account for approximately 70 % of value added and employment by SMEs (Romanian National Office for Commerce 2013).

The Romanian SME sector accounts for over 58 % of the turnover experienced by the Romanian economy and employs two-thirds of the active workforce in the marketplace. Between 2008 and 2009, Romania's SME sector was affected by the global recession and although it experienced a recovery from the brutal hit it lost its momentum in 2012. The sector's performance is evaluated as below average for seven out of nine Small Business Act principles issued by European Commission. In 2013 and 2014, SMEs are expected to return to precrisis levels in terms of their overall numbers and employment (European Commission—SBA Fact Sheet 2013).

	Number of enterprises			Number of employees			Value added		
	Romania		EU27	Romania		EU27	Romania		EU27
	Number	Share	Share	Number	Share	Share	Billion €	Share	Share
Micro	389,206	88.7%	92.1%	889,271	23.1%	28.7%	7	13.6%	21.1%
Small	39,928	9.1%	6.6%	804,960	20.9%	20.4%	8	16.9%	18.3%
Medium-sized	7,992	1.8%	1.1%	827,897	21.5%	17.3%	10	20.4%	18.3%
SMEs	437,126	99.7%	99.8%	2,522,128	65.6%	66.5%	25	50.9%	57.6%
Large	1,513	0.3%	0.2%	1,325,085	34.4%	33.5%	24	49.1%	42.4%
Total	438,640	100.0%	100.0%	3,847,213	100.0%	100.0%	49	100.0%	100.0%

These are estimates for 2012 produced by London Economics, based on 2008-10 figures from the Structural Business Statistics Database (Eurostat). The data cover the 'business economy', which includes industry, construction, trade, and services (NACE Rev. 2 sections B to J, L, M and N), but not enterprises in agriculture, forestry and fisheries and the largely non-market service sectors such as education and health. The advantage of using Eurostat data is that the statistics are harmonised and comparable across countries. The disadvantage is that for some countries the data may be different from those published by national authorities.

Source: European Commission—SBA Fact Sheet 2013

4.6 Family Businesses in Romania

Many businesses in Romania are in fact family business but they are not identified as such. They are neither tracked, investigated, nor included in the official statistics of the country but are simply assimilated within the large SMEs category (Szabo and Szabo 2014).

Within the Romanian national context, the official meaning of the term "family business" is regulated by Law no. 300/2004 (Art. 1–4) authorizing individuals or family businesses to begin self-employment. In Romania, entrepreneurs are those who start family businesses because they want, in the early stage of the business endeavor, to work with only those they trust, in this case their family (Vaduva 2004) (Fig. 4.1)

4.7 Description of Romanian Family Businesses in the Study

The main characteristics of the respondent family business are as follows:

- 44 % of responding Romanian family businesses have only one owner.
- 93 % of responding Romanian family SMEs employ between 1 and 4 family members.
- 64 % are in their first generation (the originators of the business still run it).
- 32 % have two generations (1st and 2nd) involved in the business activity.
- 84 % of surveyed participants are owners/partner in the business.
- 80 % of respondents have higher education (college, M.B.A., Ph.D.).
- 23 % of SMEs surveyed are in manufacturing.
- 18 % of SMEs surveyed are in retail/trade.
- 49 % of SMEs surveyed families have a turnover between 100.000 and 500.000 EUR.

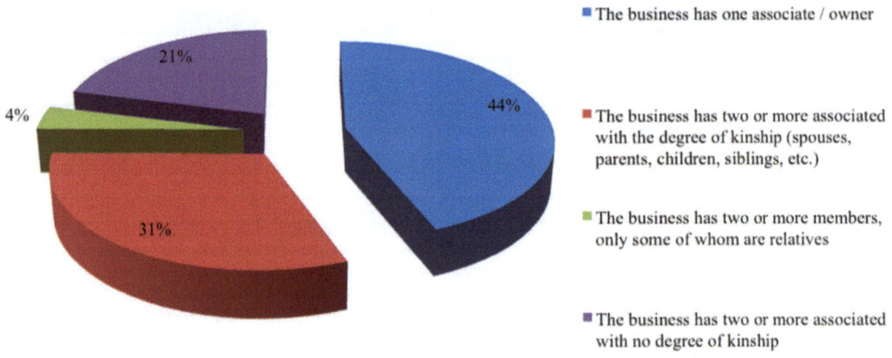

Fig. 4.1 Ownership of family business in Romania and the degree of kinship. 44 % of the responding family businesses have one associate/owner

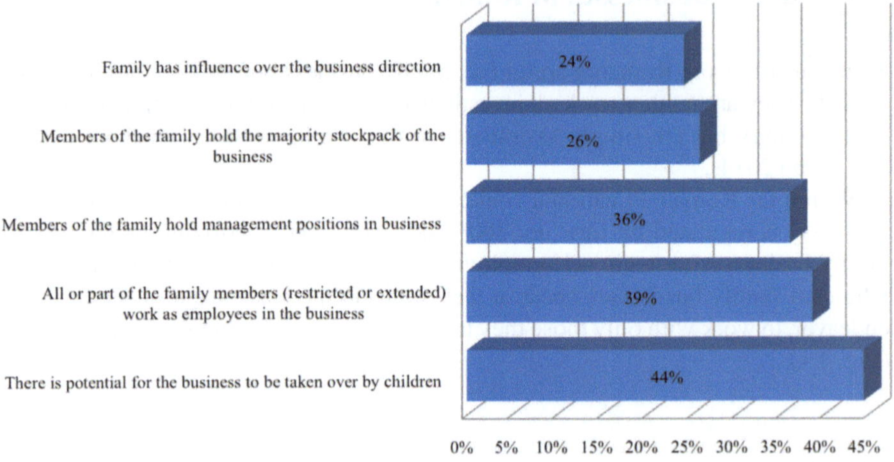

Fig. 4.2 Family-business relationship of Romanian family businesses. In 24 % of the cases the family has influence over the business direction

When it comes to the degree of family involvement in the business (Fig. 4.2), employment of family members in the business is more prevalent (39 %) than ownership (26 %) and influence (24 %).

The trans-generational perspective is present in Romanian family businesses, 44 % of the responding firms will potentially be taken over by children (Fig. 4.2).

The distribution of formal leadership roles in Romania family SMEs (Fig. 4.3) leans more towards men for the role of administrator (64 %), executive director (44 %), production manager (25 %), while the CFO is predominantly female (21 % female, compared to 5 % male).

When compared to their nonfamily counterparts (Table 4.1), family businesses are more likely to feature more owners, although nonfamily SMEs seem to involve 1 or 2 family members in the business but not at ownership level. The number of

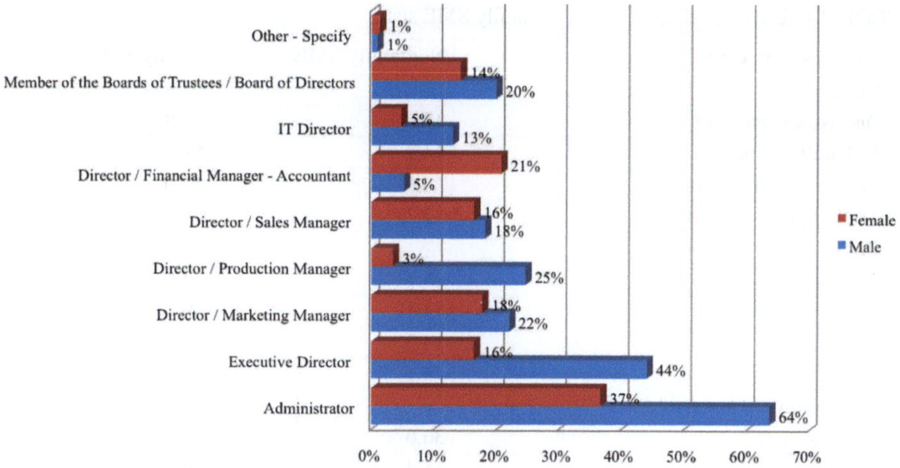

Fig. 4.3 Distribution of management positions among family members. In 64 % of the cases the administrator of a family business is a male family member

family members involved in family businesses does not differ much from nonfamily SMEs. The sample family-businesses have mostly 1–2 family members involved in the business. The main relationships present are mostly husband-wife and parents-children.

In terms of formal internal evaluations, the comparative analysis between family and nonfamily SMEs indicate that family businesses are more likely to use internal evaluation and control mechanisms such as financial plan, operational, customer satisfaction, employee satisfaction, and performance evaluation (Table 4.1).

In Romanian family firms strategic decisions are highly concentrated in the person of the owner-manager (61 % for strategic decisions—Fig. 4.4). Coupling this piece of information with the information regarding ownership (Fig. 4.1) which indicate that most of the respondent firms (44 %) have only one owner/associate we can argue that Romanian family firms pertain to the "controlling owner" generic type identified by the research literature.

"Family" as a forum for collective and collaborative decision-making and consultation is less involved in strategic and tactical decision-making. "Activation in the business" (having a formal leadership position or being formally active in the business) prevails over "family membership" as a criterion that gives the right to participate/be invited in the decision-making process (Fig. 4.4). Therefore family consultation on strategic decisions is done based on the criteria of involvement in the business and the position occupied in the business.

This rather restrained involvement of the family in Romanian family firms could be explained through the cultural context of the country. According to Hofstede analysis Romania scores high on Power distance dimension (score of 90) which means that people accept a hierarchical order in which everybody has a place and which needs no further justification. Hierarchy in an organization is seen as reflect-

Table 4.1 Business characteristics by family SME status

Business characteristics	Nonfamily SME	Family SME
Ownership		
One associate/owner	47.6	39.8
2+ Family owners	14.7	51.5
2+ Some family owners	4.6	3.0
2+ No family owners	33.2	5.6
# of involved family members		
0	36.7	3.0
1	44.4	49.8
2	14.3	37.7
3+	4.6	9.5
Relationship of involved family[a]		
Husband/wife	36.0	70.6
Children	15.4	39.8
Siblings	11.9	17.3
Parents	5.6	12.1
Family-business relationships (#)		
1	68.5	35.6
2	19.9	23.3
3	7.4	13.2
4	4.2	15.4
5	0.0	12.3
Family-business relationships (Type)[a]		
Employees	25.9	54.6
Majority stockholders	12.2	42.9
Influence business decisions	11.5	39.8
Management positions	22.4	53.3
Potential for child(ren) succession	39.2	51.1
Formal evaluations[a]		
Financial	75.5	87.5
Operational	40.6	48.1
Customer satisfaction	76.6	74.9
Employee satisfaction	47.2	57.1
Performance	66.4	66.2
Mean agreement (SD[1]-SA[5])		
Well-defined strategic plan	3.6	3.8
Appropriate communication	3.7	4.1
Clear long-term vision	3.6	3.9
Responds properly	3.4	3.8
Intentional sustainability	4.0	4.3
N	**286**	**231**
Management mechanisms[a]		
Organizational chart	64.3	56.7
Job descriptions	81.8	76.2

(continued)

Table 4.1 (continued)

Business characteristics	Nonfamily SME	Family SME
Weekly management meetings—operations	38.1	31.2
Regular management meetings—strategy	58.4	56.7
Partner written agreement	8.7	10.8
Annual member meetings	25.2	23.4
Directors/trustees meetings	27.3	21.7
Other	3.2	2.2
Control of management decisions[a]		
Target/objectives	68.2	64.5
Internal periodic evaluation	80.4	77.5
External periodic evaluation	14.3	20.8
Board of management/Directors/Trustees	26.2	31.2
Respondent company position		
Owner/associate	72.7	84.4
Member of the board of trustees/directors	2.5	1.3
CEO/Chairman/Managing Director	10.8	7.4
CFO/Finance Director/Controller	1.4	0.4
CIO/Technical Director	1.4	0.9
Manager	10.5	4.8
Other	0.7	0.9
Approximate revenue (2013)		
<100.000 EURO	12.2	15.2
100.001–200.000 EURO	15.4	15.2
200.001–500.000 EURO	31.8	33.8
500.001–1.000.000 EURO	18.2	17.8
>1 mil. EUR	22.4	18.2
Business sector		
Banking and financial services sector	1.8	0.4
Chemical	1.4	1.3
Construction/real estate	10.8	9.5
Food/agriculture	4.9	8.7
Industry/manufacturing	16.8	22.9
IT	6.3	1.7
Pharma/health	2.5	3.9
Energy/mining	2.1	2.2
Publishing/printing	1.8	0.9
R&D/new technology	0.7	18.2
Retail and wholesale trade	10.5	15.6
Services	23.8	0.4
Telecom/media	2.5	1.3
Tourism	2.1	5.6
Transport	3.9	7.4
Other—specify	8.4	0.4
N	**286**	**231**

[a]Multiple responses allowed

Fig. 4.4 Strategic decision-making process in Romanian family businesses. For 30 % of the family businesses the owner/s make strategic decision with people in leading positions

ing inherent inequalities, centralization is popular, subordinates expect to be told what to do.

The high degree of centrality in the person of the owner-manager can be observed at tactical level also (Fig. 4.5) him being the main character in the process of tactical decision-making. In this domain also the formal involvement in the business prevails over family membership as criterion for participation in decision-making at this level. Only for 16 % of the interviewed family businesses the family is collectively involved in the operational/tactical decisions (Fig. 4.5).

Nevertheless, the statistical analysis indicates that family-businesses who feature a trans-generational perspective (*have indicated that there is potential for the business to be taken over by children*) engage the family collectively in operational and tactical decisions more than those who don't feature the trans-generational perspective (Table 4.2).

When it comes to the future direction of the family business, Romanian entrepreneurs exhibit an internal focus, choosing to consult with people directly involved in the business (family members—62 % nonfamily leadership employees—38 %) rather than with external individuals such as specialists and consultants (24 %) which could bring a fresh perspective over the business (Fig. 4.6). This could have several reasons behind it: (1) the mistrust in an outsider's capability to really understand the business and answer its struggles in a meaningful way; (2) transparency issues and the low willingness to share information externally; and (3) the low willingness to pay for consulting services.

When analyzing the issue of outward focus of family businesses in Romania it seems that the number of family members involved in the business play a role. The statistic analysis indicate that family SMEs that have 3 or more family members involved in the business communicate more on the future plans of the business with

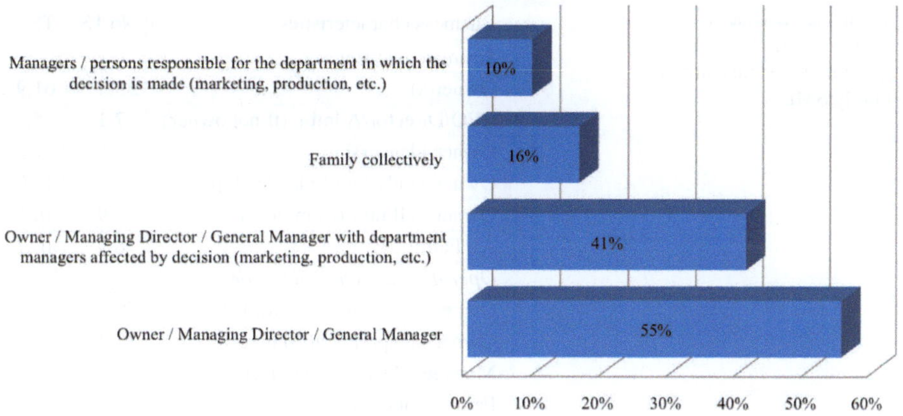

Fig. 4.5 How are operational/tactical decisions made in a Romanian family business. In 16 % of the cases operational and tactical decisions are made with a collective involvement of the family

actors outside the family circle—nonfamily leadership, business partners, specialists, and consultants, compared to those with fewer members of family involved (Table 4.3).

The trans-generational perspective is present in Romanian family businesses, 44 % of the responding firms will potentially be taken over by children (Fig. 4.2).

Succession at different levels is about to take place in many family businesses in Romania within the next 5 years with 42 % of the responding family businesses indicating that a member of the family will take over the ownership of the business (Fig. 4.7) and 63 % indicating that a succession in management will take place (Fig. 4.8). Outside succession is a less preferred option for family businesses in Romania (Fig. 4.9).

Nevertheless, there is a considerable percentage (25 %) of responding family businesses who do not know or did not think about a potential take over of the ownership of the company by a family member.

When it comes to actual planning of succession 71 % of respondent family businesses do not use a succession plan (Figs. 4.10 and 4.11), only 3 % have a methodology for evaluating potential successors and 6 % feature policies for entering the business. Nevertheless, 32 % confirm that they have already identified the person of the successor (Fig. 4.12). Although family businesses with a trans-generational perspective are more likely to implement a succession plan than those who don't poses this perspective, still this governance tool is in a draft or idea form (Table 4.2).

Communication plays a critical role in family business due to overlapping of roles. Although family businesses are characterized by a higher level of trust due to the nature of relationships between the persons involved, still communication contributes to maintaining and increasing the trust.

Table 4.2 Business characteristics by trans-generational status[a] among family SMEs

Business characteristics	No TS	TS
Strategic decisions[b]		
Owner(s)	59.3	61.9
CEO/Director/Admin. (if not owner)	7.1	5.1
Owner + leadership	22.1	37.3
Owner + only family leadership	6.2	11.0
Owner + all family employees	8.9	16.1
All Family	8.9	10.2
Operational/tactical decisions[b]		
Owner/Managing Director/GM	59.3	51.7
Owner + Department Managers	35.4	46.6
Managers/Department Heads	7.1	11.9
Family collectively	9.7	22.9
Family communication types		
Informal—as needed (Home)	29.2	29.7
Informal—as needed (Office)	12.4	14.4
Informal—regular (Home/Office)	41.6	46.6
Formal—regular	12.4	8.5
None	3.5	0.0
Other	0.9	0.9
Future plan communication[b]		
Family within SME	64.6	59.3
Family outside SME	12.4	17.8
Nonfamily leadership	37.2	38.1
Business partners	31.9	34.8
Specialists/external consultants	18.6	28.8
Family members	11.5	27.1
Friends/acquaintances	10.6	9.3
Succession plan implementation		
Written form	6.2	6.8
Draft form	2.7	6.8
Ideas	14.2	22.9
Do not yet use	77.9	63.6
N	**113**	**118**

[a]Respondents who selected response: "There is potential for the business to be taken over by children."
[b]Multiple responses allowed

Most of the information sharing regarding the life of the family business has an informal character (88 %) and the preferred medium for communication to take place is the office (58 %) (Fig. 4.13).

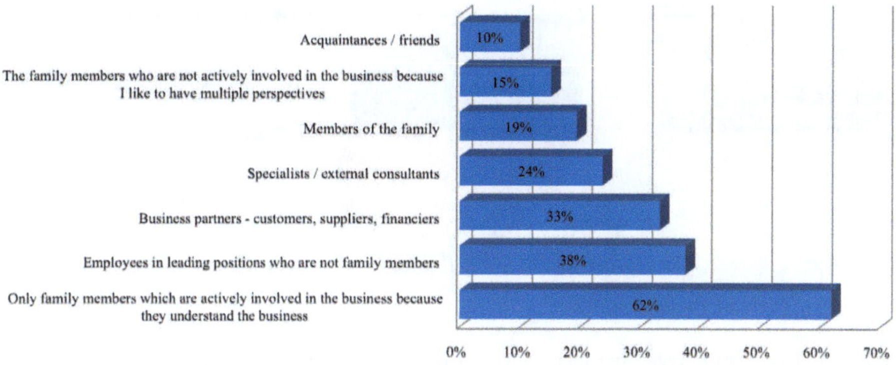

Fig. 4.6 Whom are consulted regarding future plans for the family businesses in Romania. In 19% of the cases members of the family are consulted regarding future plan for the family business

Table 4.3 Business characteristics by number of involved family members among family SMEs

	# Involved family members		
Business characteristics	1	2	3+
Family communication types			
Informal—as needed (Home)	33.9	28.7	4.6
Informal—as needed (Office)	13.0	12.6	22.7
Informal—regular (Home/Office)	40.9	48.3	50.0
Formal—regular	8.7	8.1	22.7
None	3.5	0.0	0.0
Other	0.0	2.3	0.0
Future plan communication[a]			
Family within SME	64.4	60.9	68.2
Family outside SME	14.8	12.6	13.6
Nonfamily leadership	35.7	33.3	50.0
Business partners	29.6	36.8	50.0
Specialists/external consultants	16.5	28.7	45.5
Family members	18.3	23.0	18.2
Friends/acquaintances	8.7	13.8	4.6
N	**115**	**87**	**22**

[a]Multiple responses allowed

4.8 Conclusions and Further Research

The present nation wide study was undertaken with the main objective of identifying family-businesses among other SMEs in Romania and their particular way of functioning. Therefore it was designed as an exploratory descriptive study that would yield baseline research that not even official institutions in Romania poses. Due to the lack of information regarding this type of business in Romania, the

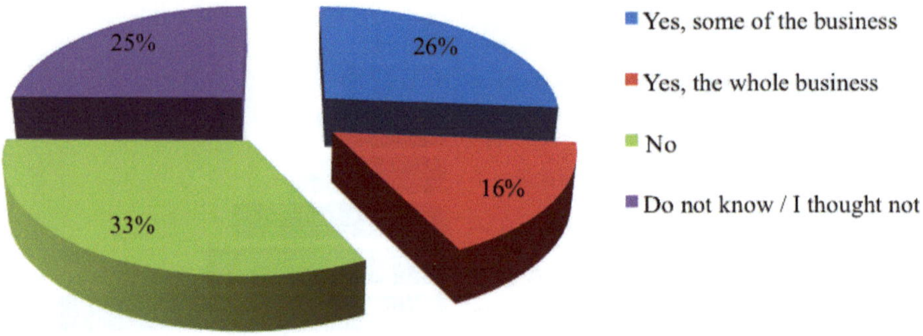

Fig. 4.7 Expectation regarding take over of a family member in the next 5 years. 16 % of the respondents are expecting that the whole business will be taken over by a family member in the next 5 years

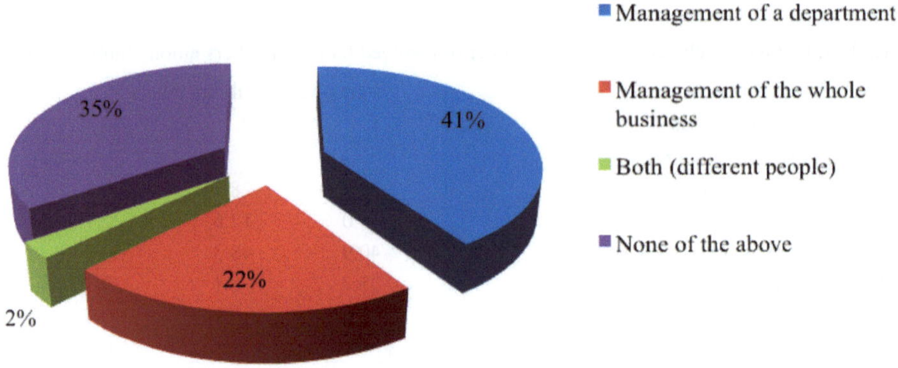

Fig. 4.8 Expectation regarding take over managing responsibility by a family member in the next 5 years. 41 % of respondents consider that in the next 5 years a family member will take over the management of a department of the business

identification of basic characteristics was critical in order to provide the background for further research .

At a first level of analysis Romanian family businesses seem to behave in many ways like a nonfamily SME. Our study didn't identify considerable differences in income level, industry preferences, internal control mechanism, or even number of family members involved in the business (Fig. 4.14).

Family businesses in Romania are closely held with a high concentration of decision-making in the person of the owner-manager both at strategic and at tactic levels. The forms and mechanisms of governance specific to this breed are present in an incipient stage among Romanian family businesses. That is, succession plans, family protocols/constitutions, and board of directors are less prevalent in managing the business.

The trans-generational perspective (desire, intention, and potential for the business to be passed to the next generation) is present among family businesses in

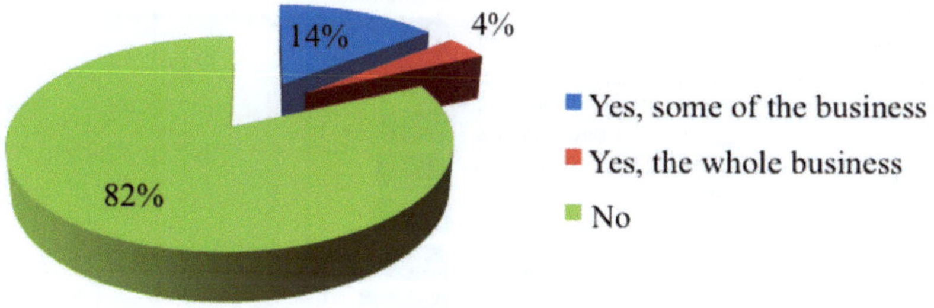

Fig. 4.9 Expectation regarding ownership take over by a person outside the family in the next 5 years. 4 % of the respondents expect that the whole business would be taken over by a person outside the family

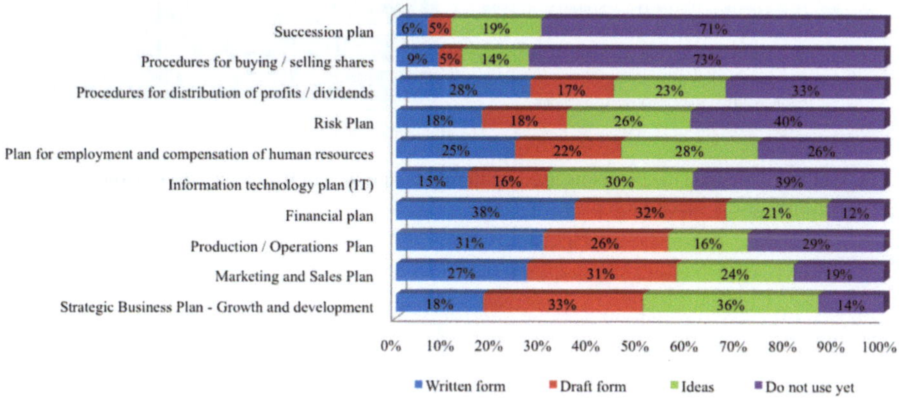

Fig. 4.10 Existence and format of planning tools in the family businesses. 71 % of respondent family businesses do not use a succession plan

Romania but it is not supported by an actual implementation of succession tools although many of the responding family businesses expect to experience succession of some kind in the next 5 years.

Romanian family businesses are characterized by a rather restrained involvement of the family in the life of the business at strategic and tactic level, participation in the decision-making process is allowed based on position in the business not necessary membership in the family.

Although exploratory and descriptive in nature this research raises interesting questions that are worth pursuing in future research endeavors. The analysis of Romanian family businesses can be further developed by investigating and evaluating the actual influence of the family on the business, the reasons for a seemingly restrained involvement of the family in the life of the business based on family membership, the influence of the national culture on the relationship dynamics within the universe of Romanian family business, the factors influencing the trans-generational perspective, and the impact of trans-generational perspective on business performance.

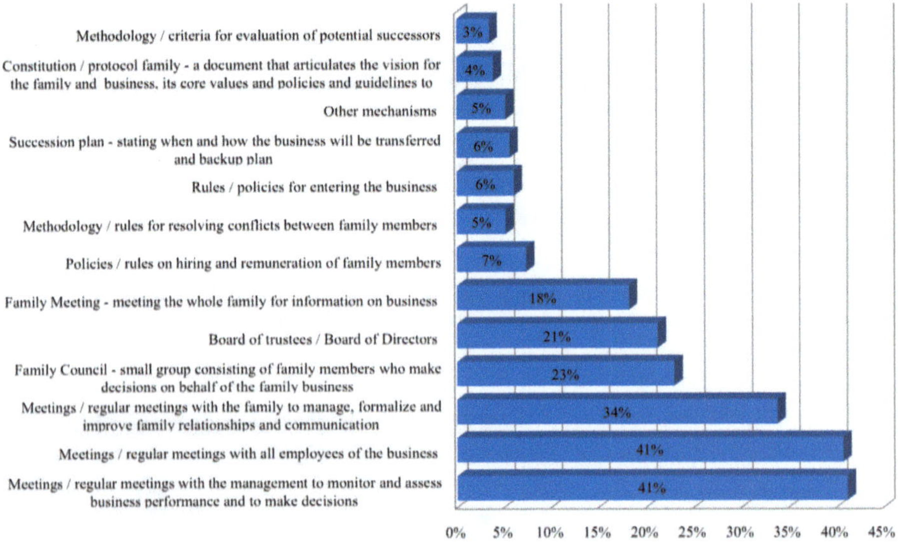

Fig. 4.11 Governance mechanisms used by family businesses in Romania. 6 % of Romanian family businesses use a succession plan

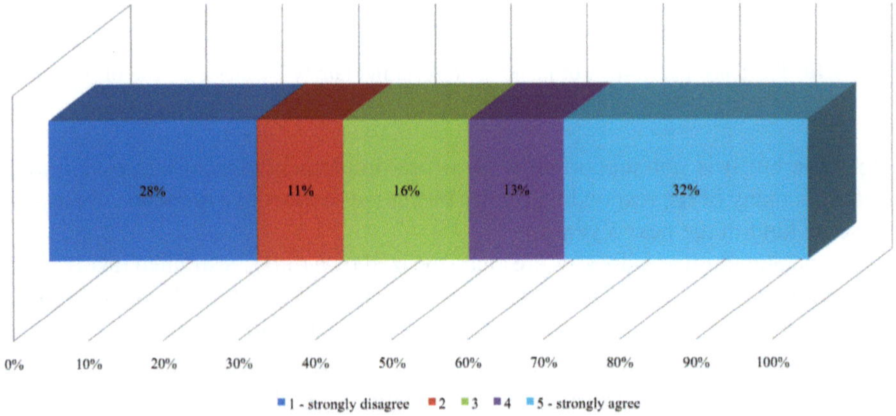

Fig. 4.12 The person who will take over the business when the current owner/manager retires has already been identified. 32 % of the respondents strongly agree with the statement

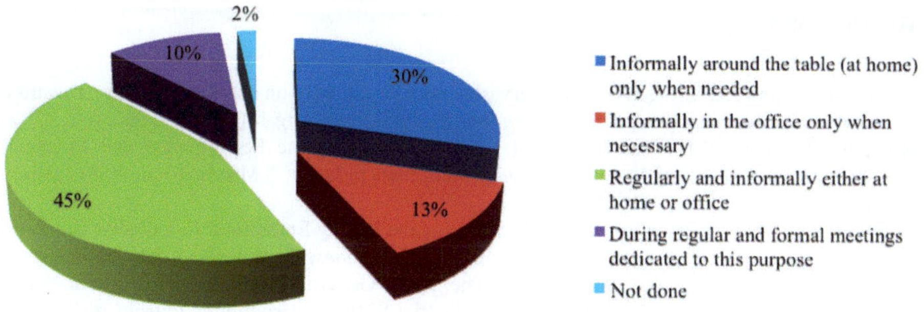

Fig. 4.13 Informing the family about the situation and direction of the business

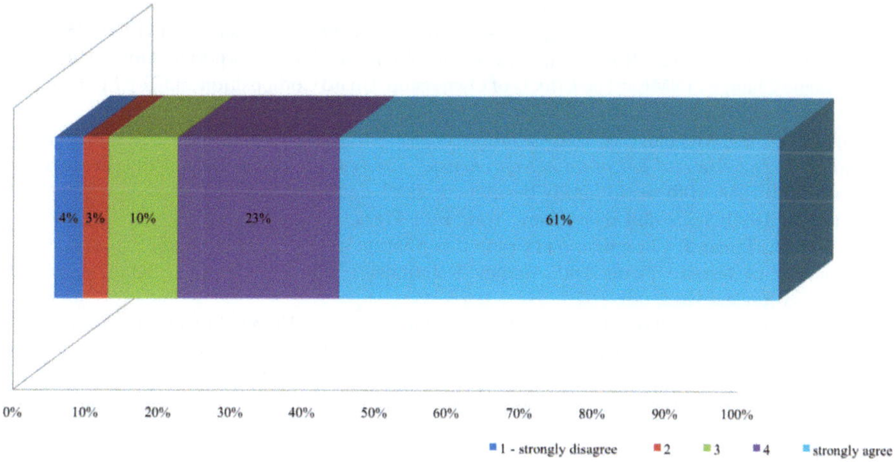

Fig. 4.14 Members of the family receive sufficient information on business activity. 61 % of respondents strongly agree that members of the family receive sufficient information on business activity

References

Aldrich, H.E., and J.E. Cliff. 2003. The pervasive effects of family on entrepreneurship: Toward a family embeddedness perspective. *Journal of Business Venturing* 18(5): 573–596.

Allouche, J., et al. 2015. The Impact of Family Control on the Performance and Financial Characteristics of Family Versus Nonfamily Businesses in Japan: A Matched-Pair Investigation. *Family Business Review* 21(4): 315–330.

Basco, R., and M.J. Perez Rodriguez. 2009. Studying the Family Enterprise Holistically: Evidence for Integrated Family and Business Systems. *Family Business Review* 22(1): 82–95.

Ben Hamad, Salah, and Afef Karoui. 2011. The SMEs Governance Mechanisms Practices and Financial Performance: Case of Tunisian Industrial SMEs. *International Journal of Business and Management* 6(7).

Bennedsen, M., Gonzalez, F.P., and Wolfenzon, D. 2010. The Governance of family firms, in corporate governance. In *A synthesis of theory, research, and practice*, eds. H.K. Baker, and R. Anderson. Hoboken, NJ, USA: Wiley. doi: 10.1002/9781118258439.ch19.

Bloom, N., and J.V. Reenen. 2007. Measuring and explaining management practices across firms and countries. *The Quarterly Journal of Economics*.

Bracci, E., and Vagnoni, E. 2011. *Understanding small family business succession in a knowledge management perspective*. http://papers.ssrn.com/sol3/papers.cfm?abstract_id=1776593.

Brunninge, Olof, Mattias Nordqvist, and Johan Wiklund. 2007. Corporate Governance and Strategic Change in SMEs: The Effects of Ownership, Board Composition and Top Management Teams. *Small Business Economics* 29(3): 295–308.

Brunninge, O., and Melander, A. 2010. *Familiness and entrepreneurship in the context of a mature industry: The rise and fall of an entrepreneurial family firm*. MoDo 1872–1990. Proceedings from the IFERA 10th world family business research conference in Lancaster.

Chandler, A. 1990. *Scale and scope*. New York: Free Press.

Chua, Jess H., James J. Chrisman, and Pramodita Sharma. 2003. Succession and Nonsuccession Concerns of Family Firms and Agency Relationship with Nonfamily Managers. *Family Business Review* 16(2): 89–107.

Claessens, Stijn, et al. 2002. Disentangling the Incentive and Entrenchment Effects of Large Shareholdings. *The Journal of Finance* 57(6): 2741–2771.

Coles, Jerilyn W., Victoria B. McWilliams, and Nilanjan Sen. 2001. An Examination of the Relationship of Governance Mechanisms to Performance. *Journal of Management* 27(1): 23–50.

Corbetta, G., and C.A. Salvato. 2004. The board of directors in family firms: One size fits all? *Family Business Review* 17(2): 119. ABI/INFORM Global.

Cowling, Marc. 2003. Productivity and Corporate Governance in Smaller Firms. *Small Business Economics* 20(4): 335–344.

Davis, James H., F. David Schoorman, and Lex Donaldson. 1997. Toward a Stewardship Theory of Management. *Academy of Management Review* 22(1): 20–47.

De Massis, Alfredo, Jess H. Chua, and James J. Chrisman. 2008. Factors Preventing Intra-Family Succession. *Family Business Review* 21(2): 183–199.

Demsetz, Harold, and Belen Villalonga. 2001. Ownership Structure and Corporate Performance. *Journal of Corporate Finance* 7(3): 209–233.

Dyer, W. Gibb. 2006. Examining the 'Family Effect' on Firm Performance. *Family Business Review* 19(4): 253–273.

Edward, G., E.G. Rogoff, and R.K. Heck. 2003. Evolving research in entrepreneurship and family business: Recognizing family as the oxygen that feeds the fire of entrepreneurship. *Journal of Business Venturing* 18(2003): 559–566.

Faccio, Mara, Larry H.P. Lang, and Leslie Young. 2001. Dividends and Expropriation. *American Economic Review* 9(1): 54–78.

Freiling, Jörg, and Steffen Grossmann. 2014. Characteristics and Managerial Behaviour of German Family Businesses.pdf. *ERENET Profile* IX(1): 3–10.

Gabrielsson, Jonas, and Morten Huse. 2005. Outside Directors in SME Boards: A Call for Theoretical Reflections. *Corporate Board: Role, Duties & Composition* 1(1): 28–37.

Gedajlovic, Eric, Michael H. Lubatkin, and William S. Schulze. 2004. Crossing the Threshold from Founder Management to Professional Management: A Governance Perspective. *Journal of Management Studies* 41(5): 899–912.

Gedajlovic, Eric, Michael H. Lubatkin, and William S. Schulze. 2004. Crossing the Threshold from Founder Management to Professional Management: A Governance Perspective. *Journal of Management Studies* 41(5): 899–912.

Haalien, L., and Huse, M. 2005. *Board of directors in Norwegian family businesses. Results from the value creating board surveys*. Research Report 7/2005 ISSN: 0803-2610.

Habbershon, T.G., M. Williams, and I.C. MacMillan. 2003. A unified systems perspective of family firm performance. *Journal of Business Venturing* 18(4): 451–465.

Howorth, C., et al. 2010. Family Firm Diversity and Development: An Introduction. *International Small Business Journal* 28(5): 437–451.

Hoy, F., and P. Sharma. 2010. *Entrepreneurial family firms*. Upper Saddle River, NJ: Pearson Prentice Hall.

Huse, Morten. 2000. Boards of Directors in SMEs: A Review and Research Agenda. *Entrepreneurship & Regional Development* 12(4): 271–290.

Jensen, Michael, and William Meckling. 1990. Theory of the Firm: Managerial Behavior, Agency Costs and Ownership Structure. *Smith, clifford w. Jr., The Modern Theory of Corporate Finance, McGraw-Hill*: 82–134.

Kellermanns, Franz, W., Kimberly A. Eddleston, Tim Barnett, and Allison Pearson. 2008. An Exploratory Study of Family Member Characteristics and Involvement: Effects on Entrepreneurial Behavior in the Family Firm. *Family Business Review* 21(1): 1–14.

Klein, S.B. 2010. Corporate Governance, family business complexity and succession. In "*Transfer of Ownership în Private Business-European Experiences*" international conference. Stockholm, Sweden.

La Porta, Rafael, et al. 2000. Investor Protection and Corporate Governance. *Journal of Financial Economics* 58(1): 3–27.

Litz, Reginald A. 2008. Two Sides of a One-Sided Phenomenon: Conceptualizing the Family Business and Business Family as a Möbius Strip. *Family Business Review* 21(3): 217–236.

Maher, Maria, and Thomas Andersson. 1999. *Corporate Governance: Effects on Firm Performance and Economic Growth*. OECD.

Mazzi, Chiara. 2011. Family Business and Financial Performance: Current State of Knowledge and Future Research Challenges. *Journal of Family Business Strategy* 2(3): 166–181.

Miladi, Abdelmoula Inès. 2014. Governance for SMEs: Influence of Leader on Organizational Culture. *International Strategic Management Review* 2(1): 21–30.

Miller, Danny, and I. Le Breton-Miller. 2006. Family Governance and Firm Performance: Agency, Stewardship, and Capabilities. *Family Business Review* 19(1): 73–87.

Miller, Danny, et al. 2007. Are Family Firms Really Superior Performers? *Journal of Corporate Finance* 13(5): 829–858.

Pardo-del-Val, Manuela. 2009. Succession in Family Firms from a Multistaged Perspective. *International Entrepreneurship and Management Journal* 5(2): 165–179.

Romanian National Office for Commerce. 2013. *White charter of Romanian IMMs*. Bucharest. http://ittrends.ro/wp-content/uploads/2013/08/Prezentare-carta-alba-a-imm-urilor-din-romania-2013.pdf. Accessed 18 July 2013.

SBA Fact Sheet Romania. European Commission, 2013.

Shleifer, A., and R.W. Vishny. 1997. A survey of corporate governance. *The Journal of Finance* 52: 737–783. doi: 10.1111/j.1540-6261.1997.

Szabo, Z.K., and Szabo, K.D. 2014. *Family business in Romania*. Final Workshop Report on "Family Businesses and SMEs in the Black Sea Economic Cooperation Region" organized by Organization of the Black Sea Economic Cooperation (BSEC) and Konrad-Adenauer-Stiftung (KAS) 7–9 October 2014. Istanbul, Turkey, 163.

Taylor, P. 2013. Effects of corporate governance mechanisms on the performance of publicly traded SMEs in developing economies. *International Journal of Economics, Commerce and Management*, 1(1): 2013. Available at SSRN: https://ssrn.com/abstract=2381213.

Vaduva, S. 2004. *Entrepreneurship: Applied practices in Romania and other transitional nations*. Bucharest: Editura Economica. ISBN 973-590-978-2.

Vaduva, S., L. Vaduva, I. Fotea, and S. Fotea. 2011. *Afaceri de familie: cum să îţi transformi familia dintr-o povară într-o comoară*, 1st ed. Oradea, Romania: Editura Universitatii Emanuel din Oradea.

Ward, J.L. 2004. How governing family businesses is different. In *Mastering global corporate governance*, eds. Ulrich Steger, Peter Lorange, Fred Neubauer, John L. Ward, and Bill George. Wiley.

Zahra, S.A., J.C. Hayton, and C. Salvato. 2004. Entrepreneurship in family vs. non-family firms: A resource-based analysis of the effect of organizational culture. Entrepreneurship Theory and Practice 28: 363–381. doi: 10.1111/j.1540-6520.2004.00051.

Chapter 5
The Power of Multinational Companies in a Global World: The Focus of Corporate Governance and Its Impact on Business Ethics

José G. Vargas-Hernández

Abstract The aim of this work is to identify the conditions of globalization that have led to suppose that transnational corporations are economic agents that negatively impact on business ethics from the perspective of corporate governance. The method of study was based on a thorough theoretical and literature review and the results obtained confirm the negative impact, since the use of corporate social responsibility programs are strategies to increase profits and global power rather than to achieve social impact.

Keywords Transnational firms • Business ethics • Globalization • Corporate governance • Corporate social responsibility

JEL Classification D43F02 • F23 • M14

5.1 Introduction

History has been a determining factor in the evolution of economic systems between nations, as all the nations in the world can turn to patterns that project and define their interests in the future.

These actors have been diverse and their intervention within the economic system has been remarkable, the degree of influence on economic policies creating a diffusion of authority and the power centers of society.

At the beginning, the main actor was the nation-state. However, because of capitalism and globalization phenomena, actors from the private sector, such as transnational

---

J.G. Vargas-Hernández, Ph.D. (✉)
University Center for Economic and Managerial Sciences, University of Guadalajara, Guadalajara, México
e-mail: jvargas2006@gmail.com

S. Vaduva et al. (eds.), *Business Ethics and Leadership from an Eastern European, Transdisciplinary Context*, DOI 10.1007/978-3-319-45186-2_5

corporations, have had a significant intervention. This was done mainly by the conditions that the current economic system has given them to increase their power, such as the opening of trade markets, cross-border investment flows, changing financial schemes, development asymmetries between nations, and the evolution of communications networks. So now, the presence and mastery of various companies of this size have led to a significant impact on global society.

Therefore, the present study aims to identify the conditions of globalization which now have led the TNCs to be considered power actors in the international system, in order to understand how this behavior has affected business ethics and the welfare of society through a corporate governance approach.

Content is integrated as follows: in the first instance, there is an account of the background that gave rise to the phenomenon of globalization from the economic point of view. This is done in order to understand how transnational corporations have been key players in the private sector and even the political sphere, derived from their influence and power over various nations in the world. Secondly, this chapter shapes the problem to be studied, using statistics and data on the presence of these companies in the global context over the last 20 years to find the social impact that transnational corporations have developed because of their global power. Later, these phenomena are described from the perspective of Global Governance regulation, starting from the external environment, using ethics as the key variable to understand the relationship of transnational corporations to the society of their host country.

Finally, the results confirm the proposed course, since the impact of transnational corporations on society is negative, when it can be inferred that the goals of the owners along with those of the agents are to obtain greater wealth, to which end they opportunistically make use of ethics and social programs. As such, they consolidate their presence in the global environment and generate dependence for their receiving states that have been unable to overcome the strategic actions and social impact developed by transnational corporations.

5.2 Background of the Problem

Historically, it was the breakdown of the bipolar East–west balance after the fall of the Berlin Wall that set the tone of the "New World Order." Thus, the dominance of capitalism ushered in a period of great turmoil, even though, after the toppling of the communist system, the world was reminded of the United States. In 1944, the country embodied, through the Treaty of Bretton Woods, to the affected nations of Europe and beyond the image of a nation committed to ending authoritarianism and economic uncertainty around the world.

Initially, the replacement of the gold standard for the dollar standard was presented, and, to regulate the change, the International Monetary Fund (IMF) was created, as well as the World Bank (WB), in order to cover the war disasters, and the General Agreement on Tariffs and Trade (GATT), leading to the proliferation of free trade areas (Aranda 2008). The economic agreement described was spearheaded by developed countries, which committed to check the validity of the capitalist system, with developing countries "forced" to join gradually, which led to the phenomenon of Economic Globalization.

From the economic point of view, authors such as Friedman (1970) emphasize that globalization is a phenomenon characterized by technological innovation and its appearance in the world has been consolidated in stages. Although some scholars of the phenomenon cite the Industrial Revolution as the event that gave rise to it, most state that consolidation occurred with a trade integration process dating from just about 30 years ago (Carbaugh 2005). It was the 1990s when globalization accelerated through the privatization of the public assets. Privatization is the action in which a state sells public property, putting it in the hands of the free market (Eun 2007a, b). While privatization can be seen from different perspectives, it is a clear example of how this phenomenon transcends borders, contracting the national control to the economic benefits provided by foreign corporations.

Therefore, the presence of multinational companies in the private sector was quick to follow, because the conditions of global markets represent great improvement opportunities. It allowed MNCs to install their production complexes anywhere in the world, being comparatively advantageous to use resources and production factors, while in their countries of origin the same employers would not be allowed to minimize costs to consolidate scale productions. Another form of globalization promoted by multinational companies is foreign direct investment, action that over the years has driven economic growth in underdeveloped economies through job creation and technology transfer.

While it can be inferred that transnational corporations have been a private actor that has driven the economic growth of most nations in the world, the same can be said of the development of global business. Not all companies in the world have the capacity, resources, or adequate instruments for the system to act in their favor, in the detriment to the creation of competitive companies, that being due, largely, to transnational corporations seeking to meet their own private gains by leveraging market asymmetries and forgetting their social origin. Consequently, and due to the rapid changes that occurred after globalization, the reliability and the positive impact of the system toward the behavior and ethics of multinational companies has been critically questioned.

5.3 Definition of the Problem

The distinguishing feature of transnational corporations, compared to multinational companies, is that the former have subsidiaries in different parts of the world without keeping a parent or residence, as it is the case with multinationals. For the purposes of this research, we will focus on transnational corporations, TNCs, since, through their nature and structure, they have greater freedom to develop on the global market, to the extent that the combined sales of the top 200 corporations in the world are much larger than a quarter of the world's economic activity (Anderson 2005).

These companies developed a capacity of influencing the decisions or policies governments create, limiting the control of formal institutions in the absence of regulatory schemes. TNCs induce the dependence of host countries in exchange for the economic benefits, even if privately; TNCs, like any other businesses, seek to maximize their individual benefit, in most cases, by the exploitation of the resources of the host country. This leads us to ask ourselves the following question and research issue: how has the power of transnational corporations, supported by the economic changes of globalization, managed to influence business ethics?

The importance of this research consists in discovering the social impact transferred by TNCs on business ethics and how they have been (mis)representing themselves and the phenomenon of globalization to the individualistic nature of the capitalist system. As such, we are reminded of the theoretical underpinnings of welfare economics, as described by Friedman in 1970, "... the responsibility of the executive is to manage the business according to its owners, who generally want as much money as possible, not to mention compliance of the basic rules of society established both in law and those embodied in ethical custom."

5.4 Justification

The economic power of transnational corporations is undisputed. In this respect, we emphasize some facts: in 2000, an average of 40,000 transnational companies identified by the Global Policy Forum that had more than 250,000 international subsidiaries (Anderson 2005). In 2008, the United Nations Conference on Trade and Development noted the existence of an average of 79,000 TNCs with over 790,000 affiliates (UNCTAD 2008), suggesting an increase of almost 50 % in just 8 years, highlighting the involvement of oil companies, investment banking, and manufacturing.

Multiple authors mention how these companies often own greater economies than those achieved by some countries. For example, by 2000 it was estimated that of the 100 largest economies in the world, 51 are global corporations and only 49 are countries (Anderson 2005). By 2009 there were 44 companies in the top 100, however, their position in the ranking had significantly improved, as in the case of Wal-Mart, which held position 22, being the company with more economic influence than even nations like Sweden, Saudi Arabia, and Venezuela (Malnight 2010).

The major transnational companies are from different sectors and nationalities, such as, mainly, American, Japanese, German, and English, to name a few. Although one should think that the TNCs' management is diverse in its origins, the results point to a kind of being unique that derives from the global environment in which they developed. This condition has allowed them to lower any initial barriers and reach different corners of the world, using their power to achieve maximum benefits without abusing the social impact that such measures may cause.

That is, since the beginning it was hoped that the phenomenon of economic globalization would generate social cohesion through the elimination of borders that enclose ideologies and the possibility of having more resources, technological and operational capabilities toward the rapid flow of information. However, the public has discovered that, to the contrary, there is a remarkable social segregation perceived at the macro level by the presence of strong asymmetries or market failures, with TNCs considered the key actors for the emergence of such behavior.

For example, in the financial sector, banks boast new global banking facilities, because the 31 largest banks in the world hold assets totaling $10.4 billion and carry out private sales of more than $800 million. Without considering the difficulties that most of the world's population face in obtaining a small loan. About 4.8 billion to 5.6 million people in the world still live in countries where the average GDP per capita is less than 1000 dollars a year, and only a few of these people have access to credit from transnational banks (Anderson 2005).

5.5 Theoretical Assumption

The phenomenon of economic globalization created a negative impact on society when transferring great economic power to TNCs. The assumption of this chapter considers that, as catalysts of such power, the mandated agents of the owners controlling these corporations take business ethics as an opportunistic means to obtain higher individual profits.

5.5.1 The Behavior of Transnational Corporations in the Context of Globalization and the Impact They Have on Society

The reality in today's economies is that there is no longer the need to promote an efficient allocation of natural and human resources in a way that is beneficial to everyone in the society. Rather, so far transnational corporations and the insatiable desire of their owners to make money and increase market position have driven the economy. TRNs conceal this desire via job creation and growth of national income in recipient countries (Jobson 2006).

Therefore, Table 5.1 reveals a comparison of the effects caused by economic globalization, its impact on TNCs, and their beneficial or detrimental drive of society.

As can be corroborated by the results of Table 5.1, the globalization from the economic environment has been a complex phenomenon, the net result of many different forces, some integrative and others disintegrative, mainly in the area where TNCs operate.

So on the one hand there is a convergence trend, when effects such as FDI boost the host country's labor activity. On the other hand, they may lead to segregation, when resources are exploited, or the competitiveness of local producers is limited, or in the way that these companies develop strategies based on economies of scope

Table 5.1 Effect of economic globalization, ETNs' impact, and social impact in the host country

Effect of globalization	Impact for ETNs	Social impact in host country
Opening of commercial markets	Developing strategies of intra industrial trade (IIT, commercial interactions between subsidiaries)	Intervention of oligopolistic structures that limit competition from small producers
	Trade regulations imposed by the WTO have limited the ability of governments of less industrialized countries to modify the behavior of TNCs operating in their territories	Influence on local trade policies
	Two-thirds of the world trade is carried out by transnational corporations and half of that trade is done via IIT (Díaz n.d.)	
Foreign direct investment (FDI)	Are a source of FDI and its main growth has led major developing economies such as China and India	Creation of jobs. Economic spill over in the host country
	In 2006, global FDI flows reached, according to preliminary estimates	Exploitation of natural resources and exploitation of cheap labor
	1.23 billion, representing an increase of 34 % over the previous year (CEPAL 2006)	
Changes in financial schemes	Diversification of risks associated with changes in domestic rates and interest rates	Generation of competitive disadvantage to local producer
	Development of the carry trade and arbitrage of change	Development of footloose capital
	Decreasing tax burden	
Evolution of communications network	Fast and efficient access to different regions in the world	Development conditional to economic growth in the host country
	Improve interactions with customers	

Source: Own elaboration

(interaction between subsidiaries), leading to deficiencies in the market structure. The development of global oligopolies generates dissemination of ethical principles in order to maximize their profits. Therefore, TNCs' practices tend to converge to local corporate globalization model.

5.6 Who Regulates Transnational Corporations?

As it was mentioned before, the ETNs have developed a major economic power, derived from the conditions created by globalization and their own intervention in the development of economic policies of the less developed nations for their very own particular benefit, thus becoming actors with an impact on society. The question that arises is who and what are the mechanisms that regulate them?

In 1999, the Organization for Economic Cooperation and Development (OECD) introduced The Principles of Corporate Governance. These precepts are based on the agency theory proposed by Ross in 1973.

Unlike it was suggested by neoclassical economics, not all agents involved in the market have complete information, i.e., know the state of technology, factor costs, quality of goods, and market prices. It is appropriate to acknowledge that since markets are not perfect, profit making largely depends on the agents' ability to benefit from the information, which is generally incomplete and asymmetric between agents, which may lead to market failures. This can be defined as Corporate Governance; the institutional, legal, and economic context within which the distribution of control rights and cash flows to shareholders, managers, and other stakeholders of the company takes place (Eun 2007a, b).

That is why, while corporate governance, from a conventional perspective, seeks to control, it does not reflect accurately the conflicts of interest between owners, managers, workers, and consumers. Thus, corporate governance must be interpreted in two areas: internal—through the problems that arise when the agent breaks the mandate of the owners or shareholders to generate greater economic benefits for the company in compliance with a particular interest—and external, as the impact of the organization on the global market trends, local politics, or lobbyists (Denis 2003).

The mechanisms shareholders should use internally to control the agent are known as "monitoring costs" and may refer to contracts or equity incentives. However, there is a gap in how the external environment as a part of corporate governance has evaluated and created means of control for companies, especially large corporations, to address economic trends affecting its stability, while on the global level (emphasizing the nature of TNCs) they have not defined the mechanisms to control the socially detrimental effects of these corporations.

Therefore, self-regulation is the key factor to understanding the degree of power that economic units have currently reached through the reframing of their activities and the strategic use of the gaps created by the governments of the states in which they operate. For instance, one of the strategies employed by TNCs has been the incorporation of, or the establishment of, nongovernmental organizations (NGOs), and the cooperation with organizations of civil society, creating social interest groups that advocate common goals to fulfill social needs, with the sole purpose of counteracting the caused damage.

Working with common goals to maintain order and the human security of a nation, TNCs are reincorporating the ethical principles that have given rise to social welfare, taking advantage of the fact that the objective of any state's political system is to support the growth and consolidation of its own causes, even at the expense of incorporating various international links. That is, states must not forget that TNCs, through these tasks, will continue to seek international links through trade and foreign investment, to sustain their economic position. Only now, these activities are framed by social causes, such as the cultural and academic exchange strengthening internal, cultural, and educational institutions.

5.7 The Ethical Implications for TNCs

Based on the study of TNCs, a prominent element in their external environment is the interest groups, formed at the base by a hierarchical society of the host country, who were harmed or who benefited from the decisions made by companies' officials. With this, ethics is used for a turn effect, if agents fail to respect the rules and moral principles of the society in question. Therefore, it can be inferred that ethics is part of governance, because the morality of the agent, shareholders, and board members can generate responsible practices with dual purpose, where on the one hand shareholders gain economic benefits and the process gives back to the society through good deeds, on the other.

In order to comply with the ethical principles of corporate governance, the ETNs have developed codes of ethics; the principles were created with the introduction of the Sarbanes-Oxley Act in 2002 to monitor US companies listed on the stock market and protect investors (Eun 2007a, b). Since then the codes of ethics were identified as a separate written document, provisioned by the owners to a previous study of the environment, in order to be adopted on a voluntary basis and containing the ethical standards to guide the agent and the employee to correct behavior in national and international contexts (Schwartz 2002).

Ideally, it could establish global codes of ethics; these codes feature regional characteristics such as conditions for compliance, formal rules set by legislation or even informal rules, cultural or traditional. These codes leave transnational corporations the freedom to pursue particular strategies for the continued growth of the company within the recipient country.

Once one understands TNCs' behavior in the global environment, and the key concepts that define ethical practices, one can make use of them in order to understand the strategies—according to the economic conditions of the system—TNCs can incorporate, using their power and position to develop positive overall impact on society. Table 5.2 displays the social practices based on ethical principles that helped the top five world corporations world improve their image and global presence. International Monetary Fund originally published this list in 2010; the information was extracted from companies' web pages.

5.8 Social Responsibility and Corporate Citizenship. Social Contribution or Economic Expansion Strategies?

The actions reviewed in the previous table can highlight social responsibility practices and their contribution to corporate citizenship. Both have proved positive strategies for expansion and dominance for many companies with global features. On the one hand, social responsibility in most definitions is assumed as normative, also regarding legal obligations. That is, it claims to be scrupulously following the legal framework, so that social responsibility would be, essentially, a series of voluntary agreements that the company is committed to meet and which generate benefit for the company (Hernández 2008).

Table 5.2 Examples of transnational social work

Transnational	Sector	Social work at global level
Wal-Mart Stores	Retail food sales	Environmental sustainability
		Hunger and nutrition
		Women's economic empowerment
		Veterans and military families
		Diversity and inclusion
		Ethical sources
Royal Dutch Shell	Oil	Shell eco-marathons
		Our neighbors
		Social investment
		Nigeria
Exxon Mobil	Oil	Exxon Mobil Foundation
		Malaria
		Mathematics and Science
		Economic opportunities for women
		Human rights
		Corporate citizenship
Toyota Motor	Automotive	CSR initiatives
		Environmental responsibility
		Corporate citizenship
ING Group	Insurance	Sustainability policy
		Social responsibility

Source: Own elaboration

As for corporate citizenship, it is a term created by Klaus Schwab, founder of the World Economic Forum, in order for companies to generate organizational social support to regions with lower incomes. However, the term was coined by TNCs, with basic economic purposes in mind, as a society with poor or low income is a society that does not consume. Therefore, the contributions those TNCs have made for social purposes lead to the generation of new consumers.

Therefore, currently many researchers in the field have struggled to define such concepts, as both partly emanate from the intention of doing something for the benefit of a vulnerable social group, yet their ends, as already demonstrated, go beyond compliance. Companies that develop social programs have been used as mechanisms to achieve better strategic and economic position as the ideal way to reduce the tax burden, turning such actions into an international marketing trend.

Thus social responsibility and corporate citizenship continue to be but a strategic leap forward in the model of economic relations between enterprises and society, with which, showing the "human face of global market" mentioned by Kofi Annan, the TNCs have been able to convince everyone of the benefits of economic globalization (Ramiro 2009).

5.9 Analysis of Results

It is easy to describe the solution to social conflicts generated by polarization derived from the free market system with words like cooperation or integration, which are only the correct key principles, not the solutions to the problems our world faces today. However, the difficulty to generate important changes for the benefit of a better society lies in the ability to achieve collective action and widespread interest. This resulted largely due to the lack of own collective values or ethical principles.

Globalization thus is no longer a phenomenon to channel the integration, welfare, and prestige demanded by any state at global level, as it omits many principles based on the community. It is also faced with great difficulty because of some problems, such as conflicts over resources like water and fossil fuels. These generate more harm for the environment every day, a progressive increase in overpopulation, the excessive growth of poverty, and an international system that provides for the individual interests of private entities gains greater power each day, as is the case of TNCs.

As shown throughout the present work, the initial assumption we raised is met, thus it can be said that the effects of the phenomenon of globalization have caused a negative impact on society by being immersed in activities that TNCs develop daily for the sake of their own benefit. Thus, three key results can be inferred:

(a) The power of TNCs stems from its false defense of the free market system, essentially constituted by social programs that aim to create a solid mask to improve their public image. However, its real face is constituted by economic strategies that generate global structures benevolent to their daily particular activity allowing them to extend their influence over governments and international institutions, including through reducing their tax burdens.

(b) The ETNs usually influence the handling of international policies to promote their profit-oriented activities within international organizations and emerging economies, whose economic conditions in most cases are worse than those of such entities generating actions that hurt the country's society receptors, such as:
   1. Exploitation of natural resources.
   2. Capital pintails (short-term investments that exploit resources of a host country and then move to another country).
   3. Economy scope-based strategies (intra-industry trade between subsidiaries).
   4. Creation of oligopolistic market structures.

(c) The behavior of self-regulation and greed-driven practices of agents has repeatedly shown concern only for their benefit and not the betterment of society, as stipulated in the corporate governance model based on the agency theory. Therefore, the laws and agreements created for its regulation are still for the exclusive use of the well-being of those entities.

5.10 Conclusions and Recommendations

Despite the TNCs appetite for profit regardless of the cost, it must be recognized that the ETNs are instruments used for the good of the society. Since they have access to a variety of resources and technologies that improve the standard of living of millions of people, and are better structured and more efficient than the bureaucratic system for handling certain social issues such as oil spills, natural disasters, and distribution of food and medicines for the poor or the people in vulnerable states.

The problem, however, is self-regulation of the activities of TNCs, their size limiting local competition, the development of scale economies favored by the exponential accumulation of wealth, the ability to move and their infiltration into the political arena that have allowed them to evade any substantial regulations. Therefore, the shortcomings of corporate governance in controlling TNCs should be noted, followed by some recommendations.

(d) No action mechanisms have been developed to balance the struggle for power, wealth, and knowledge. This means that states have not yet implemented strategies for competitive promotion that regulate the growth and concentration of oligopolistic market structure, as a priority states should have to provide the guidelines for economic development. Although some strategies have increased the level of income of some nations, they also generate conflicts resulting in social decline, led by inequality, exploitation of the environment, and poverty.

(e) The regulation strategies should follow four fundamental principles for corporate governance, comprising responsibility, accountability, fairness, and transparency. The responsibility for TNCs to obey the rules without coercion, but with the equity and accountability that go along with the increased transparency should be applicable not only to the public organization, but also to private companies derived from their influence and social impact and finally use equity as a means of fostering competition. However, the TNCs behavior stays away from these principles.

Therefore, it is clear that in the absence of control mechanisms on the international stage, a new economic system is emerging as the dispersion of power and authority of the states has fostered the growth of transnational private entities which, in spite of their ultimate goals, engage in social and political movements, not only on a regional scale but globally. This is derived from the lack of action through public institutional means, achieving the empowerment of a network of activists that certainly can wrest control of conflicts arising at the state level.

References

Anderson, S.A. February 18, 2005. *The Rise of Global Corporate Power*. http://globalpolicy.igc.org/socecon/tncs/top200.htm.

Aranda, J. L. (15 de Noviembre de 2008). ¿Qué fue Bretton Woods? El país. 15 november 2008 retrived from http://economia.elpais.com/economia/2008/11/15/actualidad/1226737974_850215.html.

Carbaugh, R.J. 2005. La globalización de la actividad económica. In *Economía Internacional,* ed. R.J. Carbaugh, 4–8. Rio de Janeiro: Thomson.
CEPAL. 2006. *Inversión extranjera directa y empresas.* Santiago de Chile: CEPAL.
Denis, D.A. 2003. International Corporate Governance. *Journal of Financial and Quantitative Analysis* 38: 1–36.
Díaz, G.V. n.d. *Globalización y comercio.* Obtained from Eumed: http://www.eumed.net/libros-gratis/2008b/389/GLOBALIZACION%20Y%20COMERCIO.htm.
Eun, C.A. 2007a. La globalización y la empresa multinacional. In *Administración Financiera Internacional,* ed. C.A. Eun, 10–16. Mexico: McGraw Hill.
Eun, C.S. 2007b. Gobierno Corporativo en el Mundo. In *Administración Financiera Internacional,* ed. C.S. Eun, 78–99. Mexico: McGraw Hill.
Friedman, M. 1970. The Social Responsibility of Business Is to Increase Profits. *The New York Times Magazine.*
Hernández, Z.J. 2008. La Responsabilidad Social Corporativa. *Centro de Documentación HEGOA.* Bilbao. HEGOA.
Jobson, I. 2006. The Unseen World of Transnational Corporations' Powers. *The Neumann Business Review,* Vol. 1, Spring 2006, 23–30.
Malnight, T.K. 2010. *Corporate Clout: The Influence of the World's Largest 100.* Global Trends.
Ramiro, P.Y. 2009. *Análisis de la Responsabilidad Social Corporativa de las empresas Transnacionales Colombianas.* Observatorio de Multinacionales en América. Bogotá, Colombia
Schwartz, M. (2002). A Code of Ethics for Corporate code of Ethics. Journal of Business Ethics, 27–43.
UNCTAD (2008). Trade and Development Report 2008. Commodity prices, capital flows and the financing of investment. United Nations Conference on Trade and Development. Switzerland. Retrived from http://unctad.org/en/pages/PublicationArchive.aspx?publicationid=2155.

Chapter 6
Talent Management and the Quest for Effective Succession Management in the Knowledge-Based Economy

Mihai-Florin Talpoş, Ioan G. Pop, Sebastian Văduva, and Liciniu A. Kovács

Abstract The chaos and uncertainty of the actual global economy create a tremendous pressure on companies' board of directors. In addition to this, there are other aggravating factors, such as the stakeholders' attitude (who demand continuous improvement of the leadership's capacity to increase the performance of the employees). There is also the growing demand for workers with specialized skills (given the influence of the Internet and IT revolution) and the increasing involuntary losses of high-performing workers or managers (because of the intensive headhunting initiatives that occur in the highly specialized personnel segments). The key to overcoming successfully such challenges is an active succession and knowledge-based talent management. A systematic effort to retain and develop the company's intellectual capital for the future will be the only sustainable differentiation in the competition strives of the next years and it will be the way to unlock the potential of a certain business direction, which has to be fully in line with the strategic vision of a company. The chapter aims to demonstrate that an organization's long-term performances depend—to a large extent—on the depth, breadth, and effectiveness of its Succession Management and that the efforts to ensure leadership continuity and proper retention of high-value talent are imperative in the attempt to outpace the competition. The chapter starts from revealing the main steps of effective human resource planning, among which succession planning plays an important role, and it continues with advancing a new knowledge-based leadership model that will increase the likelihood of obtaining sustainable business

M.-F. Talpoş, Ph.D. (✉)
Emanuel University of Oradea, Oradea, Romania

Center for Entrepreneurship Promotion in the Field of Sustainable Development, Cluj-Napoca Technical University, Cluj-Napoca, Romania
e-mail: mihai.talpos@scoalainformala.ro

I.G. Pop, Ph.D. • S. Văduva, Ph.D.
Emanuel University of Oradea, Oradea, Romania
e-mail: ioan.pop@emanuel.ro; sebastianvaduva@emanuel.ro

L.A. Kovács, Ph.D.
Babeş-Bolyai University of Cluj-Napoca, Cluj-Napoca, Romania
e-mail: liciniu@yahoo.com

S. Vaduva et al. (eds.), *Business Ethics and Leadership from an Eastern European, Transdisciplinary Context*, DOI 10.1007/978-3-319-45186-2_6

effects in the actual economy. The discussion leads to several study cases that are relevant for the importance of succession planning, namely: Aldis, Edy Spedition, Banca Transilvania, or Tarom.

Keywords Succession Management • Career development • Performance management • Recruitment • Leadership

6.1 Introduction

By definition, Succession Management is a "purposeful and systematic effort made by an organization to ensure leadership continuity, retain and develop knowledge and intellectual capital for the future, and encourage individual employee growth and development" (Schein 2011).

From the procedural side, Succession Management is an important element of the human resource planning process (as seen in Fig. 6.1). The idea presented in the below pictograph is that human resources planning starts with fully understanding the vision and the mission of the company and it is directly influenced by the environmental interactions (both external and internal) and by the availability of future personnel.

The development of various human resource plans (recruitment, training, replacement, succession, etc.) has to take into account the main factors of influence, because they directly condition and affect the abovementioned plans. Among the most important factors of influence, we mention technical progress, labor market, government regulations, the general economic situation, the policies of the external partners, etc. (inspired by Mathis, Nica, and Rusu's model 1997: 26).

Given the fact that there are multiple dynamics at play, which are making human resource planning a critical business issue, many companies are now struggling to find better ways to face the talent mismatch that manifests on the labor market (35 % in 2013, according to ManpowerGroup Romania) (Nechifor 2013). In spite of its importance, effective human resources planning cannot be found in most companies, because the exercise of good HR planning strongly depends on the individual abilities and strength of motivation that each CEO has. The probability of obtaining good results in the corporative human resources administration also depends on the type of leadership model that the CEOs embrace.

6.2 A New Leadership Model

A knowledge-based leadership model that will increase the likelihood of obtaining sustainable business effects in the actual "glocalized" (Norberg-Hodge 2009: 210) economy and high-impact Succession Management is the one presented in Fig. 6.2.

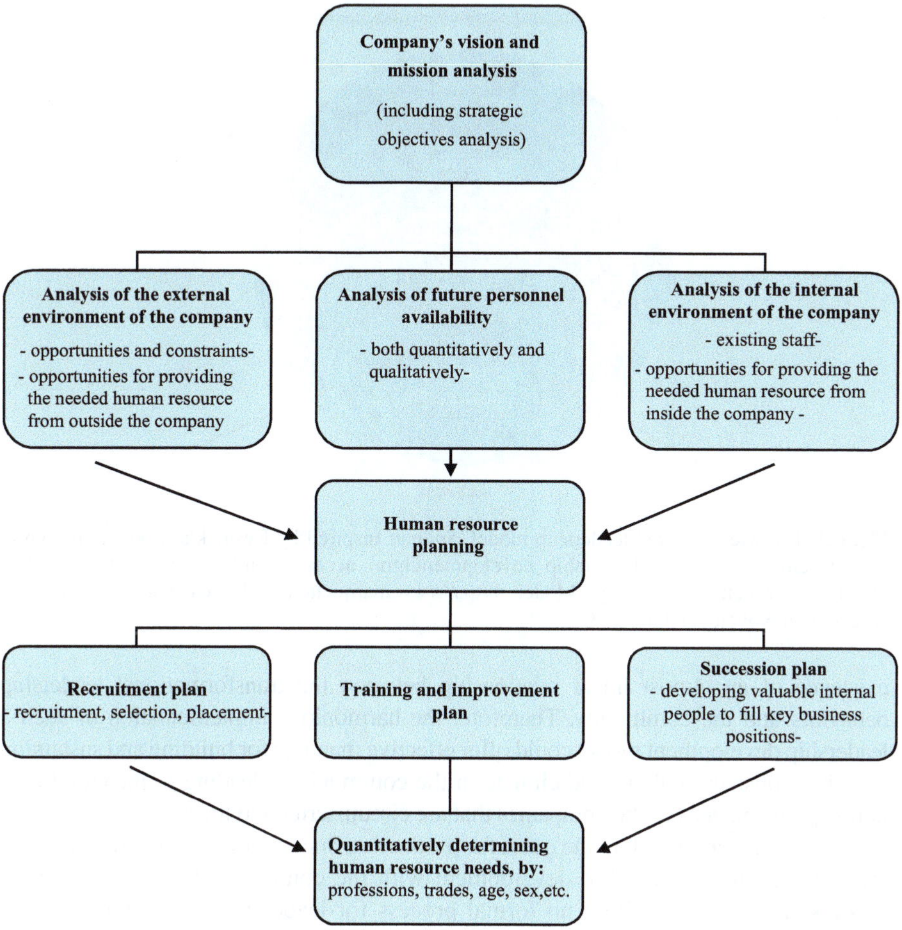

Fig. 6.1 Human resources planning stages (inspired by Mathis, Nica, and Rusu's model 1997: 26)

Such a knowledge-based leadership model is based on rational principles that value simplicity, personal abilities, and effective strategic thinking, in a special manner that highlights the idea that any business arises, in fact, from the community and it is a part of a connective temporal sequence (Šlaus 2003: 3–19; Hall 1959; Pop and Mătieş 2011). STC—*time wise* "think long-term and act now," and both on global and local dimensions, representing *spatiality*—participative space sequence, SSP—*space wise*—"think globally and act locally." In a networking relationship working as interactive action sequence, SAI—*act wise*—"be aware that your act produces consequences globally and your thoughts are rooted locally."

As such, both the leading process of a modern company and the Succession Planning and Management of that company have to be circumscribed to the community, in order to gain real sustainability. Well-executed Succession Management cannot be done without linkage with the "tacit knowledge" of the community, no matter how unique the needs of a company can be. The above presented leadership model also shows the

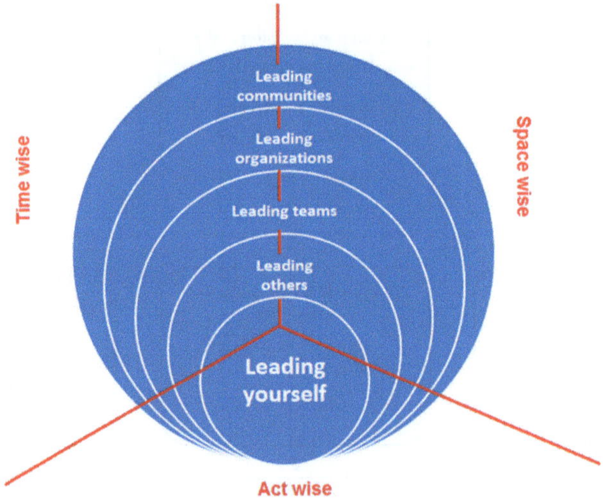

Fig. 6.2 Knowledge-based leadership model. *Source*: Inspired by Resnick's Model http://www.worksystems.com/services/leadership_development.html, accessed on November 1st, 2013. And by the Marquette University Model http://www.marquette.edu/dsa/leadership/model.shtml, accessed on November 1st, 2013

existence of an almost linear relationship between the transformational leadership behaviors and the community. Therefore, the harmonious implementation of such a leadership development model could offer effective manners for building and sustaining a positive business culture and climate in the communities, leading to increased economic performances of the companies that are circumscribed to those communities.

An effective approach in the quest for productive Succession Management implies the integration of leadership development with the company's talent-management process (Bersin 2008). With no formal process for leadership development, many companies fail in applying the principles of the above described leadership model. They underutilize or inconsistently apply those principles, with direct negative effects on meeting their business objectives (Bersin 2008). Even more disturbingly, many companies have no process for succession planning at all (Bersin 2008).

As a result, if the need arises, those companies cannot immediately name a successor to their CEO. This translates into erosion of the stakeholders' trust, inability to put into practice the business strategy, lack of customer focus and, eventually, into important operational gaps inhibiting the success of those companies (Schroeder-Saulnier 2010).

6.3 Succession Management, from Blooming to Maturity

There are five levels of maturity for succession management (as shown in Fig. 6.3), (Lamoureux et al. 2009) that can be associated with five different stages of evolution, from the blooming of Succession Management to its maturity.

Fig. 6.3 Succession management, from blooming to maturity (inspired by Lamoureux, Campbell, and Smith's Management Maturity and Model 2009)

The first stage is the one that involves the realization of the problem, the realization of the fact that the company does not have succession planning at all, and the understanding of its role and importance. This stage may include the identification of successors for the executive-level positions (Lamoureux et al. 2009).

The second stage involves the development of a replacement plan that will help the company in identifying senior-level positions and high-potential employees, but it will not clarify the aspects concerning the development of those employees (Lamoureux et al. 2009). The third stage is one that allows a better business-unit focus, talent reviews, and, last but not least, the conceiving of articulated development plans for the key positions in the company (Lamoureux et al. 2009).

The fourth stage entails business strategy alignment and talent management integration (Lamoureux et al. 2009), which means that several connected organizational processes are conceived to attract, motivate, develop, manage, and retain key valuable people. The fifth stage is the most complex one, because it involves highly transparent HR dynamic processes, in the context of a board of directors that consciously and professionally assumes Succession Management roles (Lamoureux et al. 2009). The integrated cross-processes set that the maturity stage includes important activities such as talent acquisition, learning and capability development, career management, performance management, leadership development, succession management, and, last but not least, rewards management.

6.4 Succession Planning in Terms of Selecting the Right Leadership for a Company

Depending on its stage of evolution in matters of Succession Management, a company and its board of directors will differently react to a certain challenge, such as the selection of the right leader. Nowadays, the stakes are higher than ever, when the need of selecting the right leadership for an important company arises (Ogden and Wood 2008).

According to Ogden and Wood (2008), there are three main types of situation in which the need to select a new leader for a company arises, namely (Ogden and Wood 2008):

1. When the board of directors has to immediately replace a CEO that was suddenly incapacitated or a CEO that died. For such situations, the companies should have a so-called "name in the envelope" succession plan.
2. When the board of directors has to face the announced departure of a CEO. This is probably a simpler case, because the board is being warned, so it has the chance of properly starting the process of finding a successor. For such situations, the companies should have a so-called "targeted retirement" succession plan.
3. When the board of directors has to face the changing of a CEO sooner than planned, because of the faltering of the business. For such situations, the companies should have a so-called "deteriorating situation" succession plan.

In any of the cases listed above, if the boards of directors did not put in place the right processes for succession management, great risks are involved (as can be seen in Table 6.1).

As showed in the examples presented above, real life brings into attention various situations that exceed Ogden and Wood's three types of model, because such situations involve the combination and integration of different succession plan categories (for instance the Edy Spedition case, which raised the necessity of having—at the same time—both a "name in the envelope" succession plan and a "target retirement" succession plan).

6.5 Conclusions

Succession management is an immature and relatively new process for most companies in Romania, even multinational companies. According to the EY study: "Your Talent in Motion: Global Mobility Effectiveness Survey 2013," 56 % of executives responsible for the mobility of the personnel in the Romanian multinational companies say their management teams are involved only in the implementation of mobility services without paying any role in the talent management nor in defining the general objectives of the business (Voncick 2013).

Table 6.1 Romanian case studies relevant to succession management planning

Type of succession plan	Studied company	Case description	Considerations regarding the quality of the applied succession plan
Name in the envelope	Aldis	Aldis, the second largest sausage manufacturer in Romania, was ravaged after the death of George Naghi (in August 2011), the administrator of the company. Salaries of employees were delayed, as well as the payments to the state budget. Because of that, the Ministry of Finance initiated the foreclosure of the company	Catastrophic failure
Name in the envelope and targeted retirement	Edy Spedition	In August 2012, Alin Popa, the administrator of Edy Spediton (a company with a turnover of more than 520 million lei) died in a terrible car accident, shaking and weakening the company's activity, given the fact those 2 weeks before the accident, the CEO of Edy Spediton (Mircea Tiplea) resigned and left the company	Failure with important consequences
Targeted retirement	Banca Transilvania	In January 2012, Robert Rekkers resigned as CEO of Banca Transilvania (the third Romanian bank in terms of market share) and the member of the Board of Directors, after leading the bank for 9 years. Although Robert Rekkers's departure was announced in advance, the bank needed over 15 months to find a replacement in the person of Omer Tetik, who took over as late as May 2013	Failure
Deteriorating situation	Tarom	In 2012, Gabriela Bordea, the CEO of Tarom (the flag carrier and oldest currently operating airline of Romania) was replaced by the Board of Directors, after having found that the company had losses (accumulated in 4 years) of a quarter of its turnover. The Romanian state, the main shareholder of Tarom, came to take such measures after its plans to put up for sale 20 % of Tarom's shares on the stock market had been postponed numerous times	Failure with important consequences

Source: Adevărul (2012), Chirileasa (2013), Ziare.com (2012)

Here is another form of evidencing the fact that organizations should indeed integrate succession management with other HR/talent management functions. Only a strong and sustainable knowledge-based leadership model, built in a new form that orbits around concepts like, can nurture this integration: self-leadership, glocalization, community, and connective temporal sequence (timewise, spacewise, act-wise). Such a knowledge-based leadership model will contribute, in a transdisciplinary synergistic-generative way, to the achievement of real sustainability.

A transdisciplinary approach involves the following knowledge chain integration: *hands-on* (passive knowledge), *hands-in* (passive–active knowledge), *hands-off* (active knowledge), and so on as a cycle (Pop 2011). As such, the quest for effective succession and talent management reduces (in a way) to finding the difference between *know-what*, as an explicit managerial act, and *know-how*, as an implicit set of knowledge procedures being known as a codified form of *know-what* (Brown and Duguid 2000: 207–241).

Succession management passes through five stages of evolution, from blooming to maturity: problem realization (no succession planning); replacement panning; traditional succession planning; integrated succession management; and transparent talent mobility. Well-executed and mature Succession Management cross-processes allow important activities such as talent acquisition, capability development, career, and performance management, leadership development, and, last but not least, rewards management.

Depending on their stage of evolution in matters of Succession Management, companies react differently to the challenge of selecting the right leader. Examples from the Romanian market, such as Aldis, Edy Spedition, Banca Transilvania, or Tarom, are relevant for the importance that the putting in place of the right processes for succession management has. Without clear and tested succession management processes, companies face great risks which may culminate in bankruptcy.

References

Bersin, J. 2008. Talent Management: State of the industry. Human Resource Executive Online. http://www.hrexecutive.com/HRE/story.jsp?storyId=98598263&query=talent%20management. Accessed 02 November 2013.

Brown, J.S., and P. Duguid. 2000. Re-education. In *The Social Life of Information*, ed. J.S. Brown and P. Duguid, 207–241. Boston: Harvard Business School Press.

Chirileasa, A. 2013. Omer Tetik este noul CEO al Bancii Transilvania. Bancherul turc va conduce instituţia financiară până la finalul anului 2016. *Ziarul Financiar*. http://www.zf.ro/banci-si-asigurari/omer-tetik-este-noul-ceo-al-bancii-transilvania-bancherul-turc-va-conduce-institutia-financiara-pana-la-finalul-anului-2016-10875877. Accessed 02 November 2013.

Hall, E.T. 1959. *The Silent Language*. Greenwich, UK: Fawcett Publications. (Le langage silencieux, Seuil, 1984).

Lamoureux, K., M. Campbell, and R. Smith. 2009. High-Impact Succession Management. http://www.ccl.org/leadership/pdf/research/HighImpactSuccessionManagement.pdf. Accessed 02 November 2013.

Mathis, R., N. Panaite, and C. Rusu. 1997. *Managementul resurselor umane*, 26. Bucureşti: Editura Economica.

Nechifor, E. 2013. *Comunicat de presă—deficitul de talente*. ManpowerGroup Romania. https://candidate.manpower.com/.../2013_Comunicat+de+presa+Deficitul+de+talente. Accessed 01 November 2013.

Norberg-Hodge, H. 2009. *Ancient Future*, 210. San Francisco, CA: Sierra Club Books. http://www.worksystems.com/services/leadership_development.html, http://www.marquette.edu/dsa/leadership/model.shtml. Accessed 01 November 2013.

Ogden, D., and J. Wood. 2008. Succession Planning: A board imperative. http://www.businessweek.com/stories/2008-03-25/succession-planning-a-board-imperativebusinessweek--business-news-stock-market-and-financial-advice. Accessed 02 November 2013.

Pop, I.G. 2011. Contributions to Transdisciplinary Approach of the Mechatronics in the Knowledge Based Society. Thesis, Technical University of Cluj-Napoca, Cluj-Napoca.

Pop, I.G., and V. Mătieş. 2011. Transdisciplinary Approach of the Mechatronics in the Knowledge Based Society. In *Mechatronics*. Rijeka: Intech Open Access Publisher.

Schein. 2011. http://dcb9maxnxelio.cloudfront.net/wp-content/uploads/2012/06/Succession-Planning-and-Management.pdf. Accessed 01 November 2013.

Schroeder-Saulnier, D. 2010. Succession Management: Positioning Your Organization's Leadership for Business Success. http://www.right.com/thought-leadership/e-newsletter/succession-management-positioning-your-organizations-leadership-for-business-success.pdf. Accessed 02 November 2013.

Šlaus, I. 2003. Political Significance of Knowledge in Southeast Europe. *Croatian Medical Journal* 4: 3–19.

Voncick, O. 2013. Multinaţionalele nu îşi implementează eficient programele de mobilitate. *Manager Express*. http://www.managerexpress.ro/decizie-2/research-atentie/multinationalele-nu-isi-implementeaza-eficient-programele-de-mobilitate.html#!.

Internet Resources

Adevărul, Cotidianul. 2012, 27 August edition. Moartea patronului zdruncină afacerea Edy Spedition. http://adevarul.ro/economie/stiri-economice/moartea-patronului-zdruncina-afacerea-edy-spedition-1_50b9fe0a7c42d5a663ae7642/index.html. Accessed 02 November 2013.

Ziare.com, 2012, 8 August edition. Tarom a avut pierderi de un sfert din cifra de afaceri. http://www.ziare.com/tarom/airlines/tarom-a-avut-pierderi-de-un-sfert-din-cifra-de-afaceri-1183140. Accessed 02 November 2013.

Chapter 7
A Transdisciplinary Approach of Ecological Economy and Sustainability in Eastern Europe

Igor Prisac

Abstract This chapter researches the issue of ecological economy and sustainability in the countries of Eastern Europe as a complex phenomenon that requires a transdisciplinary approach for the strategies and economic policies behind their political acts and processes. Starting with the analysis of the evolution of these desires and the current situation in this field, this study stresses the role and importance of having a society that strives for a sustainable economy and well-being. The scientific problem to be solved in order to reach this social objective is to find ways of balancing bioeconomy and consumerism, a big challenge for the whole world, especially for the Eastern European countries. Applying the transdisciplinary approach in tackling this social and ecological problem, we discovered that positive feedback in political decisions and international cooperation—such as the investment in education, human resources development, society susceptibility, and the promotion of innovation and technologies—is the key in having an ecological system and sustainable economy for the developing countries of Eastern Europe. The practical implementation of these concepts to society and its economic components is another issue discussed in this chapter. For a better understanding of this phenomenon, it is imperative to understand that this process is a dynamic one that needs complex study.

Keywords Complexity • Transdisciplinarity • Ecological economy • Sustainability • Human development • Economic policies • Bioeconomics • Consumerism • Entropy • Dynamic equilibrium

7.1 Introduction

From the classical approach of the English economist Pigou, one of the founders of ecological economy, to nowadays, we can observe a continuous development of knowledge that tried to bring human progress and the natural environment in a dynamic equilibrium. More and more scholars support the paradigm of transdisciplinarity

I. Prisac, Ph.D. (✉)
Divitia Gratiae University, Chisinau, Moldova
e-mail: ida@uni-dg.md

S. Vaduva et al. (eds.), *Business Ethics and Leadership from an Eastern European, Transdisciplinary Context*, DOI 10.1007/978-3-319-45186-2_7

as an unstoppable tendency in finding new effective approaches in tackling the challenges the humanity has to face in the long term-future in order to step in a sustainable development direction. This phenomenon involves many factors, interactions and historical heritages (economic, social, and cultural) for the Eastern European countries that stand to deal with a complex investigation of the problem and with integrative ecological politics.

Therefore, quantitative figures and methods, as Negrei (1996) states, are not able to give results to this issue; thus we need to apply the qualitative level of approaches (1969: 24) due to the complexity that ecological economy and sustainable development involve. This investigation also covers geographical, political, philosophical, and ethical ways of approach, stressing again the need to have a transdisciplinary dimension in elaborating and implementing the policies necessary for a better future. As Fiodorov states, ecology knowledge is transformed from a fundamental science into a complex, synthetic, and interdisciplinary science given the conditions of a permanent human activity that changes the planet's landscape (Florea, 2000: 5).

The economies of the Eastern European countries have a specific background concerning sustainability and economic development because of their having been part of the socialist block, as well as to the continued intensive transition toward the free market economy. The communist teachings that promoted equality and massive industrialization at that time, in order to compete with the West at any cost, had little to do with ecological care and education in this part of the world.

The aggressive promotion of equality in those days had nothing in common with bringing society and the consumption of bio-resources and the environment in a state of balance. In other words, the communist doctrines of equality and well fare were not able to bear fruit towards economic efficiency, much less for sustainable development. Because of a closed political and economic system, this European region was in an entropic state (Avery 2012: 169), with a low level of social information that led to a high waste of energy, high militarization, and low quality of goods, and all types of pollution. In addition, in the twenty-first century, the majority of these countries inherited part of this entropy due to the geopolitical influence (*Republica Moldova. Programul național strategic de acțiuni în domeniul protecției mediului înconjurător* 1995: 3), the low economic development that restricts administrative resources, and the ways to follow the international agreements and national strategies on environment protection.

This high level of entropy in the Eastern part of Europe, at the phenomenological level, was expressed in the increase of ecological catastrophes, which need a very thorough investigation at all levels in order to make progress in sustainable development. Here we can call to attention a few examples that illustrate this phenomenon: the vast flood in Romania due to extensive forest clearing (1970–1975), or the accident at the nuclear power plant in Chernobyl (1986). Another example is the high level of pollution because of the oil extraction in the Russian Federation. Moreover, public intoxication from the lead wastes at the "Acumulatorul" enterprise in Romania (1998) (Găldean and Staicu 2000: 4) and the damaging and poisoning experiment with pesticides and herbicides on the Moldovan and Ukrainian agricultural lands during the Soviet Union's reign caused consequences still present nowadays, on both humans and the economy. Ecological issues were of little interest for politics and were a topic of debate mostly within universities and research institutions. Ecological risk management was a feebly developed field and generated a culture unable to take risks and social responsibility, as well as to avoid catastrophes and negative consequences for the society and the environment. In this respect, some of the Eastern European enterprises assumed that European integration, with its economic and ecological standards, would put an end to the high ecological entropy and inefficiency inherited from the socialist culture. This would not be the case if we tried to analyze the violations of security rules and ecological responsibility, and the lack of risk culture at Ajka alumina plant on October 4, 2010, in Hungary, a member state of the European Union.

Even though these regional accidents take place once every 10 years, these phenomena lead to a long-term big demographic change, which is one of the biggest problems especially for former soviet republics. It is expressed in higher mortality and morbidity rates, a decrease in population, an increase in cancer and lung diseases, in mass emigration, and a lower quality of life in the last two decades (Cuznețov, 1996: 6–9; *Starea mediului în Republica Moldova în 2007–2010*: 28–31). This emphasizes again the importance of the strong and efficient regional policies and strategies the Eastern European countries have to follow in a responsible way, by abiding by the European standards on ecology and sustainable development and to repair the mistakes of the past and to minimize the consequences for the future generations.

Another important issue specific to the developing countries from Eastern Europe consists in production inefficiency. This region needs more investments in tackling the losses and waste along the production process (FAO, 2014). In developing countries, the waste and loss of crop after harvest go as high as 40 %. In Europe, there is 280–300 kg of waste per capita accumulated each year. In this respect, we can observe another sustainability dimension where the state's policies must be oriented in optimizing and improving the production process. A potential approach for this issue would also contribute significantly to the solution of the food problem in the future, considered the main global problem.

This European region is accustomed with borrowing models of sustainable development, even though we have the UN principles and approved convention for the environment to follow and implement in our countries, we have elaborated national policies, strategies, and tariffs, as well as being part of EU standards, directive, decisions, and resolution for the member states. These norms and strategic frames are very important to be considered, but they become very complex to implement because of the economic specifics of Eastern Europe: countries here are developing countries that need direct intensive development and in which it is very common to promote consumption and feel the "comfort" of consumerism. Even the transition phase for us translates in significant economic growth; as Avery states, we need to lead a successful transition to sustainability (Avery 2012: 170). This model means that there should be a dynamic equilibrium between consumption, which is driving the economy, and the protection of biodiversity, energy efficiency, environment protection, and investment in the quality of people's lives.

China is a good model of economic growth for many national economies through its fundamental economic policies, finding an extraordinary balance between autocratic political power and the free market economy based on their culture, tradition, and historical context. However, China remains a bad example, has a lot to do in order to improve its sustainable development, and needs to find the right equilibrium between economic growth and environment protection. The USA is the biggest economy of the world, but with the highest quantities of energy use per capita, that demands consumption rationalization.

Eastern European countries need to learn from the European states that, throughout their history, were able to establish a rational system of interaction between economic development and ecology promotion, such as Iceland, Switzerland, and Sweden. These economic models are prominent for having found the right industries, services, and energy sources to live in a productive socioeconomic and socio-ecological realm, proving a natural dynamic equilibrium.

We take into consideration Georgescu-Roegen's representation of economic processes, which in transdisciplinary terms refers to the entropic transformation of valuable natural resources (low entropy) into valuable waste (high entropy) (Avery 2012: 169). In observing the economic evolution of the developing countries of Eastern Europe, we need to follow the right dynamic equilibrium in regard to these two types of entropic states (see Fig. 7.1). It is impossible to renounce entirely to the production of goods in order to be economically strong (that brings a high entropic state) and concentrate all effort on providing services and intellectual work. For example, producing computer software requires few resources and results in less waste. Thus, this is an activity with a very small ecological footprint. Similarly, education, research, music, literature, and art are all activities that do not weigh heavily on the carrying capacity of the global environment.

Furthermore, cultural activities lead in a natural way to global cooperation and internationalism, since the people of the entire world (Avery 2012: 170) share cultural achievements. This is one of the main dilemmas that transdisciplinarity is called on to solve, because economic and social systems are consuming and transforming natural, energy, and information resources and the first two we find in nature. The right dynamic equilibrium is called on to find the necessary sustainability order in the system, able to satisfy human needs, as well as the capacity of reducing entropy to its minimum (see Fig. 7.1).

Knowing that the ecological economy needs to be approached from the points of view of dynamic equilibrium and a natural development, we need to find ways using political, legislative, educational, and international mechanisms to have this phenomenon happen. In addition, good synergies in achieving this objective come in form of human development as the main catalyst in developing higher technologies and innovation as well as higher responsibility in having a rational consumption of goods and resources and environment protection. Of course, this would be one of the biggest challenges developing countries in Eastern Europe face and in our modern age, we have quite enough mechanisms, international and regional collaborations, the involvement of NGOs and central authorities, as well as ways to measure the environmental

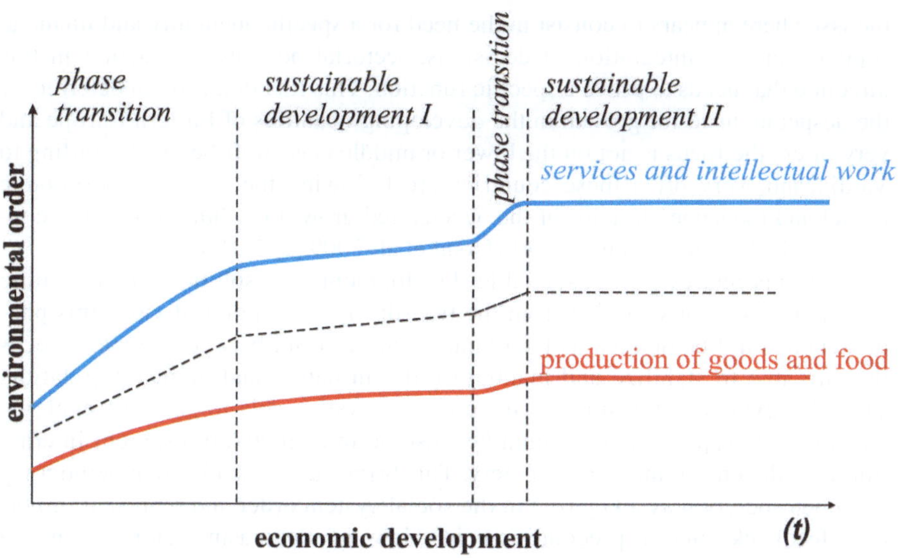

Fig. 7.1 Dynamic equilibrium between high and low entropy economic activities

situation. In other words, in the last two decades, we have developed institutional structures and legislation frames, but our society needs to concentrate on how to create functional structures to bring harmony between humans and the environment.

A transition from the space–time structures that consist in any kinds of tools, institutions, administrations, and standards to the functional ones must take place. At this level, we reach the highest point where the transdisciplinary approach can help in achieving functional structures, having an adequate sustainable development. This should be started with what has been achieved in conventional ways and to continue to connect them at all levels of society to obtain functional structures that enable the decrease of entropy in the economic system and obtain a dynamic equilibrium regime.

After the Rio de Janeiro conference, where the concept of sustainable development was officially accepted, it was found that the achievement of this objective is to some extent limited because of both its interpretation and the absence of an operational infrastructure. In addition, it is because of the fact that in the intersectorial process the social component has been neglected (Ursul et al. 2009: 173). As Ursul et al. (2009) state, the classical view on reaching this goal is by social projection and the construction of a new socio-natural model for further development in the form of a normative forecast of our sustainable and common development (2009: 50). Pop and Mătieş (2011) formulate the definition of sustainable development as "creative and responsible stewardship of resources (human, natural and financial resources management) in order to generate stakeholder value while contributing to the well-being of current and future generations of all beings" (2011: 292). The integration of the norms and ecologic policies of all levels is another approach to a successful sustainable development. However, the issue here appears to consist in the need for a specific mentality and financial support, and the integration of decisions, sectorial policies, and action in this direction that needs to prove a specific function. This function is often deterred by the desperate need for growth in the developing countries of Eastern Europe and very often, the focus is not on the lower or middle class well-being. According to Vardineanu, very often these countries are following the same socioeconomic model and the same attractor of the accelerated growth rhythm, outside the context and the human capital support (Ursul et al. 2009: 182–183).

With this analysis on sustainable development as a solution for the future generation, we can state that from the transdisciplinary point of view, this phenomenon could be defined as the dynamic equilibrium between people's needs that are able to stabilize and maintain order in nature and human population. This also expresses the state of an economic system able to keep the ecologic and social entropy to its minimum because of an open and transparent interaction with the environment and society. This brings us to the idea that democracy and open society play a key role in the social system order and represent important feedback and a precondition in view of decreasing entropy in the environment.

In the last two decades, the international community and the majority of the countries have analyzed possible ways to preserve the environment through sustainable development concepts. There are countries that served as models that succeeded in sustainable development. That means that we have the necessary *thesaurus* for the sustainability of the Eastern European countries. In addition, national states and the international society have approved many strategies and norms for the preservation of the environment, also because in twenty-first century this idea has become a universal value that most of the populations accept, being expressed in political and scientific conferences and pro-environment demonstrations. In transdisciplinary understanding, we can say that the necessary *social selector* is already taking place, also in the Eastern European countries. What our socioeconomic system needs to prove is, as Bransky states, that the necessary *social detector* that consists in a configuration of *positive feedback* happening over a certain period can enable this phenomenon to pursue the dynamic equilibrium track (Бранский 2000: 116).

The dynamic equilibrium in the economic system must demonstrate certain order parameters of the production of goods (the big natural resources consumer and high entropy source) and the providing of services, education, scientific and technologies research, and human capital development (the lower consumer of natural resources and a much lower entropy source). This optimum state is dynamic along its evolution and must contribute to the high environmental order and less accumulated entropy during the time of development (see Fig. 7.2).

On a practical aspect, this configuration of positive feedback would consist in a minimum of four dimensions: human development, social capital development, economic sustainability, and environment sustainability (Ursul et al. 2009: 35) (see Fig. 7.2).

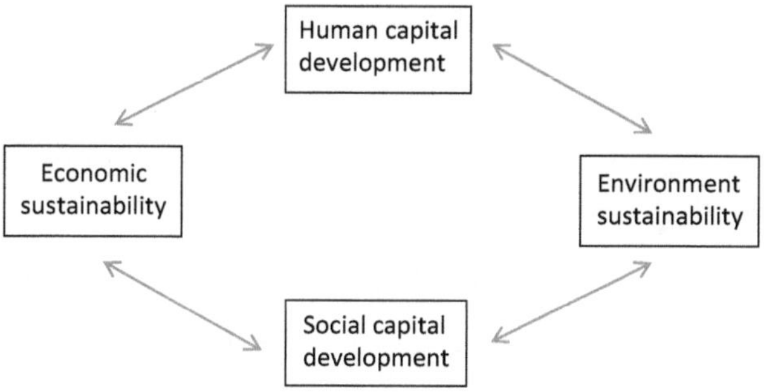

Fig. 7.2 Sustainable development detector. *Source*: Inspired from Goodland, Robert (2000)

7.2 Human Capital Development

There is a direct link between sustainable development and human capital. Šlaus and Jacobs mention "that development of human capital is the critical determinant of long-term sustainability and that the efforts to accelerate the evolution of human consciousness and emergence of mentally self-conscious individuals will be the most effective approach for ensuring a sustainable future" (Šlaus and Jacobs 2001: 97). However, the challenge of today's society is "to find ways to harness all available forms of capital in a manner that promotes human welfare, well-being, and sustainable development for all" (Šlaus and Jacobs 2001: 100).

Our educational systems must encompass deep approaches to how the future human capital will contribute to economic sustainability. The high school and university programs of all future specialists could have a vital impact on the sustainable economy based on a transdisciplinary approach, able to change the environmental situation. The investment in human capital leads to a variety of positive feedback in our society, contributing, during history, to high technologies and innovations that were very productive both for the development and for the economic sustainability. The productivity of the future human capital must be oriented towards the decrease of irrational natural resource consumption and overcapitalization of the economy to a higher possible conservation of nature by providing quality services and promotion of innovations that would contribute to sustainability.

In this respect, higher levels of education and human capital in developed countries such as Japan, Austria, and the UK have led in the last century to a decrease in the intensity of energy, contributing in an efficient way to economic sustainability in its environment (Šlaus and Jacobs 2001: 111) (see Fig. 7.3). In addition, the results of human development investment should lead to discoveries and innovations able to create resilient alternatives of ecological energy, having the capacity to cover at least the human needs of contemporaneity.

A positive element in the recent past is that human work is undergoing an accelerated transition from manual work and industrial jobs to intellectual human activity, leaving part of the input to the latest technologies and automated machines.

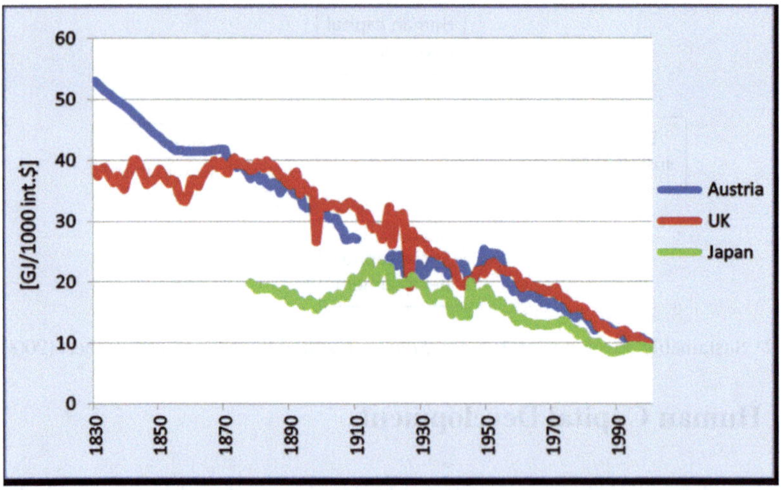

Fig. 7.3 Decrease in energy intensity 1830–2000. *Source*: Šlaus and Jacobs (2001)

This is a good tendency towards development because humans have a lot to explore and use the planet's resources and possibilities requiring more knowledge, even though the classical economy had another view (Avery 2012: 171). Avery proves that the limit factors in the production of goods and food are the shortages of human capital while the land, forest, fossil fuels, minerals, oceans filled with fish, and other natural resources are assumed to be present in large quantities, thus being not a limiting factor (Avery 2012: 171).

7.3 Social Capital Development

The Eastern European states need to keep investing in the social services and public goods in order to develop the social capital, a very important catalyst in the development of other capitals, such as the human one and the functionality of the necessary dynamic equilibrium of sustainable development. This important element reduces work costs as a whole and facilitates cooperation in economy and society, as well as promoting more values and benefits: patience, friendship, love, commonsense, discipline, morality, and ethics (Goodland 2000). The state must promote the adequate laws in order to contribute to the necessary input in developing this capital and make this positive feedback happen. In other words, well-being in society is not promoted only by the economic development but also the social understanding in society, a high cooperation between its individuals and transparency, facilitating the opening of the system, a key property for the entropy to decrease.

Another important aspect of the social capital is that this level significantly influences society's culture and the people's mindset. Social capital increases/decreases the susceptibility of the population to state reforms and economic policies and complying with the norms. The decision makers at all levels have a big responsibility in developing this social dimension, but this is not the only one. The representatives of the civil society have played a big role in the Eastern European states in order to develop the social capital, and it needs more national and international financial and administrative resources in continuing to be involved in making the sustainable development functional. The civil society is the meso-level of a social system and it facilitates positive feedback between the macro and micro levels of society. Without this component, it is very difficult to develop the social capital alone through the government.

7.4 Economic Sustainability

In bringing human and social capital into a sustainable economic system, there is another challenge ahead that is important to be faced in order to generate the right positive feedback and create dynamic equilibrium. By definition, economic sustainability represents a set of conditions and elements that allow the maintaining, and the increasing of income and well fare involving the control of demographic stabilization, resource monitoring, production and consumption improvement in order to keep the scarce resource stocks at an adequate level (Ursul et al. 2009: 37). Using consumerism to stimulate the economy is becoming a greater challenge in Eastern Europe as well, but we have to take the lessons of the 2008–2009 financial and economic international crisis and perceive this as a systemic dangerous stimulus that is unfair on the long term for both the economy and the environment. A sustainable economy must be driven by a rational and environment-oriented vision and strategy of the countries in this region. The term *economic capital* includes the capacity of the economy that is based on the *interest benefit* and not on the *capital benefit* (Goodland 2000). Knowing that the amount of financial and fixed capital is reduced in many Eastern European countries, creating goods, providing services on real economic capital is a big opportunity, and they need to concentrate production and services on a sustainable future based on interest consumption.

Our state economic policies must create the mechanisms of monitoring and facilitating the right production chains in order to contribute to the sustainable development by promoting creativity and transdisciplinary approaches. Pop and Mătieş state that

> only the transdisciplinary knowledge achievement, as a new methodology, can explain the way creativity, with a synergistic significance, works as an intentional action through ideas, design, modelling, prototyping, simulation, incorporating *informergically* the information in *matt-ergy*, to obtain *smart products*, *sustainable technologies* and *specific integrative methods* to provide solutions to the emerging problems (Pop and Mătieş 2011: 289).

Even the real experience is not replaceable by learning, so by simulations we need to create virtual tools such as design and modulations, to build smart mechatronic products (Pop and Mătieş 2011: 287) by taking into consideration the competitive environment and the international trends.

To these analyses, we have to add that at the micro level enterprises must develop their culture values. The culture values enable the creation of positive feedback for the economic sustainability and consist in responsibility and a culture of risk. As it was discussed above, Eastern European companies must develop this detector in order to build its sustainable development. There should be an investment of both the macro level and the micro level in developing this culture. The ecological management of the enterprises' efficiency is part of the first input for sustainable economy. The ecological management represents a complex approach with regard to the elaboration of an integrated system including organizational structure, the rights and obligations of the personnel, methods, procedures, and the necessary resource (*Starea mediului în Republica Moldova în 2007–2010*: 149). Here we have to specify that this is not just the responsibility of the state, but of all the economic and social actors including enterprises.

7.5 Environment Sustainability

Our environment is a source of all the natural resources that our economy is transforming into goods and food. The problems that are raised here consist in the fact that people and governments must understand and ensure our consumption is maintained according to our necessities and that we have sustainable waste and pollution management. We have to save our natural capital and concentrate our efforts on innovation to find the necessary dynamic equilibrium which is able to limit to its minimum the emissions and pollution and rationalize to its maximum the consumption of natural resources. This is possible if our economies are able to produce in a way not exceeding the regeneration of the resources that we consume (Goodland 2000).

In the last decade, a lot was invested in large quantities of resources of all kinds, especially in Central Europe, which gave a significant boost to these economies. In the next decades, it is time to create the dynamic equilibrium of a sustainable economy and orient investment in a wise way such that the new applications, ecological technologies and innovations, as well as the economic activities, could put our economic system on this evolution track. We have models of developed countries that succeeded in achieving this, we have scientific and political support, and there is a new accumulation of human and financial capital. In the next transition phase, in the context of European integration and globalization, we need to concentrate our programs and efforts on sustainable development, which is accompanied by transdisciplinary approaches and knowledge.

7.6 Conclusion

Sustainable development represents a dynamic equilibrium between the people's needs of being able to stabilize and maintain order between nature and the human population. There are more models of how this connection could be achieved and one of these is the equilibrium between providing services and goods, to which extent these phenomena could be applied by the state economic development strategies. Intellectual work and promotion of innovation are important positive feedback types to stimulate this type of equilibrium to meet our society's needs. The lessons we learned from the former socialist system show that industrialization without innovation, freedom of choices, and new technologies in a free economic market does not bring social and environmental success. Because these consequences cost the Eastern European countries too much, the right model and strategy of sustainable development model must be on our agenda for all social and economic policies.

In broad terms, the economic system must contribute to the decrease of ecological and social entropy to its minimum and create open and transparent interactions with the environment and society. This brings us to the idea that democracy and open society play a key role in the social system order and represent important feedback types and a precondition to decreasing the entropy in the environment. This fact we observed in countries with democratic development, which are good models of sustainable development for the Eastern European economies. That is why we need to create the right functional structures based on the success models and the international trends.

References

Avery, John. 2012. Entropy and Economy. *Cadmus: promoting leadership in thought that leads to action* 1(4): 166–179.

Cuznețov S. Problemele ecosociomane în perioada de tranziție în Republica Moldova. In: Management ecologic şi dezvoltare durabilă. Tezele conferinței internaționale consacrate zilei protecției mediului înconjurător şi aniversării a 5-a a Institutului Național de Ecologie (5–6 iunie, 1996), 208 p.

Găldean, Nicolae, and Gabriela Staicu. 2000. *Curs de ecosisteme*, 155. Bucharest: Universitatea Ecologică Bucureşti.

Goodland, Robert. 2000. Social Environment Assessment to promote Sustainability—an informal view from the World Bank. In *World Bank*. http://www-wds.worldbank.org/external/default/WDSContentServer/WDSP/IB/2000/10/21/000094946_0010130548139/Rendered/PDF/multi_page.pdf.

Agriculture officials condemn unnecessary loss and waste of good food. In: FAO 2014 [online], viewed 28 April 2014.

Florea, Serafim. Factorul ecologic şi dezvoltarea socioeconomică teritorială durabilă a Republicii Moldova. Chişinău: Şearec-com, 2000, p. 315.

Negrei, Costel. 1996. *Bazele economiei mediului*, 170. Bucureşti: Editura didactică şi pedagogică.

Pop, Ioan, and Vistrian Mătieş. 2011. Transdisciplinary Approach of the Mechatronics in the Knowledge Based Society. In *Advances in Mechatronics,* Rijeka: In Tech, 2011, 271–300.

Republica Moldova. Programul național strategic de acțiuni în domeniul protecției mediului înconjurător. 1995. Chişinău: Editura Uniunii Scriitorilor, 147.

Šlaus, Ivo, and Garry Jacobs. 2001. Human Capital and Sustainability. *Sustainability* 3: 97–154.

Ursul, Arcadie, Ion Rusandu, and Arcadie Capcelea. 2009. *Dezvoltare durabilă: abordări metodologice şi de operaționalizare*, 251. Chişinău: Ştiința.

Бранский, В. 2000. Теоретическое основание социальной синергетике. In *Вопросы философии*, vol. 4, 112–129. Москва: Наука.

Chapter 8
Artificial Intelligence and the Concept of "Human Thinking"

Dan Aurelian Botică

Abstract The twentieth century may indeed be called the century of "scientific revolutions," evidently, depending on how one understands the notion of "revolution." Yet, apart from the debate on terminology, advances in medicine, computer science, and communication technology have indeed been astounding. Even more remarkable are the revolutionary changes in computer science and information technology that have taken place in the first 16 years of the twenty-first century. In particular, one area that has experienced promising developments is the field of robotics and AI—Artificial Intelligence. The science of AI itself has been active for many decades now; at least ever since advances in computer programming have helped the fields of "robotics" achieve some promising results. In this context, a number of philosophers have raised the question of whether the human mind could be mirrored by a computer program. More specifically, can scientists replicate—via a computer program/robot—the mechanisms and operations that run the human brain? This debate has given birth to a number of collateral questions about the nature of *human intelligence*, *self-awareness*, and the phenomenon of *consciousness*. In other words, philosophers and scientists have been interested in knowing whether advances in science can produce an artificial mind, or the "mind" is a unique human entity that cannot be recreated. In this essay, we will review the issues of the debate on Artificial Intelligence and argue in favor of the view that the human mind is a far too complex and elusive entity for the claim of "complete reproduction" to be valid.

Keywords Artificial Intelligence • Mind • Consciousness • Awareness • Spirituality

8.1 Strong and Weak Artificial Intelligence

Artificial Intelligence (AI) is the concept behind science's attempts to create machines that will mimic human intelligence. AI works on a rather wide functional spectrum. Some proponents aim very optimistically at achieving a level of

D.A. Botică (✉)
Emanuel University of Oradea, Oradea, Romania
e-mail: dabotica@gmail.com

S. Vaduva et al. (eds.), *Business Ethics and Leadership from an Eastern European, Transdisciplinary Context*, DOI 10.1007/978-3-319-45186-2_8

intelligence that will allow machines to purpose and feel, not only think. John Searle characterizes this school of thought as Strong AI (1990: 27).

Such "a program would not merely be a model of the mind; it would literally be a mind." From Steven Spielberg's *A.I.*, to *The Terminator* and *Avatar*, this worldview has metamorphosed into several Hollywood productions about robots with undistinguishably human traits; including emotions.

The other theory considers AI the object of a branch of science in the service of humanity, not necessarily one that aims at creating an alternative form of humanity. Searle coined this approach the Weak AI. The argumentation presented in this chapter will take a more philosophical approach and will evaluate the claims of Strong AI against several important criteria. It starts with the underlying assumption that there exists something special about the human person—"Special" in the sense that human beings are unique. Evidently, this does not downplay the amazing intelligence of say, dolphins or apes (White 2009: Chap. 4). In fact, multiple studies have attested that some animals bear some traits in common with us on the level of intelligence (McFarland and Bosser 1993: 9–11).

Nevertheless, the achievements of human beings in arts and sciences bear the marks of superior human imagination and reflect the greatness of human reason. So much so, that the human mind has gone on to further prove its unique capability in attempting to create another "intelligence" in its image and likeness. That is, a quasi-being capable of "doing everything a human mind can do" (Penrose 1991: Foreword).

8.2 Challenges to Strong AI

The science of AI has advanced so much that predictions made a few decades ago have now become reality and the predictions that are being made today seem more realistic than one would be willing to concede. This evidently raises the question of whether AI will succeed in creating the hardware and replicating the processes of human intelligence in all its complexities. Scholars have argued that the human being is characterized by certain processes such as consciousness, memory, creativity, planning, and imagination, a sense of aesthetics, and humor, which essentially cannot be explained by resorting to epiphenomenal categories.

In addition, they assume that the human mind itself may be too limited to create with absolute accuracy an identical copy of itself. It is improbable that, unless one is able to access the human mind in all its dimensions, he or she might produce another equally intelligent being. Finally, a number of scholars have argued that the notions of "purpose" and "understanding" play out on different levels in the perception of a human being and that of a computer. The theories will be presented in the following pages.

8.2.1 *Strong AI, Reductionism, and the Artistic Makeup of the Mind*

One of the philosophical currents that have brought a critical contribution to this debate is reductionism. Anchored in a strong scientific foundation, reductionism has also influenced the fields of philosophy, religion, and culture in general (Jones 2000: 13–14). Essentially, it attempts to reduce all mental states to physical phenomena. According to Hilary Putnam, materialist reductionism assumes that "we are, as wholes, just material systems obeying physical laws" (1991: 242–243). In essence, our mental states are identical with the physical and/or chemical states that govern our bodies. If mental states can be reduced to physical processes, and if one could map and simulate these processes, mental states may be predicted. In other words, the body is to the brain what hardware is to software.

Putnam, however, argues that certain human states can neither be predicted nor explained by simply appealing to reductionist or materialist explanations. He uses the example of the Turing Machine (TM), a device invented by the mathematician Alan Turing in 1936. Turing created the Machine as a hypothetical device that would compute and predict certain outcomes based on what today scientists employ as algorithms. The Machine employed an "infinite tape" as its unlimited memory and a "tape head" that could "read and write symbols and move around on the tape" (Sipser 2012: 165–166). In this sense, the TM served as a precursor to modern computer programs. While most scientists have acknowledged the limits of the TM in calculating and predicting all types of scenarios, Turing's contribution set an early stage for the development of Artificial Intelligence (McCorduck 2004: 59–84).

Pointing to the TM argument in favor of AI, Putnam shows that, for the claim to work, TM ought to roughly predict a certain chronology of mental states. For example, "if I am a Turing Machine, then my present 'state' must determine not only whether or not I am having [a] particular kind of pain, but also whether or not I am about to say 'three,' whether or not I am hearing a shrill whine, etc." (1991: 245). In addition, there seem to exist certain psychological states like joy, love, or jealousy that are not instantaneous states. Geoffrey Jefferson, an early pioneer in the field of neurosurgery, raised the problem of the limitations of any machine that people claim to mirror the processes of the human mind. Though a bit outdated in terms of the current technological advances, Jefferson's point remains poignant to this day:

> Not until a machine can write a sonnet or compose a concerto because of thoughts and emotions felt, and not by the chance fall of symbols, could we agree that machine equals brain—that is, not only write it, but know that it had written it. No mechanism could feel…pleasure at its successes, grief when its valves fuse, be warm by flattery, be made miserable by its mistakes, be charmed by sex, be angry, or depressed when it cannot get what it wants (1949: 1110).

Jefferson's views have not remained unchallenged (see Turing 1950: 433–460) but, overall, his line of argumentation still stands. In other words, the predictions of the TM do not fit the category of states "which determine, along with learning and memory, what the next state will be, as well as totally specifying the present condition of the human being." Since one may not identify these as "machine" states, in the sense that the explanatory power of a TM can satisfactorily account for them, it follows that there exist certain "states" that have little or nothing to do with the framework within which a TM operates. If this were true, one would have to conclude that the TM has a limited range of explanatory power when it comes to dealing with human psychological states. In order to be successful, the AI scientist would have to produce another complete intellect, be it made out of "silicon chips or vacuum tubes" or cheese and toilet paper (Putnam, 1991: 276). It does not suffice to reproduce only "several," or "most" of the mental states that appear in the brain.

Now, in fairness to Putnam, one must realize that he is not a dualist and does not necessarily reject the worldview of reductionism in all of its dimensions. Even so, the arguments Putnam raised have remained valid. For, in order to be able to at least claim it is possible to duplicate the activity of the human intellect, one must first gain knowledge of its blueprint, that is, the original model based on which the intellect was constructed. Jefferson followed a similar line of argumentation when he formulated one of the earliest arguments recorded against Artificial Intelligence. In the paper "The Mind of Mechanical Man," Jefferson called attention to the difficulty of the premise with which the AI proponents start. Namely, that AI begins with the assumption that somehow, one has gained understanding of the model of the human mind, which he or she attempts to simulate (1949: 1109). According to Jefferson, science simply lacks full access to the blueprint of the human brain, to be able to use it as a model in the first place. One would have to admit that, even though Jefferson wrote his piece almost 65 years ago, neuroscience has not yet invalidated his observations.

8.2.2 *The AI Machine and the Aging of the Brain*

AI arguments must also take into account the fact the human brain changes its makeup and, implicitly, its processes with the passing of time. A large percentage of the brain cells (neurons) that make human thinking possible are not only dying, but are never replaced by new ones either. Scientists have observed this phenomenon not only in the case of people who suffer from neurodegenerative diseases (e.g., Parkinson's, Huntington's, Alzheimer's), but all across the spectrum of healthy men and women who are merely aging (Gould and Oppenheim 2006: 271–282; Montagnier et al. 1997: 472–476).

What this means for the AI scenario is that, firstly, the machine must take into account and reproduce the process of brain cell loss, and then predict accurately how the losses will affect thinking, the emotions, and the like. Secondly, the fact that each human brain is unique makes neuronal loss an unpredictable phenomenon as well. This means that one ought to customize AI machines on the bases of the individual makeup and of the neuronal loss of each brain. Thirdly, for the first two conditions to be met, the AI scientist must start with the assumption that he or she has complete knowledge of the human brain, in general, and of the individual makeup of each brain, in particular. In addition, the AI scientist must consider the fact that neuronal losses vary according to the age, DNA, and health of each individual. That may in turn depend on external factors such as a personalized environment, dieting, stress, and the like. Thinking may be a process of the brain, but the brain itself is an organ of the body, which in turn reacts to the external environment in which it lives. It is hardly conceivable that AI science can solve all these problems.

The fact remains that science has not even mapped out the complete configuration of the brain, with all its chemical/electric reactions to the internal and external environment. In order to build a car that functions properly, one needs a complete set of plans and materials. However "when we are not even at the level of an idealized description of the functional organization of the brain, to talk about the importance of small perturbations seems decidedly premature" (Putnam, 1991: 248). One certainly needs to know himself/herself first before creating other identical "selves."

8.2.3 AI and the Phenomenon of Thinking

Scholars have also raised the question of what exactly means for a human being to *think*, and whether a computer program can replicate genuine human thinking. In this sense, John Searle defines "computer program" thinking as the manipulation of the symbols that the programmer uses in order to achieve a given outcome (1990: 26–31). Symbols are abstract notions that only require a context and rules that will govern their arrangement. What differentiates between *human* and *program* thinking is that the human mind infuses values and meanings into the process, whereas the program merely combines the 0's and 1's into operations.

As with Penrose, Searle rejects both strong dualism and strong AI arguments. He makes the case for "physicalism," that is, the view that the mind does not function independently from the brain. However, this is a claim that AI scientists cannot make, since the program is ran, but not produced, by the computer hardware. Now, we do not necessarily accept all the implications of Searle's "physicalism" here. There are scholars who have argued persuasively that emotions and thoughts depend on the brain, without necessarily implying that the mind cannot exist independently from the brain (Jeeves 1994). However, in the present context, the specifics of Searle's argument remain valid. In contrast to the AI scenario, if emotions and thoughts depend on the brain—thus the "mental context"—they make not only *syntax*, but also *meaning* (semantics) possible. Moreover, even if one agreed that the manipulation of symbols (syntax) may be considered a form of thinking, in itself thinking is more than symbol manipulation. It is *semantics*, that is, reasoning through, and discovering, *meaning*, not only following *syntax* (similarly, Jaki 1989: 278).

In the same context, one may also note the argument of Quine (1968: 185–212). According to Quine, "meanings are, first and foremost, meanings of language," which Quine describes as a "social art which we all acquire on the evidence solely of other people's overt behavior under publicly recognizable circumstances."

This construct makes it possible that, due to sociocultural and historical factors, an experience may accumulate different meanings at different times. True, Quine's argument may become vulnerable, if it can be shown that certain meanings have retained their original sense throughout time and in spite of sociocultural changes. At least in the context of the debate on AI, Quine's argument still stands: meanings require a community of practice that functions independent of them. On the other hand, the AI scenario, with its claim of merely replicating human thinking, cannot account for this dimension. Thinking—that is, arriving at "meaning"—requires a behavioral and a communal dimension. In addition, this is precisely what the AI machine is not programmed to do. The program can only follow the algorithmic structure that has been written for it.

8.2.4 AI, Consciousness, Will, and Aesthetics

One other factor that has come up in this debate is the issue of "consciousness." As Penrose argued, "consciousness is needed in order to handle situations where we have to form new judgments and where the rules have not been laid down beforehand" (1991: 411). Firstly, the criterion of "laying rules beforehand" raises an extremely difficult problem for AI. For a machine to solve problems, the "rules," that is, the formulae of the program itself must be spelled out from the beginning. True, the programmer could conceive and write formulae that would solve ever emerging and unexpected scenarios. A "chess" computer is a proper example for this problem. Nevertheless, even these scenarios must fit the paradigms for which the program was written in the first place, no matter how comprehensive they are. In this sense, the difference between human judgment and computer programs is that the latter must be externally/artificially modified in order for them to be able to solve problems that had not been anticipated by the programmer.

Secondly, one may still raise the question of whether or not AI programs/machines may be conceived as possessing consciousness. In an AI machine program, the "thinking" takes place by virtue of algorithmic processes. These would handle the input data in order to imitate all the mental functions that occur in the human brain. Supposing that the program possesses the necessary data and algorithms to make "thinking" possible, does the process itself produce genuine consciousness? One must seriously doubt that this is so. According to Penrose, for a system to be conscious, it requires possessing "awareness" of something, if it has a model of that thing within itself. Similarly, as Baker argued, "What makes a human person a person is the capacity to have a first-person perspective" (2000: 91). In light of this definition, the subject can distinguish between himself "from a third-person" perspective and himself "from a first-person point of view" (Baker 2000: 69). Such a person "can conceive of her thoughts, attitudes, feelings, and sensations as her own. And the ability to conceive of one's thoughts…as one's own is a form of genuine self-consciousness." Using the illustration of a video camera aimed at a mirror, Penrose concludes that, even though the camera "forms a model of itself within itself," the reception of its own image does not make the camera aware of itself, or "self-aware" (1991: 411). What is different now from its immediate past is only that new data has been recorded on the tape. In Penrose's view, the presence of *consciousness* makes possible the act of discernment in matters of common sense, judgments of truth, understanding, and artistic appraisal.

Now, one must acknowledge that the absence of consciousness does not necessarily mean the impossibility of performing an operation. As we noted above, computer programs employ algorithms in order to obtain a given result. However, as a mathematician, Penrose believes that one must also "'see' the truth of a mathematical argument to be convinced of its validity. This 'seeing' is the very essence of consciousness" (1991: 418). In other words, human thinking may be characterized by an intuitive power that leads to discovering the "truth of an idea." Consciousness, then, makes possible the experience of being "convinced" that one has experienced "truth." Evidently, Penrose operates here with a narrow understanding of "consciousness," since the context in which he defines it does not necessarily require "moral" truth. Still, for the sake of the argument, one can understand the reason why AI must replace expressions such as "discovering truth" with "correct input" or "sufficient data" (Penrose 1991: 419).

The factor of "aesthetics" has been another dimension of the debate concerning the validity of AI. Penrose argues that a number of mathematical and scientific laws (Poincaré, Dirac, etc.) were discovered in a "flash of inspiration" (1991: 421). What made this experience unique was the feeling of "conscious awareness" that one found "truth." As Weizenbaum pointed out:

> We are capable of listening with the third ear, of sensing *living truth*, that is, truth beyond any standards of probability. It is that kind of understanding, and that kind of intelligence that is derived from it, which I claim is beyond the abilities of computers to simulate (Weizenbaum 1976: 76, op. cit. in Paden 1992).

While here Penrose limits the notion of aesthetics to the context of science, he uses language that could equally describe the emotional experience of a painter, writer, or composer. Both the inventor and the artist had the awareness of "inspiration" and experienced the emotion of discovering beauty in their craft. In addition, it is precisely this experience that the AI system, "where algorithms and computation reside," cannot replicate. As Thomas Nagel pointed out, "at present we are completely unequipped to think about the subjective character of experience without relying on imagination" (1991: 254).

In the same context, scholars have also raised the question as to whether AI discourse can objectively make sense of the notions of "purpose" and "will." For example, Stanley Jaki insists that "purposeful action involves not only an intellect whose nature is to know things, but also a will, another primary datum that cannot be circumvented or leapfrogged" (1989: 270). Now, not all scholars agree that human beings possess genuine free will (see Lemos 2013; Williams 1980, for the various schools of thought involved in this debate). In fact, if Putnam is right, that AI works best on the philosophical/scientific premises of Reductionism, then the AI proponents may a priori reject the dilemma of free will (1991: 242–243). They would have to. Computers simply do not possess the freedom to choose whether they will follow the program that has been written for them. However, if one agrees that human beings possess even a limited amount of free will, then one must ask how he or she can reconcile this belief with the basic assumptions of the AI worldview. Namely, that all mental states are reduced to predetermined physical phenomena. The only alternative to reconcile the AI assumptions with the view that humans possess a certain amount of freedom is to admit that the AI machine falls short of imitating human thinking. In addition, this is the position that is taken throughout the chapter. AI research remains an incredibly effective branch of science. It is "being applied to pattern recognition, robotics, user interfaces, expert systems, and the like" (Paden 1992: 9). What it may not do, however, is to claim that it can grasp the universe of the human brain in its complexities and, in doing so, that it can use this pattern to create an artificially intelligent system equal on all levels to human thinking.

References

Baker, L. 2000. *Persons and Bodies: A Constitution View*. Cambridge, MA: Cambridge University Press.

Gould, T.W., and R.W. Oppenheim. 2006. Neuronal Death and Rescue: Neurotrophic Factors and Anti-apoptotic Mechanisms. In *Textbook of Neural Repair and Rehabilitation*, vol. 1, ed. S. Michael, 271–282. Cambridge: Cambridge University Press.

Jaki, S. 1989. *Brain, Mind, and Computers*. Washington, DC: Regnery.

Jeeves, M. 1994. *Mind Fields: Reflections on the Science of Mind and Brain*. Grand Rapids, MI: Baker.

Jefferson, G. 1949. The Mind of the Mechanical Man. *The British Medical Journal* 1: 1105–1110.

Jones, R.H. 2000. *Reductionism: Analysis and the Fullness of Reality*. Lewisburg, PA: Bucknell Press.

Lemos, J. 2013. *Freedom, Responsibility and Determinism*. Cambridge, MA: Hackett Publishing.

McCorduck, P. 2004. *Machines Who Think: A Personal Inquiry into the History and Prospects of Artificial Intelligence*. Natick, MA: A K. Peeters.

McFarland, D., and T. Bosser. 1993. *Intelligent Behavior in Animals and Robots*. Cambridge, MA: MIT.

Montagnier, L., R. Olivier, and C. Pasquier. 1997. *Oxidative Stress in Cancer, AIDS, and Neurodegenerative Diseases*. Boca Raton, FL: CRC Press.

Nagel, T. 1991. What Is It to Be a Bat? In *Metaphysics*, ed. N. Oaklander, 249–256. Belmont, CA: Wadsworth.

Paden, R. 1992. Artificial Intelligence: From the Foundations of Mathematics to Intelligent Computers. http://ict.aiias.edu/vol_07/07cc_173-187.htm. Accessed 02 June 2014.

Penrose, R. 1991. *The emperor's new mind*. New York: Penguin.

Putnam, H. 1991. *Representation and Reality*. Cambridge, MA: MIT Press.

Quine, W. 1968. Ontological Reality. *The Journal of Philosophy* 65(7): 185–212.

Searle, J. 1990. Is the Brain's Mind a Computer Program? *The Scientific American* 262: 26–31.

Sipser, M. 2012. *Introduction to the Theory of Computation*, 3rd ed. Florence, KY: Cengage Learning.

Turing, A. 1950. Computing Machinery and Intelligence. *Mind* 59(236):433–460. New Series.

Weizenbaum, J. 1976. *Computer Power and Human Reason: From Judgment to Calculation*. San Francisco, CA: W.H. Freeman.

White, T. 2009. *In the Defense of Dolphins*, The New Moral Frontier. Hoboken, NJ: Wiley.

Williams, C. 1980. *Free Will and Determinism*. Cambridge, MA: Hacket Publishing.

Chapter 9
Utilizing Data from Social Media to Inform Business Decisions: The Case for Facebook

Daniel S. Neagoie, Thomas M. Smith, and Ioan S. Fotea

Abstract We argue that the true power behind social media lies in its ability to provide data for business decisions. This chapter presents a framework and mapping process for extracting data from social media into the various marketing functions. We use Facebook as the particular social media and show how the data from Facebook maps into the four major functions of marketing. We then show how this data can provide information that is new, more genuine, more efficient to obtain, and more readily available than data obtained from traditional marketing research tools. Finally, we provide a simple example of how this process was used for an educational institution.

Keywords Social media • Facebook • Data

9.1 Introduction

Given the staggering rate of change within the business environment, it is no surprise that the importance and necessity of marketing information, and thus the importance of marketing research, has also greatly increased.

This trend has seen companies, entrepreneurs, and organizations using marketing research to a much greater extent in their attempts to identify new needs and opportunities, to increase sales, and to provide additional information at all stages of the decision-making process.

A second trend that is making its way into the business environment is the massive increase in the use of social media. In the last few years, this phenomenon has literally exploded in terms of the number of people using social media and in the variety of platforms that are available.

D.S. Neagoie (✉) • I.S. Fotea, Ph.D.
Griffiths School of Management, Emanuel University of Oradea, Oradea, Romania
e-mail: sorin.neagoie@emanuel.ro; ioan.fotea@emanuel.ro

T.M. Smith, Ph.D.
Hope College, Holland, Michigan
e-mail: tsmith@hope.edu

S. Vaduva et al. (eds.), *Business Ethics and Leadership from an Eastern European, Transdisciplinary Context*, DOI 10.1007/978-3-319-45186-2_9

One of the fields that is starting to feel the impact of social media is in the area of marketing research. Alongside these trends is the observation that people have little to no knowledge of how data from social media can be extracted and converted into information that can be useful for business decisions. Within this state of events, we have tried to design a framework that can be used to assist managers and marketers on how to understand and extract the data found in social media and convert this data into information that can be used to assist in business decision-making.

Given this motivation, there are four objectives for this chapter. First, we will identify the data that is available from social media. For our purposes, this will be done with the specific platform known as Facebook. Second, we will construct a framework in order to map the data available in Facebook into the corresponding marketing functions. Third, we will evaluate the information found in Facebook in terms of new, genuine, efficient, and available relative to traditional methods of marketing research. Finally, we will provide examples of how the data can be used to assist specific marketing/business decisions.

In order to achieve these objectives, we will begin by providing a brief introduction and definition of marketing research. We will then proceed in giving an insight into social media, how it can be used in marketing research, and where the gains can be made vis-à-vis traditional marketing research tools. Once this is accomplished, we will provide a deeper dive into one outlet of social media (Facebook) in order to understand the data that is available, develop and utilize a framework to map this data into functional information, evaluate the information, and provide examples on how this information can be used in decision-making. We will end with several conclusions and ideas for future research.

9.2 Marketing Research

Given the state of the business environment, marketing research has taken on an even greater level of importance within any business organization, especially for those businesses that sell directly to the end user. The most common explanations for this increase include globalization, mass customization, the speed of technological advancements, and consumer preferences that have become both more demanding and more rapidly changing (Christodoulides and Jevons 2011; Poynter 2010; Sevec 2011).

Marketing research is defined as the systematic and objective identification, collection, analysis, dissemination, and use of information that is undertaken to improve decision-making related to identifying and solving problems in marketing (Malhotra 2012). Companies must continually engage in marketing research in order to provide goods and services that better satisfy the needs of their customers, and do it in such a way that provides better value than their competitors. By engaging in this research, companies need to focus on both the present and the future. They need to understand the current needs of their customers and their opinions on current goods and services. At the same time, companies need to work on reducing the risk of both product and business failure by more accurately forecasting future trends. Marketing research serves four primary functions:

1. The ***exploratory*** function of marketing research occurs when researchers have a limited understanding or no knowledge at all about a marketing situation or a particular outcome.
2. The ***descriptive*** function refers to the gathering and presentation of information about a marketing phenomenon or situation.
3. The ***diagnostic*** function utilizes data analysis techniques to investigate relationships and phenomena within data that has been gathered through various marketing research methods.
4. The ***predictive*** function of marketing research allows data to be used to predict or forecast the results of a marketing decision or consumer action (Clow and James 2013).

Traditional marketing research can be categorized as primary or secondary research (Kotler 2000). Primary data is data that is collected to address a specific marketing problem. This type of data is further divided in two categories: quantitative and qualitative data. Secondary data is defined as data that has already been collected for purposes other than the problem at hand (Malhotra 2012). The main types of primary research methods used to gather this data include surveys, observation, experiments, focus groups, and in-depth interviews. In terms of secondary research, sources include customer databases, data warehousing and data mining, customer relationship management and database marketing, syndicated services, government data, business data, and social media (Malhotra 2012).

9.3 Social Media

The source known as social media is a fairly new and rapidly growing phenomenon. It is quickly beginning to have an impact on how marketing research is done. Social media is the media we use to be social (Safko 2012). Mayfield defines social media as a group of new kinds of online media, which share most or all of the following characteristics: participation, openness, conversation, community, and connectedness (Mayfield 2008). Social media can be categorized into six types:

- Collaborative projects which enable the joint and simultaneous creation of content by many end users (e.g., Wikipedia)
- Blogs and microblogging which are special types of websites that usually display date-stamped entries in reverse chronological order (e.g., Twitter)
- Content communities which has as its main purpose the sharing of media content between users (e.g., YouTube)
- Social networking sites are applications that enable users to connect by creating personal information profiles, inviting friends and colleagues to have access to those profiles, and sending e-mails and instant messages between each other (e.g., Facebook)
- Virtual game worlds are platforms that replicate a three-dimensional environment in which users can appear in the form of personalized avatars and interact with each other as they would in real life (e.g., World of Warcraft)

- Virtual social words which allows inhabitants to choose their behavior more freely and essentially live a virtual life similar to their real life (e.g., Second Life) (Kaplan and Haenlein 2010)

In terms of marketing research, social media can be used in two ways. First, it can be a tool for traditional marketing research methods. For example, social media can simply be used to facilitate primary research. An example of this is using a social networking site, like Facebook, in order to do survey research. One could do this by posting the link of your survey allowing people to complete the survey online. The second way in which social media can be used in marketing research is the huge pool of data that can be used as a source of information to help in decision-making. This is the real power of social media in marketing research and is the focus of this chapter.

There are several reasons why social media can be so interesting and so important for marketing research. First, it can provide **new** types of information that cannot be gleaned from traditional marketing research. Second, social media can provide more **genuine** information than traditional methods of marketing research in the sense that traditional marketing approaches are based on asking questions and waiting for the respondents to answer. With social media, listening becomes the main focus in doing research. Since social media provides such a platform for listening, people share their feelings and opinions in a more genuine, open, and honest way. Third, social media can provide information in a more **efficient** way in terms of quicker access. Finally, the data on social media can be extracted, and thus it is **available** to everyone.

Although much has been written regarding the use of social media as a tool for traditional marketing research (Patino et al. 2012; Quinton 2013; Smith 2009; Kearon and Earls 2009; Poynter 2010), less is known about what data is available and how the data that is generated from social media can be used as a source of information to aid in decision-making. Therefore, the purposes of this chapter are to (a) identify the data that is available through social media, (b) map a process that converts this data into information that is both useable and useful, and (c) evaluate the data in terms of the categories described above—new, genuine, efficient, and available. Since Facebook is probably the most commonly known type of social media, it will be the media used in order to pursue these purposes.

9.4 The Mapping Process

After analyzing the Facebook platform, we created three main categories of data. All the data that can be gleaned from Facebook can be separated into (a) data about the page of a company, (b) data about the posts of a company, and (c) demographic data. The specific data within each of these categories is provided in Table 9.1.

A conceptual process was designed in order to identify the types of information that can be gleaned from the data. We used a framework developed by McKinsey

Table 9.1 Type of data available on Facebook

Data from users		
Page	Posts	Characteristics of fans
• Number of visits on the page	• Number of people who saw	• The hours when fans are on Facebook
• Number of likes	• Number of likes	• Gender
• How people who liked the page found the page	• Number of unlikes	• Age
• Number of unlikes	• Number of comments	• Country
• Number of evaluations and ratings	• Positive/negative content of comments	• City
• Number of people who discuss the company	• Number of likes on a comment on a post	• Language
• Number of people who have actually been to the company	• Number of shares	
• Number of times others have posted on the page	• Positive/negative content of a share	
• Number of times referenced through external references	• Number of people who hide a post and/or report post as a spam	
	• Total impact	
	• Number of participants at a posted event	

called the "consumer decision journey" (Divol et al. 2012). It was created in order to understand how consumers interact with companies during the purchase decision. The framework is presented in Fig. 9.1.

This framework can be used to understand the four main steps that a company must take regarding social media in order to increase its demand. The first step involves monitoring what is said online about the products and services that a company has on the market. This step is akin to the exploratory function of marketing. This step should take place constantly in order to glean insights on consumer's opinions (Divol et al. 2012).

The second step has to do with responding. The company needs to take time to respond on a personal basis to the information they have discovered in the first step. These activities fall into the descriptive function of marketing. This kind of response can certainly be positive if it is done to provide customer service or to uncover sales leads (Divol et al. 2012).

The third step involves amplification. This step focuses on designing marketing activities used as a social motivator to spur broader engagement and a sharing of the company's products and services. These activities align with the diagnostic function of marketing. By designing these activities, a company should use its core concepts for campaigns in order to invite customers into an experience that they can choose to extend by joining a conversation with the brand, product, fellow users, and other enthusiasts (Divol et al. 2012).

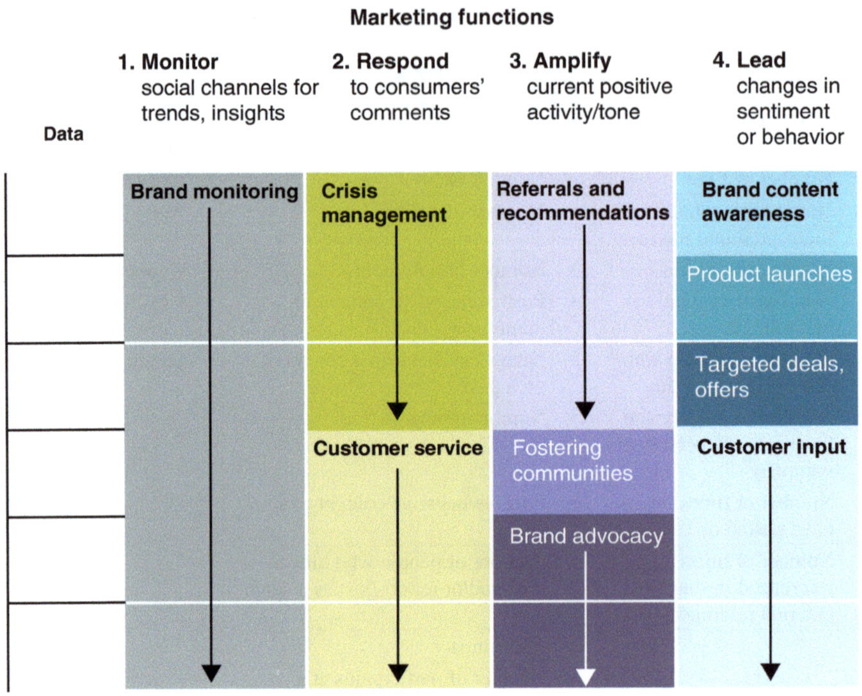

Fig. 9.1 Consumer decision journey framework

The fourth and final step of the framework is leading. Companies can use social media most proactively in order to lead consumers toward long-term behavioral changes. In terms of the primary functions of marketing, this is similar to the predictive function. Marketers should use social media to generate buzz through product launches and also solicit consumer input after the purchase. This ability to gain product-development insights from customers in a relatively inexpensive manner is emerging as one of social media's most significant benefits (Divol et al. 2012).

As part of our conceptual process to identify the types of information that can be gleaned from Social Media, we first converted the four steps from the McKinsey framework into the four primary functions of marketing. Once this was accomplished, we took the data that could be gleaned from Facebook and mapped it to the appropriate marketing function. The results of this mapping process are presented in Table 9.2.

By observing the table, it can be seen that almost all the data can be included in the exploratory, diagnostic, and predictive functions of marketing. However, it is only the data related to the posts on a page that provides with information for the descriptive function of marketing. Thus, a company should be able to find data from Facebook that relates to all the different functions of marketing, or for those identified by McKinsey in the consumer buying process.

Table 9.2 Facebook data mapped to the specific function of marketing

	Exploratory	Descriptive	Diagnostic	Predictive
Page				
• Number of visits on the page	X		X	X
• Number of likes	X		X	X
• How people who liked the page found the page	X		X	X
• Number of unlikes	X		X	X
• Number of evaluations and ratings	X		X	X
• Number of people who discuss the company	X		X	X
• Number of people who have actually been to the company	X		X	X
• Number of times others have posted on the page			X	X
• Number of times referenced through external references			X	X
Posts				
• Number of people who saw	X	X	X	X
• Number of likes	X	X	X	X
• Number of unlikes	X	X	X	X
• Number of comments	X	X	X	X
• Positive/negative content of comments	X	X	X	X
• Number of likes on a comment on a post	X	X	X	X
• Number of shares	X	X	X	X
• Positive/negative content of a share	X	X	X	X
• Number of people who hide a post and/or report post as a spam	X	X	X	X
• Total impact	X	X	X	X
• Number of participants at a posted event	X	X	X	X
Characteristics of fans				
• The hours when fans are on Facebook	X		X	X
• Gender	X		X	X
• Age	X		X	X
• Country	X		X	X
• City	X		X	X
• Language			X	X

As an example, a company could analyze the number of likes on its Facebook page in order to monitor its brand and to also get an idea about its brand content awareness. In the same way, by analyzing the positive/negative content of comments from the consumers, a company can use the feedback in order to develop new products and services or to improve the existing ones. By analyzing the number of likes for each post, a company will be better informed when it comes to understanding consumer interest in certain areas or ideas of the company.

All the information that a company could glean by analyzing the data offered by the consumers on its Facebook page can play a major role in the decision-making of the company and on its strategy regarding the future. At the same time, by utilizing the data that can be obtained from social media, a company will have additional information that could be used when addressing issues with its major stakeholders—customers, suppliers, stockholders, employees, the community, and the government.

The power of social media, and in this case Facebook, has to do with the fact that much of the information that can be gleaned from analyzing the different types of data have a certain advantage when compared with the information a company could obtain by doing a traditional marketing research. We have identified four ways in which this kind of information can have an advantage—it can be **new** information, it can provide more **genuine** information, it can be obtained in a more **efficient** manner, and it can have greater **availability**. We have analyzed each category of data that can be extracted from a company's Facebook page and have assigned the advantage of using social media based on these four categories. This analysis is found in Table 9.3.

As can be seen from Table 9.3, much of the data that can be retrieved from Facebook will allow the company to construct new kinds of information that was not available in the past. Not only is the information new, it tends to be more genuine in the sense that the company has not solicited this data and customers are providing this data without prompting. Caution must be used in terms of understanding the sample that is providing this data. It is very difficult to perform any sort of reliability testing on samples based on Facebook. Having said this, the cost of obtaining this information is quite minimal and the data can be retrieved in real time.

A simple example can be used to see how information obtained from data available on social media, in this case Facebook, can be used for future decisions within a company. In the spring of 2013, Emanuel University organized an event called Quo Vadis. This event targeted high school students in order to help them decide about their future, in particular their future plans regarding higher education. After the event, Emanuel University was able to extract data from its Facebook page and posts (primarily through the number of likes, of comments, the content of the comments, number of shares) regarding the general reaction and reception of the students toward the event.

Using this kind of information, together with the information obtained through traditional research, Emanuel University has decided to do another event this year called Quo Vadis Juvenis. By using the feedback from the initial Quo Vadis event in order to implement suggested improvements, the Juvenis event was

Table 9.3 Facebook data mapped to the characteristic

	New	Genuine	Efficient	Available
Page				
• Number of visits on the page	X	X	X	X
• Number of likes	X	X	X	X
• How people who liked the page found the page	X	X	X	X
• Number of unlikes		X	X	X
• Number of evaluations and ratings		X	X	
• Number of people who discuss the company		X	X	
• Number of people who have actually been to the company			X	
• Number of times others have posted on the page			X	
• Number of times referenced through external references				
Posts				
• Number of people who saw	X	X	X	X
• Number of likes	X	X	X	X
• Number of unlikes	X	X	X	X
• Number of comments	X	X	X	X
• Positive/negative content of comments	X	X	X	X
• Number of likes on a comment on a post		X	X	X
• Number of shares		X	X	
• Positive/negative content of a share			X	
• Number of people who hide a post and/or report post as a spam			X	
• Total impact			X	
• Number of participants at a posted event				
Characteristics of fans				
• The hours when fans are on Facebook	X	X	X	
• Gender			X	
• Age			X	
• Country			X	
• City			X	
• Language			X	

largely a success. Claiming that this event was a "success" was primarily based on the data extracted from Facebook posts regarding the event itself. Although new to this type of medium, the University has found it to be of significant help, primarily in the easy availability of the information and the efficient way in which it can be gathered.

Even this simple example can show how information gleaned from the data that is available on social media, and in this case Facebook can really help an organization enhance its decision-making in order to provide better products or services to its customers. It begs the question on how powerful this medium can be for marketing research when given the proper attention, expertise, and resources.

9.5 Conclusions

The ethical aspects of social media, especially marketing research through social media, include the disclosure of confidential information, the unauthorized use of trademarks, and the unauthorized use of copyright-protected works (Neal and McDevitt 2010; Patino et al. 2012; Buchanan 2010). When an organization is conducting marketing research using social media as a source, it should be aware that it can provide both benefits and limitations at the same time (Poynter 2010). Heeding our previous warning, companies need to be aware of the potential sample bias for the people who actually post on social media and sample size in which the data is actually being generated.

There are two significant contributions and conclusions of this chapter. First of all, social media has the potential to provide information that can not only complement and support information obtained from traditional forms of marketing research, but it can also provide information that is currently unavailable through traditional methods. Furthermore, we make the case that not only is this information new, it is also more genuine, more efficient to obtain, and easily available and accessible. We break down all the forms of data that can be extracted from Facebook and describe them according to these four descriptives.

Second, the data that can be extracted from social media, specifically Facebook for our purposes, support the entire spectrum of marketing decisions and functions. Whether you use the exploratory, descriptive, diagnostic, and predictive categories or the monitor, respond, amplify, and lead classifications, data from Facebook can be used to support decision-making in all four of these functions. We broke down all the forms of data that can be extracted from Facebook and described them according to these four classifications. We then provided a simple example of how Facebook data was converted to diagnostic and predictive information for the decisions of (a) if to host an event, and if so, (b) the general set-up of the event.

There are two suggested paths for future work in this area. The first one involves performing an empirical study in order to validate the proposed framework and mapping process. This could be done using the Facebook page of one or more companies. The critical aspect of the study would be determining how the company specifically used the data obtained from Facebook to complement and support decision-making throughout the company.

The second area for future work would be utilizing the framework and mapping process to other social media outlets like Twitter, LinkedIn, and Youtube. It would be interesting to see the similarities and differences, and the relative strengths and weaknesses among the various social media outlets. Our impression was that Facebook was the most natural fit for marketing research purposes, but future work is needed to support this conjecture.

References

Buchanan, E. 2010. *Internet Research Ethics and IRBs*. http://www.slideshare.net/InResEth/internet-research-ethics-and-irbs-by-elizabeth-buchanan.

Christodoulides, G., and C. Jevons. 2011. The Voice of the Consumer Speaks Forcefully in Brand Identity: User-Generated Content Forces Smart Marketers to Listen. *Journal of Advertising Research* 51(1): 101.

Clow, K.E., and K.E. James. 2013. *Essentials of Marketing Research: Putting Research into Practice*. Thousand Oaks, CA: Sage.

Divol, R., D. Edelman, and H. Sarrazin. 2012. *Demystifying Social Media*. McKinsey & Company. http://www.mckinsey.com/insights/marketing_sales/demystifying_social_media. Accessed 16 April 2014.

Kaplan, A.M., and M. Haenlein. 2010. Users of the World, Unite! The Challenges and Opportunities of Social Media. *Business Horizons* 53(1): 59–68.

Kearon, J., and M. Earls. 2009. Me-to-we Research. In *From Asking Unreliable Witnesses about Themselves to Asking People What They Notice, Believe, and Predict about Others. Esomar Congress*. http://www.brainjuicer.com/xtra/Me-to-We_Research_-_ESOMAR_Congress_2009.pdf.

Kotler, P. 2000. *Marketing Management: The Millennium Edition*. Upper Saddle River, NJ: Prentice-Hall. http://www.bazaryab.net/attachments/090_Kotler-in-Marketing.pdf.

Malhotra, N.K. 2012. *Basic Marketing Research: Integration of Social Media*. Boston: Pearson.

Mayfield, A. 2008. What Is Social Media? *Scribd*. http://www.scribd.com/doc/136469371/what-is-social-media. Accessed 26 February 2014.

Neal, S., and K. McDevitt. 2010. Top 10 Legal Issues in Social Media. http://www.nealmcdevitt.com/assets/news/Top_10_Social_Media_Legal_Issues_FINAL.PDF.

Patino, A., D.A. Pitta, and R. Quinones. 2012. Social Media's Emerging Importance in Market Research. *The Journal of Consumer Marketing* 29(3): 233–237.

Poynter, R. 2010. *The Handbook of Online and Social Media Research: The New Rules and Tools for Market Research*. Chichester: Wiley.

Quinton, S. 2013. The Digital Era Requires New Knowledge to Develop Relevant CRM Strategy: A Cry for Adopting Social Media Research Methods to Elicit This New Knowledge. *Journal of Strategic Marketing* 21(5): 402–412.

Safko, L. 2012. *The Social Media Bible: Tactics, Tools and Strategies for Business Success*. Hoboken, N.J.: Wiley.

Sevec, J. 2011. Technology's Impact on Data Collection in Market Research. PAI Blog. http://info.paiwhq.com/technologys-impact-on-data-collection-in-market-research/.

Smith, T. 2009. Conference Notes—The Social Media Revolution. *International Journal of Market Research* 51(4): 559.

References

[illegible]

Chapter 10
Decoupling in Organizational Ethics: An Institutional Perspective

Călin Gurău

Abstract Institutional decoupling represents a pervasive phenomenon in modern society, one that can be defined as a gap between formalized policies and real practices, or between means and ends. Using an exploratory approach, this study investigates seven cases of decoupling between declared organizational ethics policies and managerial practices in seven medium-sized firms. The results outline the contextual elements leading to decoupling situations, the rationalization of top managers, and the strategies employed to control and exploit the decoupling situation. The chapter also discusses the influence of decoupling on the work-related satisfaction of employees, identifying several different types of perceptions and behaviors.

Keywords Organizational ethics • Institutional theory • Decoupling • Policy–practice • Means–ends

10.1 Introduction

Organizational ethics is an essential element of organizational culture, comprising the ethical values and beliefs defined, expressed and/or formalized by an organization, which are shared by its members and represent guidelines for corporate actions and personnel (including management) behavior (Ampofo et al. 2004; Key 1999). The present market environment is characterized by hyper-competition, unpredictability, and increased social pressures, forcing business organizations to develop and sustain competitive capabilities that respond to market expectations and needs. Increasingly, the values of a company and its ethical stance and actions represent important elements shaping consumer preferences and behavior. Organizational ethics is an essential element of organizational culture, comprising the ethical values and beliefs defined, expressed and/or formalized by an organization, which are shared by its members and represent guidelines for corporate

C. Gurău, Ph.D. (✉)
Montpelier Business School - MRM, Montpellier, France
e-mail: calingurau@gmail.com

S. Vaduva et al. (eds.), *Business Ethics and Leadership from an Eastern European, Transdisciplinary Context*, DOI 10.1007/978-3-319-45186-2_10

actions and personnel (including management) behavior (Key 1999). Organizational ethics are most times in a state that is formalized and communicated internally and externally, by the members of the organization. The aim is developing a positive market reputation. A positive ethical reputation engenders trust in a company's statements and behavior, representing an important asset in developing and maintaining good relationships with various categories of stakeholders: customers, government, nongovernmental organizations, other companies, etc.

The importance of ethical and responsible behavior is demonstrated by the rising importance of Corporate Social Responsibility (CSR) practices, which nowadays are even the object of an ISO standard, the ISO 26000 international certification for CSR practices.

However, ethics is more about actions than about words. When corporate actions and the behavior of a company's personnel and leader contradict the declared ethical values and beliefs, we experience a decoupling situation. Decoupling is an essential concept in Institutional Theory and represents a gap between policies and practice (Tilcsik 2010), between intentions and actions (March and Olsen 1976), or between means and ends (Bromley and Powell 2012).

Considering these two forms of decoupling, this study provides a qualitative analysis of five medium-sized business organizations, in which institutional ethical principles and policies were formally declared to improve their market reputation, but with little impact on internal procedures, and on the behaviors and attitudes of the top management. The findings outline a series of important social phenomena developed within these organizations, in order to legitimize the use of decoupling: the emphasis of the managerial discourse on fierce market competition, accentuating the difference between organizational members and the external "Others," the fragmentation of social relations within the organization. Another social phenomenon was the total control of the official discourse by the top management. On the other hand, the second type of decoupling is identified in two business organizations that sought ISO 26000 international certification for their CSR practices: in these cases, the organizations focused on fulfilling the accreditation requirements, without making real changes in their internal procedures. The chapter concludes with a summary of the main findings, and with several propositions for future research.

10.2 The Concept of Decoupling in Institutional Theory

Institutional Theory explains the behavior of various actors (states, organizations, individuals) as a result of external pressures to adopt, apply, and conform to social rules, norms, and regulations that define the structure and functioning of a specific institutional environment or field (Scott 2008). Behaving in accordance to existing institutions provides social legitimacy and allows the social integration of the participating actors (Grewal and Dharwadkar 2002).

This process is expressed through three different mechanisms (Connelly et al. 2011; DiMaggio and Powell 1983): coercive isomorphism (conformity to laws and norms enacted and enforced by regulating organizations or actors that control essential resources). There is also the normative isomorphism (adoption of voluntary standards developed by trade or professional associations and certification agencies) and mimetic isomorphism (imitation of other social actors to reduce cognitive uncertainty).

Meyer (2008, 2010) argues that the phenomenological aspects of sociological institutionalism enrich and sometimes even contradict some of the established principles of traditional institutional theories. The presentation of these aspects can clarify the way in which environmental ideas and practices have emerged in the globalized society, and explain some of the paradoxes related to their application in green marketing channels.

A central element of the new institutionalism is the vision that actors (states, organizations, individuals) are constructed in and by the wider environment, not only influenced by it. From this sociological perspective, actorhood and action are not connected by a simple causal relation, becoming roles scripted by institutional structures, which, in specific circumstances, are automatically enacted by institutional actors with no, or very limited, rational choice.

On the other hand, the global wave of cultural rationalization developed after the Second World War determined an unprecedented increase in the rights and powers attributed to people, which, alongside the increased access to education, science, and information, has created the institutional role of "Others." These "Others" represent actors that, by adopting a legitimated posture of disinterest, develop and transmit opinions on various social issues, telling more interested actors how to be and what to do. Good examples of such "Others" are NGOs or activists that militate for different causes.

The diffuse, but pervasive power of "Others" creates institutional pressures towards interested actors, so they may adopt specific postures of actorhood that promote the greater good and disinterested action. Unfortunately, these symbolically constructed postures are often loosely coupled with practical action, resulting in obvious inconsistencies, which reveal the contradiction between the unrealistic standards developed and promoted by "Others" and the real capacity of actors to implement or enact them (Brunsson 1989, 2006; Meyer 2010).

Therefore, decoupling represents a central concept of Institutional Theory, generally defined as a gap between policies and practice (Tilcsik 2010), or between intentions and actions (March and Olsen 1976). Faced with institutional pressures, organizations may adopt formal policies, signaling their social compliance, but then they fail to adapt their practices accordingly (Scott 2008). Meyer and Rowan (1977) outline that organizational decoupling can be considered as a rational behavior that has a twofold purpose: on one hand, to reinforce the social legitimacy of the organization, and on the other hand, to preserve a level of internal flexibility which allows the organization to address specific situations using pragmatic considerations. Other possible explanations of decoupling practices are the attempt of organizations to access specific resources, to protect their technical core from environmental pressures (Bromley and Powell 2012), or to preserve the interests of organizational leaders (Westphal and Zajac 2001).

In a recent article, Bromley and Powell (2012) expand the meaning of this concept, suggesting that decoupling in modern organizations takes place at two levels: policy–practice and means–ends. While in policy–practice decoupling formal rules are systematically unimplemented or violated, means–ends decoupling is characterized by an implementation of formal rules and policies that have an uncertain relationship with the declared outcomes. The emergence of this new type of decoupling is determined by the fragmentation of the external environment into multiple, highly rationalized domains, and the spread of various evaluation models and procedures. In their attempt to fulfill the (often contradictory) expectations of an increasing number and variety of external stakeholders, organizations create increased internal complexity and inconsistency (Greenwood et al. 2011; Lok 2010; Pache and Santos 2010), by implementing formal practices that contradict or neglect their core goals (Bromley and Powell 2012; Chatterji and Toffel 2010; Sauder and Espeland 2009).

On the other hand, Tilcsik (2010) outlines the importance of analyzing decoupling as a specific phase of an organizational transformation process. Sometimes, the symbolic adoption of new policies may determine, in time, the development of procedural routines that close the initial gap between organizational policies and practices through habituating and recoupling (Bromley and Powell 2012; Espeland 1998; Grewal and Dharwadkar 2002; Kelly and Dobbin 1998; Tilcsik 2010).

In this chapter, we apply the analytical framework associated with various forms of decoupling, in order to investigate the manifest incongruity between ethical declarations and real actions, in seven companies registered and active in the European Community. Although the concept of decoupling in itself is very interesting, we aim to go further into our analysis, attempting to identify the reasons, strategies, and outcomes of the decoupling phenomena in the investigated firms.

10.3 Research Methodology

Taking into account the importance of organizational ethics as an evaluation and signaling element of the trustworthiness of firms in the modern economy, and the ethical controversies stirred by Enron or Arthur Andersen, in this study we attempt to investigate several cases of organizational ethical decoupling, the managerial strategies applied to justify them, and their effect on the employees' satisfaction.

The cases presented in this chapter were identified during a research project conducted several years ago regarding work-related satisfaction and the factors influencing it, which investigated medium-sized companies from several European Union countries. The employees of these firms were very concerned by the possibility that their answers could be identified by the top management, and lead to negative repercussions on their professional career. To address these concerns we promised strict confidentiality of their provided data, and therefore, we will not disclose any further information regarding the country of origin, the name, the business profile, or the industrial sector of these companies. However, it is important to emphasize that although these companies were active in various economic sectors, they were all subjected to hyper-competition and high social pressure regarding ethical and CSR issues.

To investigate the decoupling situation in organizational ethics, we interviewed, in each of the seven investigated firms, at least two employees or middle managers, and the top manager. The interviews lasted between 30 and 45 min, and were conducted at each company's headquarters. The data collected was then analyzed using discourse analysis techniques, which consist in identifying the main convergent themes in the answers of various respondents, which were then codified into ten anchor concepts: ethical values, CSR, corporate communication, managerial strategy, differences between statements and actions, social and individual justice, corporate reputation, market competition, work satisfaction, and corporate loyalty. These anchor concepts were then used to identify and describe recurrent situations, and to structure the narrative regarding the decoupling phenomena.

10.4 Results

10.4.1 Background

At the time of the data collection, these firms were all medium-sized, having between 50 and 250 employees. They were relatively young firms, having between 4 and 10 years of activity, and their markets were characterized by hyper-competition, instability, unpredictability, and a strong reliance on consumers' perceptions. In terms of competitive strategy and performance, their management can be considered successful, but, from a social point of view, it can be described as highly centralized, autocratic, this being the characterization of a strongly hierarchized structure based on high power distance.

10.4.2 Policies–Practice Decoupling

To answer to the consumers' and the market's pressure regarding CSR standards, all these firms developed internal codes of ethics, which were posted on their website and used as marketing communication assets to signal a corporate ethical stance. Unfortunately, the internal and external managerial practices were not aligned with these formal policies: "It is really weird. We all know the ethical principles declared by the management, but we easily recognize almost weekly infringements" (Employee, Company B).

Decoupling took place in external practices, by encouraging employees to achieve forced sales and put significant psychological pressure on clients. On the other hand, the sales team was instructed to abide by but a few simple rules, which were easily recognizable and used as proof of corporate ethical behavior, such as the interdiction to use comparative advertising, or to change the negotiated price without prior and due notice. As one of the salespeople declared, "The situation is confusing, because on the one hand we are encouraged to use any possible trick to get more sales, but on the other hand, we have clear indications to behave ethically in a few punctual elements. It is like a shop window—you put a few very nice items out there to attract clients, but in the shop you have a real mess" (Salesperson, Company D).

On the other hand, the ethical values were also neglected internally, especially in what concerned the professional evaluation and evolution of employees. The bonus and the promotion systems were completely informal. There was a lack of transparency regarding career evolution or salary increase, which had to be negotiated individually by each employee. The employees were not affiliated to any labor union, since this was seen from a negative perspective by the top management, although it was not formally forbidden.

10.4.3 Means–Ends Decoupling

To further reinforce their competitive advantage in terms of corporate image and reputation, two of the investigated firms initiated the process of getting the ISO 26000 certification. To achieve this, the management team created a task-force commission, which had as mission to study and implement the standards required by the certification body. This task force developed a conformity plan, including objectives, deadlines, priorities, and responsibilities. However, despite the amount of human and financial resources spent on the certification process, the internal application of ethical principles was not improved: "We have the impression that they are doing this only for the inspectors. Nothing changed in reality…" (Employee, Company A).

10.4.4 Managerial Strategies to Justify and Control the Consequences of Decoupling

In line with Meyer and Rowan's (Meyer and Rowan 1977) claim that most decoupling situations represent the result of rational (or rationalized) choices, we found that the management of some of the investigated firms was not even aware of the decoupling situation. In comparison, others rationalized it by saying that it was necessary to develop a positive corporate image, but without "destroying" the internal cohesiveness and efficiency of the present organization: "Our firm is highly productive, and internal control is the price we have to pay for maintaining this efficiency" (Manager, Company A).

Some managers were even convinced that they act in the best interest of the firm's employees: "It is a harsh world out there [...] plenty of competition and opportunistic clients. We just do what we have to do to survive, and somebody needs to make and implement the difficult decisions..." (Manager, Company E).

To ensure the smooth functioning of the firm, even in decoupling situations, the management of the investigated firms used three main internal strategies:

1. The emphasis of the managerial discourse on fierce market competition, accentuating the difference between organizational members and the external "Others"
2. The fragmentation of social relations within the organization
3. The total control of the official discourse by the top management

10.4.5 Work-Related Satisfaction

As many previous studies (Elçi and Alpkan 2009; Schwepker 2001; Yates 2014) demonstrate, there is a clear and direct link between the ethical behavior of the management team and the job satisfaction of employees. The personnel turnover of these seven investigated firms was quite high, but, interestingly, the management justified this situation in a completely different way: "This is normal. There are always people who cannot find their place in our organization. They may have family problems, or personal issues that determine them to resign" (Manager, Company D).

As many of the interviewed employees indicated, the internal situation was tense and difficult, which negatively influenced their job satisfaction and the overall work climate. The main problem they identified was the attempt to deny and hide the decoupling situation, which put an additional strain on their everyday behavior: "I always have to be careful what I can say and what I cannot... There is internal politics and too many lies for one to feel secure and relaxed. It is like a code that has to be applied to anything you say or do" (Employee, Company B).

On the other hand, it was interesting to note that some people justified their participation in the decoupling process by adopting the views of the management: "You cannot be completely open about what and how you are doing your work. There is a lot of competition in our market and we have to defend ourselves by taking advantage of every internal asset available" (Employee, Company F). Yet other people had nothing to reproach to the management, from a personal point of view: "They are doing their job, and trying hard to develop our firm despite all the adversity. Personally, I was never treated badly, I cannot complain" (Project manager, Company G). "You cannot have a completely transparent system, because some people will exploit it. I have confidence in Mr. X [the manager], since he knows our personal situation and treats everybody according to their potential" (Team manager, Company C).

10.5 Discussion

The decoupling situations described above are clear illustrations of the institutional process described by Meyer (2008, 2010). The emergence of rules in the present society, because of attitudes, beliefs, and opinions translated into social activism by significant publics (i.e., the "Others"), creates compliance pressure and determines, in time, the development of new social institutions. The power of the significant "Others" is amplified by the globalized and pervasive media, which provides real-time connection with and between various categories of stakeholders.

In this situation, when the pressure to adopt and use the new institutions is high, but the resources and knowledge available to implement them properly are scarce, decoupling phenomena emerge as gaps between formalized policies and real practices. On the other hand, the signaling function of some institutions, which can significantly enhance corporate image and competitive advantage, is reinforced by certification procedures, which control and evaluate the correspondence between official declarations and real behavior. Unfortunately, in some cases, the extreme standardization and formalization of the certification process creates a new form of decoupling between means and ends, when companies become better not in the required behavior, but rather in fulfilling certification requirements.

The investigated decoupling situations were all determined by specific visions of the top managers, who rationalized these strategies as necessary and good for the survival and profitability of the firm. It is interesting to note that the significant "Others" are presented as threats, and the emerging institutions are not adopted because of a strong belief in their intrinsic value, but rather as means to an end (i.e., to reinforce corporate reputation and, consequently, its competitive advantage).

For the "greater good" of the company, the employees are coerced to comply with the vision and strategy of the top management. Some freely adopt the vision of the top management, suppressing any personal judgment, since "[…] the manager knows what he is doing, he has full responsibility for this strategy" (Employee, Company F). Others decide to leave the company, as they cannot deal with the dual nature of the decoupling situation. Finally, some others remain in the firm, although they are unsatisfied and uncomfortable: "I am overall happy with my position here. I considered leaving this firm in the past, but I had no guarantees that another company would be better" (Employee, Company B).

However, it would be overly simplistic to describe the decoupling situation as the exclusive fault of the top management. Although excessively controlling and autocratic, the top managers of the investigated firms sincerely believe that they do the right thing for the survival and development of the firm. By taking this stance, it is easier for them to make controversial decisions since they were considered "necessary for the greater good of the company" (Manager, Company C).

Internally, these managers try to treat all employees fairly, but their perception is biased by the level of compliance displayed by various people. However, in general, they make good judgments regarding the productive value of each employee, although individual initiative is drastically limited. Therefore, paradoxically, despite the lack of transparency and social justice, many employees have a perception of individual justice in relation to the decisions and measures taken by the top manager. This dichotomy between individual and social justice creates a deep fragmentation of the social environment, the employees of the investigated firms displaying a strong individualistic and defensive behavior.

10.6 Concluding Remarks

Decoupling represents a pervasive phenomenon in modern society due to the multiplication of social, institutional, governmental, and social pressures and standards. The importance of this study lies not in a value judgment regarding the strategies and behaviors of managers and employees, but rather in providing a better understanding of a situation that can explain many apparently paradoxical and conflicting situations.

This chapter has a number of limitations determined by its exploratory approach. The data collection and analysis adopted a purely qualitative approach. Future research should further investigate decoupling in various types of organizations and institutions, in order to validate and refine the findings of our study. On the other hand, the exploratory approach should generate elaborate studies based on in-depth individual case studies, or quantitative analyses based on large samples and validated measurement scales.

References

Ampofo, A., B. Mujtaba, F. Cavico, and L. Tindall. 2004. *Organizational Ethical Culture: A Significant Determinant of Ethical Behavior*. http://aaahq.org/AM2004/cpe/Ethics/Forum_01.pdf. Accessed January 2014.

Bromley, P., and W.W. Powell. 2012. From Smoke and Mirrors to Walking the Talk: Decoupling in the Contemporary World. *The Academy of Management Annals* 6(1): 483–530.

Brunsson, N. 1989. *The Organization of Hypocrisy*. Chichester, UK: Wiley.

Brunsson, N. 2006. *Mechanisms of Hope: Maintaining the Dream of the Rational Organization*. Copenhagen, DK: Copenhagen Business School Press.

Chatterji, A.K., and M.W. Toffel. 2010. How Firms Respond to Being Rated. *Strategic Management Journal* 31: 917–945.

Connelly, B.L., D.J. Ketchen Jr., and S.F. Slater. 2011. Toward a "theoretical toolbox" for Sustainability Research in Marketing. *Journal of the Academy of Marketing Science* 39: 86–100.

DiMaggio, P.J., and W.W. Powell. 1983. The Iron Cage Revisited: Institutional Isomorphism and Collective Rationality in Organizational Fields. *American Sociological Review* 48: 147–160.

Elçi, M., and L. Alpkan. 2009. The Impact of Perceived Organizational Ethical Climate on Work Satisfaction. *Journal of Business Ethics* 84(3): 297–311.

Espeland, W.N. 1998. *The Struggle for Water*. Chicago, IL: University of Chicago Press.

Greenwood, R., et al. 2011. Institutional Complexity and Organizational Responses. *The Academy of Management Annals* 5(1): 317–371.

Grewal, R., and R. Dharwadkar. 2002. The Role of the Institutional Environment in Marketing Channels. *Journal of Marketing* 66(3): 82–97.

Kelly, E., and F. Dobbin. 1998. How Affirmative Action Became Diversity Management. *American Behavioral Scientist* 41: 960–984.
Key, S. 1999. Organizational Ethical Culture: Real or Imagined? *Journal of Business Ethics* 20: 217–225.
Lok, J. 2010. Institutional Logics as Identity Projects. *Academy of Management Journal* 53(6): 1305–1335.
March, J.G., and J.P. Olsen (eds.). 1976. *Ambiguity and Choice in Organizations*. Bergen, Norway: Universitetsforlaget.
Meyer, J.W. 2008. Reflections on Institutional Theories of Organizations. In *The Sage Handbook of Organizational Institutionalism*, ed. R. Greenwood, C. Oliver, R. Suddaby, and K. Sahlin-Andersson, 789–809. London, UK: Sage.
Meyer, J.W. 2010. World Society, Institutional Theories and the Actor. *The Annual Review of Sociology* 36: 1–20.
Meyer, J.W., and B. Rowan. 1977. Institutionalized Organizations: Formal Structure as Myth and Ceremony. *American Journal of Sociology* 83(2): 340–363.
Pache, A., and F. Santos. 2010. When Worlds Collide: The Internal Dynamics of Organizational Responses to Conflicting Institutional Demands. *Academy of Management Review* 35(3): 455–476.
Sauder, M., and W. Espeland. 2009. The Discipline of Rankings: Tight Coupling and Organizational Change. *American Sociological Review* 74: 63–82.
Schwepker Jr., C.H. 2001. Ethical Climate's Relationship to Job Satisfaction, Organizational Commitment, and Turnover Intention in the Salesforce. *Journal of Business Research* 54(1): 39–52.
Scott, W.R. 2008. *Institutions and Organizations: Ideas and Interests*. Thousand Oaks, CA: Sage.
Tilcsik, A. 2010. From Ritual to Reality: Demography, Ideology, and Decoupling in a Post-communist Government Agency. *Academy of Management Journal* 53(6): 1474–1498.
Westphal, J., and E. Zajac. 2001. Decoupling Policy from Practice: The Case of Stock Repurchase Programs. *Administrative Science Quarterly* 46(2): 202–228.
Yates, L. 2014. Exploring the Relationship of Ethical Leadership with Job Satisfaction, Organizational Commitment, and Organizational Citizenship Behavior. *The Journal of Values-Based Leadership* 7(1). http://scholar.valpo.edu/cgi/viewcontent.cgi?article=1093&context=jvbl. Accessed April 2014.

Chapter 11
Evolving Perceptions of Romanian Workplace Motivation: An Employee–Manager Comparison

Randolph Wilt, Popa Liana, and Bonţe Adrian

Abstract During a period when incremental efficiencies are arguably more important than ever for the Romanian economy, practitioners therein stand to maintain the highest level of productivity by better understanding how workforce motivation is currently evolving rather than relying on potentially dated assumptions. Therefore, this conceptual chapter, and corresponding exploratory study, was initiated to examine specifically perceptions of workplace motivation in Romania between employees and managers. The exploratory examination was accomplished by means of a survey of Romanian workers in the Romanian cities of Bucharest (the capital) and Oradea. The survey, and the subsequent interviews of employees and managers from six companies, demonstrates that both Romanian managers and employees give the impression of having an acceptable understanding of what motivates the employee. It is from this exploratory information that we concluded that motivation in the Romanian workplace is an authentic concept, and a concept that merits future research and understanding.

Keywords Extrinsic • Herzberg • Intrinsic • Romania • Motivation • Workplace

11.1 Literature Review and Concept

Motivation can be defined as internal and external factors that stimulate desire and energy, in such a way that people are more interested and committed to do their job, perform their role, and (to) make an effort to attain their goal (Motivation n.d.). To be motivated means to be moved to do something.

R. Wilt, Ph.D. (✉)
Concordia University, Austin, TX, USA
e-mail: randolph.wilt@concordia.edu

P. Liana • B. Adrian
Griffiths School of Management, Emanuel University of Oradea, Oradea, Romania
e-mail: liana.popa@emanuel.ro; adrian.bonte@emanuel.ro

S. Vaduva et al. (eds.), *Business Ethics and Leadership from an Eastern European, Transdisciplinary Context*, DOI 10.1007/978-3-319-45186-2_11

A person who feels no impetus or inspiration to act is thus characterized as unmotivated, whereas someone who is energized or activated toward an end is considered motivated. Almost everyone who works or plays with others is, accordingly, concerned with motivation; they face the question of how much motivation the other, or oneself, has for a task, and practitioners of all types face the perennial task of fostering more versus less motivation in those around them.

There are two types of motivation, intrinsic motivation, which comes from within and describes a person's desire to complete the activities for their own benefit, and extrinsic motivation, which comes from external sources (Dewani 2012). Intrinsic motivation refers to that kind of motivation that is driven by an interest or simply enjoyment in the task itself (Isen and Reeve 2005). It is viewed to exist within the individual even when there are no external pressures on the individual. In contrast, extrinsic motivation refers to the performance of an activity in order to achieve an outcome. Intrinsic motivation is defined as the doing of an activity for its inherent satisfactions rather than for some separable consequence. When intrinsic motivation drives a person, that person is moved to act for the fun or challenge entailed rather than because of external prods, pressures, or rewards.

The phenomenon of intrinsic motivation was first acknowledged within experimental studies of animal behavior, where it was discovered that many organisms engage in exploratory, playful, and curiosity-driven behaviors even in the absence of reinforcement or reward (White 1959). Because intrinsic motivation exists in the nexus between a person and a task, some authors defined intrinsic motivation as a task that is interesting, while others defined it as the satisfactions a person gains from intrinsically motivated task engagement (SDT; Deci and Ryan 1985). Although intrinsic motivation is clearly an important type of motivation, most activities people do are not exactly intrinsically motivated. This is especially the case of the period that follows early childhood, as the freedom to be intrinsically motivated becomes increasingly curtailed by social demands and roles that require individuals to assume responsibility for non-intrinsically interesting tasks. In schools, for example, it appears that intrinsic motivation becomes weaker with each advancing grade year (Deci and Ryan 1985).

Extrinsic motivation is a construct that applies whenever an activity is done in order to attain some separable outcome. Extrinsic motivation thus contrasts with intrinsic motivation, which refers to doing an activity simply for the enjoyment of the activity itself, rather than its instrumental value. As an example, a student who does his homework only because he fears parental sanctions for not doing it is extrinsically motivated because he is doing the work in order to attain the separable outcome of avoiding sanctions. Similarly, a student who does the work because she personally believes it is valuable for the career she chose is also extrinsically motivated because she too is doing it for its instrumental value rather than because she finds it interesting. Both examples involve instrumentalities, yet the latter one entails personal endorsement and a feeling of choice, whereas the former involves mere compliance with an external control. Both represent intentional behavior, but the two types of extrinsic motivation vary in their relative autonomy (Deci and Ryan 1985).

Frederick Herzberg's two-factor theory on intrinsic/extrinsic motivation explains that certain factors determine job satisfaction. Herzberg labels these two factors as motivators and hygiene. Motivators are considered challenging work, recognition, and responsibility that gives positive satisfaction to the employee. Hygiene factors are represented by job security and salary. According to Herzberg, these factors do not motivate but, if they are not present, there may be a level of demotivation in the workplace. The reason Herzberg calls this factor "hygiene" is that, as with proper hygiene, its presence will not improve health, but its absence can cause health deterioration. According to Herzberg,

> Individuals are not content with the satisfaction of lower-order needs at work; for example, those needs associated with minimum salary levels, or safe and pleasant working conditions. Rather, individuals look for the gratification of higher-level psychological needs having to do with achievement, recognition, responsibility, advancement, and the nature of the work itself (Herzberg 2003).

Job enrichment was Herzberg's application of the motivation-hygiene theory. Job enrichment involves modifying jobs so that employees can experience more of the motivator factors. Enriched jobs offer frequent opportunities to experience achievement, opportunities to take responsibility, opportunities to be autonomous, and opportunities to learn. Herzberg stated that if managers enriched jobs, employees would be more interested in their work and, subsequently, they would exercise greater responsibility and produce higher quality (not necessarily quantity) in their output. Herzberg introduced seven suggestions for enriching jobs. These "ingredients of a good job" include:

1. Providing employees with direct performance feedback from the work itself
2. Establishing client relationships where employees have the opportunity to serve an internal or external client
3. Creating continual opportunities to learn
4. Giving employees control over their own schedules
5. Giving employees control over organizational resources
6. Granting employees the permission to communicate directly (instead of through hierarchical channels) with people in the organization
7. Providing employees with personal accountability for their own performance

Herzberg argued that managers should keep the administration of the motivator factors separate from the administration of the hygiene factors. He stated that managers should not try to motivate their employees by offering higher pay, better benefits, and performance bonuses when they can motivate their employees with training, interesting work, and greater responsibility. So concerned was Herzberg that managers would manage by manipulating rewards rather than by offering opportunities to learn that he often advocated an all-salaried workforce instead of an hourly paid workforce.

11.2 Positive Psychology

There is a prominent correlation between positive psychology and motivation in the workplace. Implementing positive psychology means to create an environment that is productive and enjoyable. It also helps to manage creatively organizational behaviors and increase productivity in the workplace, by applying positive organizational forces (Seligman and Csikszentmihalyi 2000).

Martin E.P. Seligman and Mihaly Csikszentmihalyi are noted as two individuals who mainstreamed the idea of positive psychology as an area of study. They state that "psychology has become a science largely about healing" and, therefore, its concentration on healing largely neglects the fulfilled individual and thriving community (Seligman and Csikszentmihalyi 2000: 5). According to Seligman and Csikszentmihalyi (2000), "the aim of positive psychology is to catalyze a change in the focus of psychology from preoccupation only with repairing the worst things in life to also building positive qualities" (2000: 5).

Positive emotions lead to positive intrinsic motivation for completing a task (Isen and Reeve 2005). The combination of having freedom to choose tasks and maintaining positive emotion results in better task performance. The concepts of positive psychology, such as hope and altruism, provide a positive work environment, which influences the moods and attitudes of the workers. Youssef and Luthans (2007) examined the effects that hope, optimism, and resilience had in the workplace on employees' job performance, job satisfaction, work happiness, and organizational commitment. Hope and resilience had a more direct effect on organizational commitment whereas only hope had a greater impact on performance. Hope allows employees to be better at creating realistic plans that are more realistic in order to complete tasks and not focus on the failure that accompanies an incomplete one. Optimism strengthens employee's resilience to break through barriers and causes the employee to build social support and other strengths to overcome obstacles he or she may encounter (Youssef and Luthans 2007).

Positive psychology also encourages maintaining a positive mood in the workplace in order to foster productivity and motivation. Therefore, having a more hopeful perspective on life helps one to be more optimistic about responding to opportunities (Froman 2010). In order to create a positive environment and, as a result, to increase motivation in the workplace, there are fun activities to be implemented that create a positive work environment that could attract and retain employees. Activities must be enjoyable and pleasurable. The activities also encourage employees to be more responsible and team players. These qualities empower employees to be more engaged with their work, take on more leadership roles, and experience less stress. Making work fun promotes positive, happy moods in employees, which, in turn, increase job satisfaction and organizational commitment (Chan 2010).

11.3 The Work Culture and Business Environment

A culture can be defined as people sharing similar beliefs, customs, and norms. Most definitions about culture emphasize human-made elements that are shared through communication, which increase the probability for survival resulting in greater satisfaction for those in the community (Brislin et al. 2005). The fact that culture has been linked to motivation is well established. This chapter will be presenting both motivation in the workplace in Romanian work culture, and information that describes Romania and its business environment.

Romania can be described as situated in the geographical center of Europe (south-east of Central Europe), in the north of the Balkan Peninsula, at half the distance between the Atlantic Coast and the Urals, inside and outside the Carpathians Arch, on the Danube's lower course (1075 km), and washed by the Black Sea. At the border between the Balkan Peninsula and Central Europe, Romania is a part of southeastern Europe and the Black Sea region. Its geopolitical position has had a large influence in the course of history; the Romanian people were always torn between the cultural and technological influence of Western civilization and, for a long time, the political and military domination of the Ottoman Empire (and later of the Soviet Union).

After the rebirth of market economy structures in 1990, the legal regulation of corporate entities has generally enjoyed a stability lacking in other fields. Business activities in Romania can now be carried out either by individuals performing acts of commerce as befitting their profession, or by legal entities, which, according to their statutory documents, have the capacity to engage in such activities. When incorporating a commercial company in Romania, its founders may choose between five types of companies:

- Unlimited guarantee collective company
- Limited partnership
- Limited stock partnership
- Joint stock company or
- Limited liability company

However, the most frequent forms of business in Romania are joint stock companies and limited liability companies.

The compensation and benefits policy in Romania has significantly evolved in the last couple of years, becoming a strategic part of the human resources system. Today, an important goal of Romanian companies is to have competitive compensation and benefits strategies in order to ensure employee retention and satisfaction within the labor market.

Regarding compensation, variable pay is most common, and it consists of:

- Performance-related bonuses—monthly (for workers) or annual (for specialists and management)
- Holidays bonuses
- Other bonuses (for exceptional achievements, for example)
- Paid overtime
- Meal vouchers

11.4 The Purpose of the Exploratory Study

This concept chapter specifically examines perceptions of workplace motivation between Romanian employees and managers. Through an exploratory study, we looked at evidence for a potential shift toward self-orientation, with more emphasis on lifetime employability over lifetime employment. To support the concept of

Romanian workplace motivation, this study was undertaken in the city of Oradea, a western industrial city, and Bucharest, the capital of Romania. These cities were chosen for both their accessibility and providing organizational entrance to the researcher. In these cities, six different companies of various industries were explored to determine what form of motivation was important and what effect it could have on the Romanian worker. The specific questions that we sought to answer via the exploratory study were:

1. Do Romanian managers and employees recognize what motivates Romanian workers?

   It is generally perceived in a positive light if management understands what motivates their workers (motivators/intrinsic factors) as well as what elements can eliminate job dissatisfaction (hygiene/extrinsic factors). By understanding better these dynamics, an organization can construct a balance to benefit from better worker productivity, as well as increase creativity and improve employee quality of life.
2. Regarding specific motivational elements, how do they rank in importance according to the manager and to the employee?

   This question was asked in order to see a person's assignment of importance to a listing of motivational elements in the workplace.
3. From interviewed statements of employees and managers, are there specific motivation comments or topics that can be identified with the Romanian worker that will reflect traditional aspects of lifelong employment (e.g., job security, job advancement) as significantly less important for Romanian workers when compared to more lifelong employability aspects (e.g., self-growth)?

We approached the study with no prior data or listing of motivation in Romania, so a listing of motivational elements had to be developed. From our personal knowledge of Romania, we came to consider that for the Romanian workers: the recognition of their work, being passionate about their work, and job security were important and constitute a link to the concept of lifetime employment in Romania. Therefore, a search for motivational elements commenced. After reviewing multiple peer-reviewed journal articles referring to international motivation, one article surfaced that investigated motivation in a non-Western work environment that in many ways displayed similarities to Romania. Located in the International Journal of Cross Cultural Management, the article by Brislin et al. entails motivation in the workplace of Japan, a collective culture similar to Romania. Social psychologist Geert Hofstede has concluded that employee motivation and management styles throughout the world can be attributed to a collectivist-versus-individualist mental program (Hofstede 1980). Therefore, the article on Japan, and its presentation of employee motivation, though not an exact cultural match was considered well suited to use in our exploratory study of Romanian workers. The Brislin listing of 16 motivational elements, as shown in Table 11.1, became a critical part of the survey questionnaire that was given to the participants.

Table 11.1 Listing of motivational elements

1.	Company's growth prospects
2.	Job advancement
3.	Amount of responsibility
4.	Challenging work
5.	Sense of achievement
6.	Company brand
7.	Work/job recognition
8.	Self-growth
9.	Interpersonal relationship
10.	Quality of supervision and leadership
11.	Company policy and administration
12.	Employee empowerment
13.	Job security
14.	Salary
15.	Working conditions
16.	Fair evaluation

Source: Brislin et al. (2005)

11.5 Methodology

11.5.1 Participants

As this is an exploratory study meant to investigate the motivation of employees in Romania, a small sampling was developed with the intent of leading to a future larger study. The data for this study came from a survey undertaken with six companies. These companies belonged to one of the following industries: Automotive, Professional Services, and Commercial Real Estate.

The survey was conducted by providing a survey questionnaire to multiple participants. Those responding to the survey questionnaire were then considered "respondents." Although the initial offering was to a larger population, the survey yielded seven respondents that represented each of the six companies.

Each of the responses, four belonging to the managerial level and three employees, provided insightful information into motivation and how it was perceived in the Romanian workplace. The survey was entirely web-enabled, in order to facilitate data manipulation and to target participants located in the city of Oradea and Bucharest, with company size ranging from 5 to 50 employees. Though not incorporated into this study, it was noted for future studies that there were four female and three male respondents of various ages.

11.5.2 Survey Instrument

In keeping with the Herzberg model, and following the listing of Brislin et al., the main part of the questionnaire was prepared to identify the items (extrinsic and intrinsic) that motivate employees. The same sets of questionnaires were administered to the managers' and the employees' groups. Employees were asked to assess the impact of the identified items on their level of motivation. On the other hand, managers were asked to assess these items according to what they thought the impact would be on their employees. The scale was numbered 1–7, with the following descriptors: 1 = Not at all, 2 = Almost not at all, 3 = Low, 4 = Indifferent/neutral, 5 = Medium, 6 = High, 7 = Extremely high. There were 16 motivating items based on Herzberg's two-factor motivation theory.

Following the Likert-style questionnaire, which incorporated the Brislin elements of motivation, the participants were interviewed by asking both groups what their organizations are currently implementing to enhance worker motivation and thus productivity. This was a semi-structured interview using open-ended questions. The purpose of using this interview style was to collect a group of statements and explanations regarding workplace motivation. The intent was to ask the questions in such a manner as to allow the respondents to answer from a personal viewpoint or that of experience, or based on their desire for future changes in motivational elements.

11.6 Results

The research questions were developed to explore whether Romanian managers understand what motivates their employees and what the employees consider as their motivation factors. Table 11.2 below was developed from the answers of the questionnaire given to the participants. Using the mean score, this table shows both employees and managers as they rate and rank the motivational elements that were presented to them. For comparison purposes, responses are given for the managers who were asked to predict what would motivate their employees.

A review of the table above reflects that *fair evaluation* had the highest mean score for employees, followed by *work recognition, quality of supervision and leadership,* and *work conditions*. The results from managers, who were asked to predict what motivates their employees, reflect similarities to the employee ratings. Because this is an exploratory study, no conclusion can be made; however, it is noted that the similarity of ratings may support the idea that Romanian managers demonstrate an awareness of what motivates their workforce. For the managers, *quality of supervision and leadership* had the highest rating, followed by *fair evaluation*, and *challenging work*. These areas of differences and similarities for employee and manager may hold value in understanding and improving motivation in the Romanian workplace.

Table 11.2 Ranking of motivating elements

	Employee ($n=7$) report		Manager ($n=4$) report	
Motivating elements	Mean	Rank	Mean	Rank
1. Company's growth prospects	5	9	5.28	7
2. Job advancement	5.71	6	5.14	8
3. Amount of responsibility	5.71	6	5.85	4
4. Challenging work	5.71	6	6.42	2
5. Sense of achievement	5.57	7	5.57	6
6. Work/job recognition	6.28	2	6.28	3
7. Self-growth	5.71	6	5.71	5
8. Interpersonal relationship	5.71	6	5.57	6
9. Quality of supervision and leadership	6.14	3	6.57	1
10. Company policy and administration	5.28	8	5.85	4
11. Employee empowerment	5.85	5	5.57	6
12. Job security	5.71	6	5.28	7
13. Salary	5.71	6	5.57	6
14. Working conditions	6	4	5.71	5
15. Fair evaluation	6.71	1	6.42	2

A second instrument incorporated into the questionnaire was the interview. As we interviewed employees and managers, we learned from their own point of view what motivates them as employees, and what they are doing as managers to motivate their employees. The answers are varied, but they do present an interesting picture of motivation in Romanian work culture. Subsequently, we learned that meaningful information and value potentially exist between the ideal (employees ranking the most meaningful) and the reality (what is used in the organization today).

The actual wording from the respondents participating in the survey is presented below. From these words and comments, topics and themes of motivation in the Romanian work place can be discovered. In addition, this information can help to provide new motivation elements that may not be listed in Brislin's Japanese workplace article.

1. Company 1

Employee said

1. *Recognition of my work*
2. *Autonomy granted to me by my superiors*
3. *The fact that I am very good at my job*

Manager said

1. *Recognize their contribution*
2. *Recognize their potential and provide coaching*
3. *Contribute to their personal development*

2. **Company 2**

   Employee said

   1. *Trust and loyalty*
   2. *Security and stability*
   3. *Self-indulgence*

   Manager said

   1. *I try to make their work as interesting as possible, by challenging them to achieve their best performances and create new ways to improve, and by increasing their responsibility.*
   2. *Coaching and persuading with data!*
   3. *Security and stability—I think that creating an environment of self-awareness and explaining the fact that employees have the power of securing their own jobs through constant involvement and in a productive way are the best ways to show what security and stability mean.*

3. **Company 3**

   Manager said

   1. *Personal development. We see every employee as a unique person, not a crowd. For us, it is very important to know the strengths and weaknesses of every person, and after that, we will develop their powerful skills, and cover their weaknesses with the others' strengths. Therefore, we love complementarity in our teams.*
   2. *Bonuses. We give the employees some extra money. If we give them 30 % more salary than other companies in our industry, they are more motivated, and their self-esteem increases.*
   3. *Training. Professional development is essential. You know, it is hard to be innovative, but if we learn continuously, we can make it happen. To solve problems, we should learn theories that will help us to be efficient in solving problems.*

4. **Company 4**

   Employee said

   1. *Team/colleagues*
   2. *Activity domain*
   3. *Money*

   Manager said

   1. *Encouragement*
   2. *Interpersonal relationships*
   3. *Wages*

5. Company 5

Employee said

1. *I feel that I am appreciated so my concern for the best of the company is always high.*
2. *The rewarding system is very clear, so I know exactly what I work for.*
3. *The communication I have with the top level is very open and one-to-one, so I can do my job with all the information I need.*

Manager said

1. *I focus on the employees' happiness and I try to share the company's success with them.*
2. *One-to-one coaching—I spend time with each of them.*
3. *I try to treat people fairly and to satisfy the employees' needs.*

6. Company 6

Employee said

1. *The first thing that motivates me is the fact that I enjoy certain independence when it comes to making decisions. I can freely express my opinion with regard to decision-making.*
2. *I feel that my work is valued according to the effort I put in and I usually receive positive feedback, so I may conclude that getting feedback from my employer can also be motivating.*
3. *Last but not least is the wage that I receive, as it shows to what extent I am considered an asset to the company/firm.*
4. *Chances of being promoted.*
5. *Being provided with training by the firm in order to enhance skills and knowledge.*

Manager said

1. *A fair assessment of their work.*
2. *Incentives for completing their work successfully.*
3. *Promotion according to competence and results.*

11.7 Discussion

The knowledge we gained from our exploratory study helped us to understand better motivation and the Romanian worker. From this knowledge, multiple concepts and ideas arose, which aligned with our original study questions.

The answer to the first question, about whether Romanian managers and employees recognize motivation, was reflected in both the questionnaire and the interview responses. Both survey instruments showed that managers and employees alike generally have an acceptable understanding of what motivates the employee. They show their perspective through their written answers to the interview question that reflects the topics and themes. Reoccurring comments regarding ongoing employee recognition, helping employees to succeed by supporting their actions and achievements, encouraging employee personal development, and promoting employee happiness would signify that the managers, for the most part in this study, appreciated and supported their employees. This also leads us to consider that the managers see employee achievement and happiness as a way toward employee motivation.

Employees' responses were not as succinct. Their answers varied from recognition to security and from stability to feeling appreciated. This would lead us to consider a more in-depth interview process to determine if the employee sees extrinsic or intrinsic motivation as more heavily weighted, and then how one may directly affect, or not affect, the other.

Question 2 regarded a ranking based upon the motivation elements defined by the Brislin article. Again, the responses reflect that there is much to be studied when considering which motivating elements are greater than others are. However, as we reviewed the results of the ranking, we did notice that a workplace or work culture that develops a fair and transparent employee evaluation and a working environment that links individual employee growth to the growth of the company appear to be high in both the employees' and the managers' opinion for successful workplace motivation.

The final question addressed the identification of themes and topics regarding motivation, and how they relate to lifelong employment compared to lifelong employability. Developing a conclusion about this question would be very difficult, based on the small number of respondents in the exploratory study. The information provided by questions one and two give some insight into the concepts of employment and employability; however, additional respondents and interviews that are more detailed would be required to give this question the rigor that it deserves for a sound conclusion.

11.8 Conclusions and Future Studies

Although this current effort fills some gaps in the literature covering the topics of motivation research in Romanian organizations, more research is needed. This exploratory study merely depicts the tip of Romanian motivation. There is much more to motivation than it is addressed by this exploratory study and future studies using a larger participant pool could help to further understand workplace motivation. However, what we did learn from this study was valuable. We learned that reoccurring comments regarding the value of employee recognition and achievements, helping employees to succeed by supporting their actions, and encouraging employees in the workplace could all be motivators.

This is the start, but there is much more knowledge to be studied regarding the Romanian workplace and its workers. Among the possible research questions that were not addressed in our study was the role of positive psychology in the workplace, and how demographics help researchers understand what motivates different groups. Lastly, the concept of employment and employability is an area we attempted to approach, but which would require more participation to understand. Future studies should encompass elements of this exploratory study. The concept of motivation as valued and distinct in the Romanian workplace is authentic, but to quantify and qualify a conclusion, several basic steps are required. They include a larger data set of participants, a more detailed listing of motivational elements, and a more rigorous personal interview phase that should create comments that are more expansive and "lived" narratives.

References

Brislin, R., et al. 2005. Evolving Perceptions of Japanese Workplace Motivation: An Employee-manager Comparison. *International Journal of Cross Cultural Management* 5(1): 87–104.

Chan, S.C.H. 2010. Does Workplace Fun Matter? Developing a Useable Typology of Workplace Fun in a Qualitative Study. *International Journal of Hospitality Management* 29(4): 720–728.

Deci, E.L., and R.M. Ryan. 1985. *Intrinsic Motivation and Self-determination in Human Behavior*. New York, NY: Plenum.

Dewani, V. 2012, January 12. "Motivation" slideshare. Accessed 22 March 2013.

Froman, L. 2010. Positive Psychology in the Workplace. *Journal of Adult Development* 17(2): 59–69.

Herzberg, F. 2003. One More Time: How Do You Motivate Employees? *Harvard Business Review* January, 87–96.

Hofstede, G. 1980. Motivation, Leadership, and Organization: Do American Theories Apply Abroad? *Organizational Dynamics* 9(1): 42–63.

Isen, A.M., and J. Reeve. 2005. The Influence of Positive Affect on Intrinsic and Extrinsic Motivation: Facilitating Enjoyment of Play, Responsible Work Behavior, and Self-control. *Motivation and Emotion* 29(4): 297–332.

Motivation [Def.1] n.d. Business Dictionary Online. http://www.businessdictionary.com/definition/motivation.html. Accessed 15 April 2014.

Seligman, M.E.P., and M. Csikszentmihalyi. 2000. Positive Psychology: An Introduction. *American Psychologist* 55: 5–14.

White, R.W. 1959. Motivation Reconsidered. *Psychological Review* 66: 297–333.

Youssef, C.M., and F. Luthans. 2007. Positive Organizational Behavior in the Workplace: The Impact of Hope, Optimism, and Resilience. *Journal of Management* 33: 774–800.

Chapter 12
Some Threats to the Ethical Delivery of Outdoor Management Development

Willem Krouwel

12.1 Introduction

Outdoor Management Development (OMD) has been a feature of British management learning since the mid-1970s. It has been adopted across the globe since then. Early proponents of OMD such as Creswick and Williams (1979) emphasised the imaginative use of the outdoors as a means to challenge entrenched managerial attitudes, enabling managers to become more than they were, and to steer businesses through an unforeseeable future (Fig. 12.1).

Others, such as Mossman (1982), saw the outdoors as 'real' and as a theatre for self-development (Mossman 1983; Pedler et al. 1994). Yet others, such as Ridgeway, took a different view, offering tough outdoor activities (http://www.goodwilltraining.co.uk/).

This presentation examines four challenges to the early Williams/Creswick approach to the outdoors, with some focus on the ethical implications of those challenges. Three of the challenges are relatively minor: undereducated practitioners; overenthusiastic advocacy; and aggressive, sometimes ill-informed, critique.

The fourth threat—outcome manipulation in the service of performativity—is more serious, striking at the roots of an open approach to learning.

All four are examined in terms of their undermining of the ethical stance of Mossman (1982, 1983) and Creswick and Williams (1979).

W. Krouwel, Ph.D. (✉)
University of Wales Trinity St. David (Prifysgol Cymru Y Drindod Dewi Sant), Carmarthen, UK
e-mail: krowel123@btinternet.com

S. Vaduva et al. (eds.), *Business Ethics and Leadership from an Eastern European, Transdisciplinary Context*, DOI 10.1007/978-3-319-45186-2_12

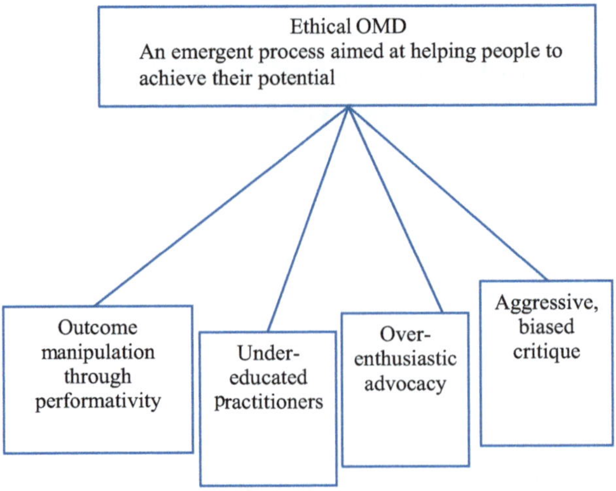

Fig. 12.1 The four threats to ethical OMD

12.2 Undereducated Practitioners and Purchasers, and Overenthusiastic Advocacy

The emergence of a body of undereducated practitioners can be ascribed to a period of inflated demand for OMD, and the reaction of traditional outdoor educators to these high levels of demand. British industry's ability to train itself was drastically reduced in 1981 when financial incentives were withdrawn by the Thatcher government (Pemberton 2001). Those training officers who remained in employment often gained funding by running programmes for the Youth Training Scheme (YTS) which ran from 1981 to 1990. YTS was a semi-obligatory 6-month in-service training programme for unemployed youth (of whom there were very many thousands), funded and content-controlled by the British government. A compulsory component was a 1-week outdoor residential.

The massive increase in demand for residents provoked by YTS could not be met by the few development training organisations existing in 1981. This resulted in the entry into the field of many new organisations, some of which were inexperienced in group process facilitation and simply offered outdoor activities (Krouwel 2002: 4). Arguably, this may have been acceptable at YTS level, but when, in 1985, the residential component was unexpectedly deleted from the YTS programme, the situation was reversed and a great many providers began to seek work within OMD. Thus, YTS, whilst providing a large number of programmes for development trainers and thus subsidising the then-nascent OMD sector, precipitated a simultaneous increase in competition and a dilution of standards among suppliers.

12.3 Fad Status

During the early years, there was much writing that unreservedly lauded OMD. Two examples illustrate this. The first (Davis 1981) is British and follows a group of managers on a programme at Outward Bound Eskdale, where they are required to impersonate secret agents, stealing fake plutonium (Davis 1981: 2). The article expresses a taken-at-face-value view of the learning, with a number of features which recur in later writing, thinking, and buying decision-making:

1. A blind acceptance of what committed proponents of OMD say it achieves: Thus, the statement that it is beneficial to place 'executives in an unfamiliar environment [that] puts them under physical, emotional and mental stress' (Davis 1981: 58) is accepted at-face-value.
2. An inappropriate use of statistics such as a survey which 'shows that around 90 % of the participants found the week to be both a helpful and enjoyable use of time' (Davis 1981: 63).
3. A vagueness as to actual learning outcomes (Davis 1981: 58).
4. A cult-like process of conversion from scepticism to belief (Davis 1981: 62–67).

A second, US, example, 'The Wilderness Lab comes of age' (Long 1987) displays similarities with the earlier British piece, particularly in relation to the bonding effect of outdoor challenge (Long 1987: 36) and the unfamiliarity of setting and tasks (Long 1987: 31). The author (Long) also recounts her own Damascus-road-like conversion to OMD. Long, like Davis, is evangelical rather than critical of the medium.

Pieces such as these helped trigger a fad for OMD which has not been wholly positive for its long-term sustenance. Glowing reports raise expectations so that, sensing a 'quick-fix', clients flocked to an explosively growing market. In this situation the seeds of commodification can germinate: If a trainer is unsophisticated, it seems simpler to sell outdoor pursuits as 'teambuilding' or 'leadership', perhaps gaining a little understanding of a few models of theory along the way (Stokes 2000a: 9). Evidence of a simplistic understanding of OMD by some purchasers and suppliers is shown by the existence of organisations which sell outdoor pursuits or even war games as teambuilding (for example, see http://www.actiondays.co.uk/mission-x).

12.4 Ethical Implications

I once asked the attendants of a conference what word they would use to describe someone who would do anything for money. I leave their response to your imagination. The ethical implications of being prepared to do anything for money are plain, an ignoring of moral and professional attitudes which can lead (and has led) to the terrorising of participants (HR Briefing 2001), and most certainly has led to provider-compliance with anything (including performativity) that the customer wants.

12.5 Aggressive Critique

OMD has suffered quite a lot of aggressive critique, not all warranted. This is an ethical issue to the extent that in the enthusiasm to critique, some interpret evidence to suit themselves and their prejudices. It does not help that OMD has no distinct theoretical basis, as this allows criticism to come from any paradigmatic position.

A critique of the criticism: the selection below illustrates the variety of paradigms from which critique is directed toward OMD.

Ethnographic Study: Burletson and Grint (1996), through a study of five OMD programmes, aim to demolish claims made by a small selection of writers (Mossman, Dainty, and Lucas; Irvine and Wilson) that OMD 'generates an entirely different form of interpersonal dynamics…' (Burletson and Grint 1996: 188).

Their task is carried out using a loaded and sardonic delivery using terms like 'touchy-feely' (Burletson and Grint 1996: 191) to reinforce argument. They also manipulate their quotations, for example, misattributing a line from a William James essay (James 1949) to Irvine and Wilson (1994) and misquoting it to such an extent that meaning is reversed. They also seem to have chosen an unusually toxic mixture of stakeholders to research: trainers who laugh at participants' problems, company development managers who spy on participants, and participants who use humour as a means of bullying. Reflecting on my own experience, it is possible that Burletson and Grint have either been deeply unfortunate in their choice of programmes, or highly selective in their observations. This critically undermines their case.

Ibbetson and Newell (1996), whose quantitative study of one weekend programme attracted a great deal of mainstream press coverage. The study demonstrated that in an OMD programme based around a competition, the effects on attitudes towards teamwork were negative for all except the winning team.

Although the evidence is persuasive (and hardly surprising), such programmes are not typical of OMD as programmes (*pace* Dainty and Lucas 1992), which can be designed around activities wherein competition against fellow-employees is not central. This critique came from a positivist perspective, and again could not be adequately repudiated by reference to any dominant perspective within OMD.

Jones and Oswick (2007: 327) attack OMD through observation/participant observation of one course. They ponder participants' complaints of lack of reflection time (Jones and Oswick 2007: 333) without taking into account that time was allowed for this (Jones and Oswick 2007: 335). Group review seems to have been contingent upon the availability of special rooms (Jones and Oswick 2007: 331) and, untypically of OMD, the programme used tasks which required nothing but physical effort. The writers make conclusions from this one programme (Jones and Oswick 2007: 338), but fail to note its unusual shortcomings.

Once more the lack of a clear paradigmatic position for OMD makes it unable to repudiate critique, this time coming from a constructivist perspective.

Badger et al. (1997) display paradigmatic confusion in their attempt to research OMD. Despite having noted Mossman's (1982) concern that '*conventional data acquisition techniques …are inappropriate to the evaluation of outdoor development*' (Badger et al. 1997: 320), they seek to generate knowledge of OMD by means of a numerically based opinion-survey. This is of a number of companies in South-West England (56 responses from a survey of 100). The results are in favour of the outdoors: 79 % believed that OMD had resulted in increased effectiveness in the workplace, and 95 % believed that the learning had been transferable to the workplace (Badger et al. 1997: 323).

Not satisfied with this, Badger et al. complain about the lack of qualitative information in their quantitative survey that '*what was not clear …was how these conclusions … were arrived at*' (Badger et al. 1997: 323). They perversely and confusingly conclude that such positive outcomes may be due to anecdote and intuition (Badger et al. 1997: 323), both of which they discount, presumably in favour of the 'proper' quantifiable data which they have generated and ignored. They unwittingly demonstrate OMD's lack of a paradigmatic basis by hopping from one position (approval of evaluation through action-research) to another (highly positivist surveys), to yet another (complaints that survey responses are 'intuitive', as if intuition were in some way not a valid human characteristic). They tend to confirm Stokes' (Stokes 2000a, b: 2) observation that *qualitative methodologies … have tended to be seen as 'anecdotal' (Irvine and Wilson* 1994*: 25), merely testimonial (Bronson* 1990*: 50) and based on 'poor' methodologies.*

'*Managers themselves have to be able to integrate and customize the relevant insight with the art and science of management*'. Badger et al. seem to see OMD through an 'engineering' frame (Schein, cited in Strebel and Keys 2005: 143). Stokes (2008) reiterates his earlier (2000a, b) view, noting that '*Many writers on OMD are* critical of approaches *they see as 'anecdotal' and are reluctant to acknowledge value in non-positivistic approaches*'.

I cannot imagine how any 'systematic' evaluation of, for example, my attendance on a 'T' group would have highlighted the powerful changes that the process of those programmes wrought on my outlook. The evidence comes later, in the turn that my life and work took, not in ticked boxes.

It seems that OMD has attracted an academic following which takes a relaxed view of critique, seeming rather to criticise through selectivity (Burletson and Grint), shifting the theoretical criteria (Badger et al.) and analysis of unrepresentative programmes (Oswick and Jones).

12.6 Outcome Manipulation Through Performativity

Outcome manipulation is an effect of the performativity agenda (Lyotard, in Bartos 1990) which has haunted management education in recent years. Performativity is Lyotard's (1984) term to describe an attitude in which performance is the main or only measure of effectiveness and which is '*fundamentally a decision-making methodology that does not care about the welfare of human beings in society … it ignores the needs of members of society to live together*' (Halbert, accessed 7th August 2012).

The conflict between whether learning appropriate to the current lives of participants should emerge from a reflective process incorporated into the programme or whether practitioners should concentrate in a performative way on objectives pre-agreed with fund-holders, is an old one. My own earlier research (Krouwel 1999: 36) unearthed vehement defences of the latter approach. Other interviewees in later research, however (Krouwel 2014) defend emergent learning as fundamental in OMD. To understand why this range of views exists, it is helpful to examine influence of performativity on HRD.

12.7 Human Resource Development: A Culture of Performativity

Since at least 1964, when the Industrial Training Act was made law in Britain, UK Government training policy has been dominated by the idea of provoking specific, measurable, achievable, realistic, and time-bound (SMART) performance improvements. An approach to HRD has thus grown in which practitioners are pressurised to ensure that learning is 'relevant' and has a commercial value (Delahaye 2012: i) (Fig. 12.2).

This state-led agenda (Broadfoot 2001: 136) has had a negative effect on OMD. Performativity '*does not care about the welfare of human beings in society … it ignores the needs of members of society to live together*' (Halbert, accessed 7th August 2012) and is thus a methodology in which the warmth of human interaction and creativity, the development of which are some of the things for which OMD is best suited, are not required. Avis strikes an appropriate note for OMD when he avers that '*Performativity … operates within a "blame culture"…*' (Avis 2005: 12) (Fig. 12.3).

Avis further notes that performance management, an expression of performativity, is at odds with the ideas underlying the free and open culture that surrounds the knowledge economy (and into which OMD can comfortably insert itself). This is confirmed through research: trainers who believe that OMD works when one '*play*[s] *an emergent-style sort of thing*' (Krouwel 2014: 439), or who '*like the organic stuff which can go anywhere*' (Krouwel 2014: 335) and who operate in situations in which '*you never know what people are going to pick up on*' (Krouwel 2014: 282).

In essence, OMD practitioners are more likely to find themselves in harmony with habitués of the knowledge economy than with the requirements of purse-string holding human resources departments. They may find that they have to make their work fit a performativity agenda by manipulating the actual group experience.

These manipulations include such things as:

Frontloading (Priest and Gass 1993: 24): In which the instructor, before a task briefing or possibly just after it

> …explains several key learning points. These points may include … sharing the learning objectives for the activity and any related motivational benefits, stressing the desired positive behaviours in advance, warning learners of the consequences of negative behaviours and asking learners to review or revisit earlier commitments to change before beginning an activity. (Priest and Gass 1993: 24)

Fig. 12.2 'SMART'—a performativity mantra

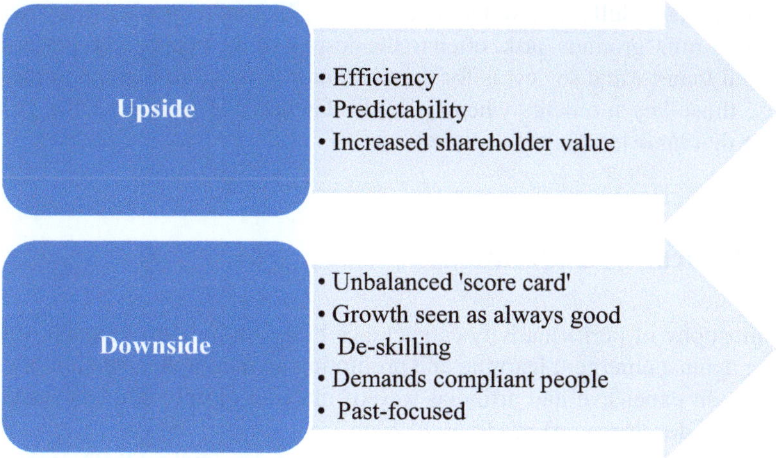

Fig. 12.3 The upside and downside of performativity

Isomorphically framing the experience (Priest and Gass 1993**: 24):** the trainer tries to turn the experience into a metaphor for work, for example, by reframing a rope spider's web as a distribution network. These are problematical. The first manipulates the experiential process, turning it from emergent learning into a set of drills whereby the participants are guided into areas of learning desired by the sponsor.

This is ersatz experientialism, substituting free group process with a procedure set up to prove the trainer's point. The main objective of such an exercise can only be to send participants home at the end of a programme carrying with them *exactly* the lessons the designer wanted for them, whether or not these are relevant to their lives and work.

Isomorphic framing is more pathetic than problematical. Telling people that a rope spider's web is a distribution network may simply not work. They can *see* that it's an arrangement of ropes and frames. If the experience does not have the capacity to be an effective metaphor, no amount of window-dressing will make it so.

Indeed, given Creswick and Williams' (1979) opinion that OMD was a place in which process learning arose from participants' interaction with real (but unrealistic) tasks, the construction of laboured metaphors seems to be counter-productive. To paraphrase Bion (1946), Creswick and Williams believed that each group was entitled to its own narrative, vocabulary, and rhetoric.

Priest and Gass's approach also encodes the 'taken-for-granted' that a sequential progression of plan-do-review (see http://www.mindtools.com/pages/article/newPPM_05.htm, accessed 12th April 2014) is *automatically* a good thing. Certainly, the conventional wisdom has become that this model is somehow more 'objective' than the rather untidy process wherein people undertake tasks without reviewing them, or review them in an ad hoc way.

This is a gross oversimplification of the experiential process. People learn at the most inconvenient of times. To think that formal, offline review is *indispensable* to learning reflects a failure to accept the complexities of the human learning process. I have spent many dull hours watching earnest facilitators reviewing every twist and turn of a 15-min 'grounds' task, often to the despair of the people who performed it. More vital than formal review is for the facilitator to be close enough to the group to sense those key moments when light has dawned and to honour the group by ensuring that *their* learning is captured.

12.8 Ethical Considerations

The philosophy of performativity can act as a brake on the development of OMD, working against emergent learning and prompting an incomplete version of experientialism, an expensive and artificial way of meeting closely defined, managerial training (not development) needs.

From a practical perspective, such programmes may make OMD deeply unattractive to anyone seeking to break out of a cycle of training which fails to suit an enterprising, creative, adhocracy (Taylor and Krouwel 2013), future-focussed attitude emphasising '*fluidity, non-hierarchical team work and high trust relations*' (Avis 2005).

From an ethical perspective, performative applications of OMD are addressed to the 'role-person' (Hall, in Mossman 1983), rather than the whole person, thus propagating a shallow attitude which undermines the medium by limiting it to short-termed, goal-centred learning which fails to address '*the unprogrammable complexities which* face [managers]' (Reynolds 1998) rather than addressing '*the distracting and specious assistance of codes, competencies, catch phrases and mission statements*' (Reynolds 1998) which bedevil the practice of management. If OMD is part of the way to solutions for our tired, damaged planet, it is truly unethical to chain it to the performative, exploitative attitudes which got us into this mess in the first place.

12.9 Concluding Thoughts

The problems outlined above have all had a negative effect on the delivery of ethical, participant-centred OMD. What might restore a more elevated OMD? The answer, in three words, is 'education, education, education'… There is no higher degree for OMD practitioners, very little in-service training, and even less first-degree provision. This is a vacuum which needs filling—the question is who, in an educational sector largely dominated by performativity, will provide it?

References

Anonymous, in HR Briefing. 2001. Issue 46 (19 July 2001).

Avis, J. 2005. Beyond Performativity: Reflections on Activist Professionalism and the Labor Process in Further Education. *Journal of Education Policy* 20(2): 209–222.

Badger, B., E. Sadler-Smith, and E. Michie. 1997. Outdoor Management Development: Use and Evaluation. *Journal of European Industrial Training* 21: 9.

Bartos, M. 1990. Performance and Performativity in Education. *Journal of Sociology* 26(3): 351–367.

Bion, W.R. 1946. Leaderless Group Project. *Bulletin of the Menninger Clinic* 10: 77–81.

Broadfoot, P. 2001. Empowerment or Performativity? Assessment Policy in the Late Twentieth Century. In *Education Reform, and the State: Twenty-Five Years of Politics, Policy and Practice*, ed. R. Phillips and J. Furlong. London: Routledge Falmer.

Bronson, J. 1990. Team Development Indicator. *Journal of Sport Psychology* 10: 32–44.

Burletson, L., and K. Grint. 1996. The Deracination of Politics. *Management Learning* 27(2): 187–202.

Creswick, C., and R. Williams. 1979. *Using the Outdoors for Management Development and Team Building*. Gloucester, Food, Drink and Tobacco Industrial Training Board.

Dainty, P., and D. Lucas. 1992. Clarifying the Confusion: A Practical Framework for Evaluating Outdoor Development Programmes for Managers. *Management Education and Development* 23(2): 106–122.

Davis, B. 1981. Outwards Leading. *Telegraph Sunday Magazine,* 8 November 1981, 57–67.

Delahaye, B. 2012. *Human Resource Development: Managing Learning and Knowledge Capital,* 3rd ed. Prahan: Tilde University Press.

Halbert, M. *Performativity, Cultural Capital, and the Internet; An Analysis of the Internet as a Proposed Medium for Scholarly Communication Using Concepts from Lyotard and Bourdieu.* http://www.service.emory.edu/~mhalber/Research/1styrpapr/ pci-internet.html. Accessed 7 August 2012.

Ibbetson, A.B., and S. Newell. 1996. Winner Takes All—An Evaluation of Adventure-Based Management Training. *Journal of Management Learning* 27(2): 163–185.

Irvine, D., and J.P. Wilson. 1994. Outdoor Management Development—Reality or Illusion? *Journal of Management Development.* 13: 5.

James, W. 1949. *Essays on Faith and Morals*. New York, NY: Random House.

Jones, P.J., and C. Oswick. 1993. Outcomes of Outdoor Management Development: Articles of Faith? *Journal of European Industrial Training* 17: 3.

Jones, P.J., and C. Oswick. 2007. Inputs and Outcomes of Outdoor Management Development: Of Design, Dogma and Dissonance. *British Journal of Management* 18(4): 327–341.

Krouwel, W.G. 1999. An investigation into the learning theories which underlie David Kolb's exposition of experiential learning, and by a process of interview and discussion, to explore how experiential learning is conducted in an established outdoor management development centre and whether it reflects these theories. Unpublished research project, University of Lancaster.

Krouwel, W.G. 2002. *Outdoor Management Development—A Critical Introduction for the Intelligent Practitioner*. Liverpool: ITOL.

Krouwel, W.G. 2014. Outdoor Management Development—A House Built on Sand? Unpublished doctoral thesis, University of the West of England.

Long, J.W. 1987. The Wilderness Lab Comes of Age. *Training and Development Journal* 41: 30–39.

Lyotard, J.F. 1984. *The Postmodern Condition: A Report on Knowledge.* Trans. Geoff Bennington and Brian Massumi. Minneapolis, MN: University of Minnesota Press.

Mossman, A. 1982. Management Training for Real. Presentation to Institute of Personnel Management National conference, 1982, Harrogate, Sectional Meeting 43, 7.

Mossman, A. 1983. Making Choices about the Use of the Outdoors in Manager and Management Development. *Management Education and Development* 14: 3.

Pedler, M., J.G. Burgoyne, and T.A. Boydell. 1994. *Manager's Guide to Self-Development*. Maidenhead: McGraw-Hill.

Pemberton, H. 2001. The Industrial Training Act: A Failed Revolution. Paper presented in the new researchers section of the conference of the Economic History Society, Bristol, 30 March 2001.

Priest, S., and M. Gass. 1993. Five Generations of Facilitated Learning from Adventure Experiences. *Journal of Adventure Education and Outdoor Learning* 10(3): 23–25.

Reynolds, M. 1998. Reflection and Critical Reflection. *Management Learning* 29(2): 183–200.

Stokes, P. 2000a. Boats, Caves, Spies and Stories: A Narrative Study of Outdoor Management Development Programmes in the United Kingdom. Unpublished doctoral thesis, Brunel University.

Stokes, P. 2000b. Perilous Journeys: The Odyssey of Narrative in Outdoor Management Development. Conference paper presented to the European Group for Organizational Studies (EGOS) 17th Colloquium, University of Lyon (2 and 3), Lyon, France, July 5–8.

Stokes, P. 2008. Theoretical Tools and Models in Experiential Human Resource Development Approaches: A View from the Field. Unpublished research paper, University of Central Lancashire.

Strebel, P. and T. Keys. eds. 2005. *Mastering Executive Education.* London: Pearson Educational.

Taylor, A., and B. Krouwel. 2013. *Taking Care of Business*. Oradea: Emanuel University Press.

Young, R.M. 2003. The Work Group Revisited: Reflections on the Practice of Group Relations. *Free Associations* 53:10, 1–13.

Internet Resources

http://www.actiondays.co.uk/mission-x.

http://www.goodwilltraining.co.uk/. Accessed 26 August 2012.

http://www.mindtools.com/pages/article/newPPM_05.htm. Accessed 12 April 2014.

Chapter 13
Financing Methods to Support SMEs in Romania

Angela Vinter

Abstract A common claim noticed in the chapters that treat the economic importance of SMEs is that SMEs are the main engine of the economic growth. However, the role of SMEs in ensuring economic growth remains a highly debated topic in literature as long as "the engine of growth" is missing the "fuel" necessary for development, namely the funding.

The financial supporting tools for SMEs in Romania involve various funding sources and mechanisms. Alongside with the financial support for SMEs development allocated by the state budget or the Structural and Cohesion Fund, the mechanisms, guarantee, and counter-guarantee funds, primarily capitalized by the Romanian government, are the main tools that facilitate SMEs' access to financing.

This chapter presents four main financial resources used by Romanian SMEs with their pluses and minuses generated by the specific context of Romanian economy aiming at supporting SMEs to perfect the instruments and methods of selecting the financing means suitable for their specific needs.

Keywords Financing • Self-financing • Small and medium enterprises • Capital • Internal resources • External resources • Profit • Credit

In order to improve the tools and methods used to select the suitable means of financing the capital of an enterprise according to its needs, there are four types of financial resources that are to be taken into consideration. These are enterprise's self-financing, external financing through equity stake, external financing through term loans, and credits and credit exchanges between enterprises, commercial loans, and bill of exchange (Bădulescu 2010).

The concept of "capital" is used for the first time in the twelfth century, having multiple meanings: fund, stock of goods, an amount of money, etc. During the fourteenth century, this concept included a broader spectrum, the term "capital" being

---

An enterprise has a good health but wishes to improve its performance—Jean Pierre Thibaut.

A. Vinter, Ph.D. (✉)
Emanuel University of Oradea, Oradea, Romania
e-mail: angela.vinter@emanuel.ro

S. Vaduva et al. (eds.), *Business Ethics and Leadership from an Eastern European, Transdisciplinary Context*, DOI 10.1007/978-3-319-45186-2_13

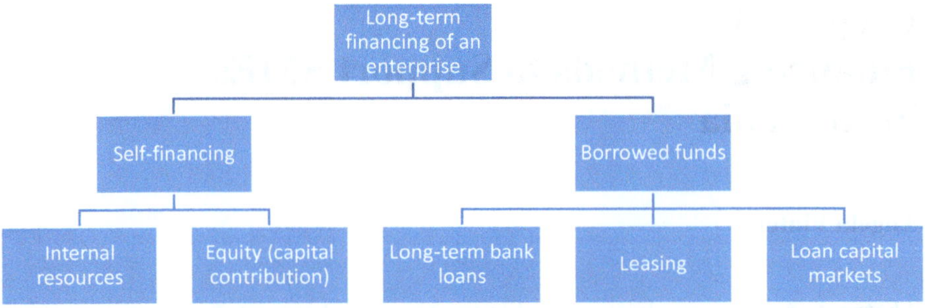

Fig. 13.1 Long-term financing of an enterprise. *Source*: Nistor (2004)

related to the state of wealth. The French economist A.J. Turgot introduced the modern approach of "capital" in the eighteenth century. From his perspective, capital means more than money and goods. Capital indicates a value, an asset that produces other new values, assets, and profits. From an economic perspective, capital stands for monetary resources and any kind of material goods expressed in money that are used by the enterprise to attain goods, activities, and services that are for sale in order to obtain profit (Nicolescu 2001).

The activities regarding the development, reorganization, and modernization within an enterprise generate important needs to be financed during the operating cycle. As a rule, investment activities are the most "resource-consuming" in the entire enterprise. Since the enterprise has more possibilities to finance its own activities, it is very important to choose those activities that best fit its needs. Resource shortfalls can be covered through banking systems, markets, non-bank financial institutions, government resources, or EU funding.

As these resources are part of the permanent capital, found in the financial mechanism of the enterprise for a longer period, a pertinent justification of the financing decision is necessary. From a strategic point of view, the decision to support the investment with financial resources is very important, due to its beneficial effects on profitability and its ability to strengthen the financial position of the enterprise, the ability of indebtedness and future cash-flow projections.

It is also important to take into consideration that the financing decision is subject to the influences of the evolution of some macroeconomic indicators, such as inflation, interest rate, exchange rate, GDP, and not least fiscal and legislative aspects (Nistor 2004). As a rule, the long-term financing of an enterprise can be designed schematically as in Fig. 13.1.

For that purpose, the relationship between debt financing and ownership equity must ensure the lowest cost of financing. The financing decision depends on the optimization degree between financing sources, allocation and use of funds, and the future realization of financial surpluses that will allow loans repayment and thus business development. Another important decision that falls under the expertise of the financial policy of the enterprise is the establishment of a financial structure. Thus, it is easier to decide the way to distribute finances between short-term credits

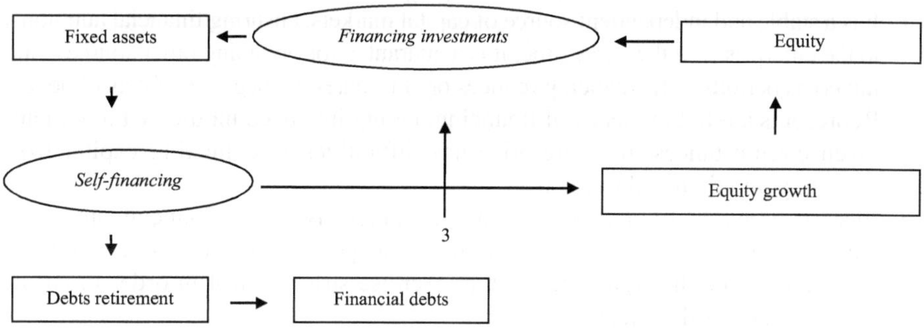

Fig. 13.2 The accumulation chain of cash resources. *Source*: Nistor (2004)

and permanent capital. The expertise should focus deeper on the structure of the permanent capital in order to choose the proportion of equity for short-term and medium-term loans (Nistor 2004). From a dynamic point of view, the accumulation chain of cash resources that contributes to the self-financing of the enterprise can be described as follows (Fig. 13.2.):

Self-financing is the process by which an enterprise finances itself from its own resources. It depends on the size of depreciations, provisions, and the unconsumed and calculated value adjustments. It also depends on the size of retained earnings and incomes from divestments. Since depreciation is a deductible expense, it means that tax savings achieved/realized in this way decrease self-financing costs to a great extent. This instrument represents the foundation of development of any nature within the enterprise and aims to cover the need for the replacement of fixed assets and the increase of operating assets. It is also an indicator of profitability because it highlights the efficiency of the capital employed. Within an enterprise, self-financing can be classified as follows:

1. Self-financing for maintenance: This requires equity allocation to maintain the performances of the productive unit. Amortization is the basic source for this type of self-financing.
2. Net self-financing development: It contributes to the expansion of the productive capacity of the enterprise. The basic resource of this type of self-financing is the net profit.
3. Total self-financing: The source of this type is the net profit, as well as the amortization.

Self-financing is the most profitable and most common financing method. It proves that the enterprise ensures its development based on its own resources, using for finance a part of the expired year's profit and depreciation funds. From all these funds, the enterprise covers its needs regarding the replacement of fixed assets, as well as of current assets used in the manufacturing process. The self-financing policy of an enterprise is a desirable financial policy but it has to be kept within boundaries in order to maintain touch with the financial market. Thus, shareholders would not become frustrated given that they rely on the income from dividends because of the reduction of profit intended for the dividends' allocation. The advantages of self-financing:

1. It is a stable and independent source of capital markets, ensuring financial autonomy to the enterprise. At the same time, it is a guarantee for obtaining other sources; during crisis periods, self-financing reduces or eliminates the negative effects of debt.
2. Represents a reliable means of financing, taking into account the fact that in any given circumstances, the enterprise has difficulties in collecting capital from monetary and financial markets.
3. Ensures freedom of activities within an enterprise. The financial autonomy gained through self-financing allows management independence towards financial and credit organizations that exercise strict control in order to ensure the guarantee of their lent capital.
4. Self-financing creates benefits for shareholders and companies as legal entities as well.

The shareholders have some advantages too, because, by capitalizing a part of the profit, the stock value of the company increases, as well as that of their shares, therefore they become more prosperous. Moreover, the reinvested profit is exempted from tax or it is subject to tax deduction, so there are more opportunities to reinvest the profit and expand the operations.

Even the enterprise as a legal entity has some advantages. It is no longer pressed to fall back on shareholders or financial markets to obtain the funds needed for development. At the same time, the financial autonomy of the enterprise towards banks increases. Nevertheless, self-financing has a number of limitations because any other financing methods rely on expectations regarding the creation of future self-financing measures. These limitations are prominent within enterprises that could have a large capacity of self-financing, but do not require big funding, while within other enterprises the phenomenon is reversed. For this reason, self-financing does not provide a real connection between the need and capacity of funding, and that is why there could be some imbalances at the level of national economy (Batrancea et al. 2006). Moreover, the capacity of self-financing can be extremely fluctuant in time, often for reasons that cannot be imputed to the enterprise in question, but to the economic environment in which it operates.

Professor Ovidiu Nicolescu, President of the National Council of Small and Medium-Sized Private Enterprises in Romania, asserts that, according to an investigation carried out on a sample of 1858 entrepreneurs from the entire country, 91.27 % of the small and medium-sized enterprises in Romania finance themselves, managing to survive, if not to develop (Nicolescu et al. 2012).

In order to fix this situation, the National Council of Private SMEs in Romania set up eight proposals which include transparency and competition growth in the banking sector, the SMEs' support through consulting services and application to a greater extent of the guarantees granted by the National Credit Guarantee Fund for SMEs and by the Romanian Counter-Guarantee Fund. The financial supporting tools for SMEs in Romania involve various funding sources and mechanisms. Alongside with the financial support for SMEs development allocated by the state budget or the Structural and Cohesion Fund, the mechanisms, guarantee, and counter-guarantee funds, primarily capitalized by the Romanian government, are the main tools that facilitate SMEs' access to financing.

As a rule, in all programs that aim to support directly or indirectly SME development, the number of submitted projects is significantly higher than the number of contracts. This fact indicates that SMEs are more interested in gaining benefits of the financial assistance of structural funds. However, according to monitoring reports, the value of the signed contracts till December 31, 2011, is far below the value of the amounts allocated to Romania between 2007 and 2013 (Oprescu et al. 2010). A common claim noticed in the papers that treat the economic importance of SMEs is that SMEs are the main engine of the economic growth. However, the role of SMEs in ensuring economic growth remains a highly debated topic in literature as long as "the engine of growth" is missing the "fuel" necessary for development, namely the funding.

The access to bank loans is restrictive for most of SMEs because banks perceive these ventures as very risky, the average non-performing loans among SMEs being of 23 %, much smaller than among medium-sized enterprises (below 5 %). Typically, banks require 120–150 % collateral as guarantee of loan repayment. The President of Banks Association admitted that the Romanian banks follow another business model and they are not bound to support Romanian economy. Ioan Mintaş, the Vice-President of the National Council of SMEs in Romania, claimed that SMEs has to ask for money from the state.

In the absence of collaterals and classical guarantees and due to recession as well, SMEs chances to obtain bank loans recently have fallen off. Nevertheless, the credit guarantee system started to improve along with the operationalizing of the Romanian Counter-Guarantee Fund, which helps more SMEs to access bank loans, increasing the exposure of available guarantees and reducing loan costs. Though the capital guarantee is still reduced towards the market demand, the newly created mechanism constitutes a major support for Romanian SMEs. Almost 20,000 enterprises are direct recipients of guarantee and counter-guarantee products.

The microfinance sector in Romania has developed in recent years and has become an increasingly useful source of support for small entrepreneurs in rural areas and small towns, managing to establish a very good connection to the European facilities and programs available in this sector. The enterprises in search for funds for various development projects have several other alternatives to the more inaccessible bank loans.

The Regional Development Agencies have published a catalog that includes almost 20 programs designed for commercial entities, which are supported by the European Union, the Romanian government or the National Credit Guarantee Fund for Small and Medium-Sized Enterprises (FNGCIMM). The novelty in the field of European funds consists of the launch of the operation 1.3.3. Support for the enterprises' integration in supply chains or clusters through POS CCE. This concept is new on the Romanian market, that is why only 40 clusters are currently active nationwide, but partnerships will be the key elements in attracting European funds between 2014 and 2020. The advantage of self-financing allows entrepreneurs to run their businesses with minimal amounts of money from other sources, to delay raising capital from external sources and to keep the company as their property. The necessary capital for carrying out the activities of the enterprise can be raised from sources such as family, friends, "angel" type investors (individuals who have the necessary capital and invest it in business receiving in exchange shares in the company or other evidence of indebtedness), or others. Self-financing is a method used by the entrepreneurs to extend the time in which the enterprise can operate with the funds they have.

Self-financing can take various forms including alternative sources of financing (personal or business) or cost reduction. Sometimes, incentives are needed to attract investments in the enterprise including shares, ownership certificates, and opportunities to buy more shares offered to employees, business partners, and even customers. Why should you self-finance your enterprise? Why should one not seek external investment resources? The answer is that such investment resources are quickly becoming very expensive methods to finance the enterprise. In addition, control of a business can be easily lost.

Within successful enterprises, the ordinary shares are beyond 100 %/year. Therefore, it is advisable to sell shares in order to raise the necessary amount of money for starting the business unless you have ensured that there is no other possible option (Herbei and Dumitru 2009). In addition, the interest rates of banks for loans allocated to SMEs are less affordable amid economic difficulties. There are several other reasons in support of self-financing rather than selling shares: fundraising lasts much longer than most entrepreneurs anticipate. This period could be spent more efficiently on selling the first product, which would generate revenues and profits. Raising the capital too early is another danger that entrepreneurs have to face. When a company fails to achieve the milestones, the value of shares increases the ownership level of the new investors. Self-financing guarantees 100 % ownership of the enterprise.

References

Bădulescu, D. 2010. Finanţarea IMM-urilor: dimensiunile nevoii şi răspunsurile diferitelor structuri de creditare. *Economie teoretică şi aplicată* XVII(7(548)): 22–35.

Batrancea Ioan, Batrancea Larissa Margareta, Batrancea Maria, Trifoi Ion-Gigi. The New Valences of Financial Analysis in Romanian Enterprises in the Context of IFRS Adoption. In *4th International Conference for Young Researchers of Economics*, 27–33. Budapest, Hungary: Szent Istvan Egyetemi, 2006.

Herbei, M., and F. Dumitru. 2009. *Gestiune financiară*. Timişoara: Editura Universităţii de Vest.

Nicolescu, O. 2001. *Managementul întreprinderilor mici şi mijlocii*. Bucureşti: Editura Economică.

Nicolescu, O., I.C. Haiduc, and D. Nancu. 2012. *Carta Albă a IMM-urilor din România—2012*. Bucureşti: Sigma.

Nistor, I. 2004. *Teorie şi practică în finanţarea întreprinderilor*. Cluj-Napoca: Casa Cărţii de Ştiinţă.

Oprescu, Gh, et al. 2010. *Analiza capacităţii de absorbţie a fondurilor comunitare în România*. Bucureşti: Institutul European din România—Studii de impact III.

Chapter 14
Ecological Policies and Their Challenges for the Economy of Eastern Europe

Igor Prisac

Abstract This chapter is a study of the ecological policy process in the last four decades, showing the system input at the international, regional, and national levels. The international community and national governments were involved in an active process in the last decades, elaborating more concepts, objectives, and strategies on the issue of sustainable development. The main challenge the economy of Eastern Europe is facing nowadays is how to put economic development and sustainability on a dynamic equilibrium track, enabling its social system to provide functional well-being. The attitude of the individuals and enterprises plays a big role and they are very important actors in tackling this problem. The methodology of this study consists in applying the systemic approach in analyzing ecological policy input at all levels. In addition, the method of historical analysis and phenomenology plays an important role in studying the evolution of the process approached in this chapter. The systematization of all input made until today represents one of the achievements of this research. An important conclusion of this chapter consists in the idea that the economic policies of the countries from Eastern Europe must take into consideration all legal and strategic policy achievements and must try to continue to develop this process towards a transdisciplinary approach in all decisions and actions by transition to new levels of sustainable development.

Keywords Sustainable development • Economic development • Ecological economy • Economic policies • Strategies • Conference • Production • Industrial development • International cooperation • Regional process • Technologies • National policies

14.1 Introduction

Industrial development started in Great Britain and the USA in the nineteenth century and advances in science played a big role in the 100-fold growth of the gross world product up to nowadays. However, very little progress has been made to find the vital

I. Prisac, Ph.D. (✉)
Divitia Gratiae University, Chisinau, Moldova
e-mail: ida@uni-dg.md

S. Vaduva et al. (eds.), *Business Ethics and Leadership from an Eastern European, Transdisciplinary Context*, DOI 10.1007/978-3-319-45186-2_14

balance between human activities and natural resource consumption and preservation, except for scientific works and research, conferences and norms. Talking about ecological policies in the context of Eastern Europe nowadays, we must approach it at the international, regional, and national levels and observe the evolution of this process throughout its history, analyzing the input at all these levels.

In the last decades, big progress has been made in the approving mechanisms to protect the environment but still many countries from Eastern Europe, especially those from the New Independent States, have to create the necessary functional structures to have this process happen.

14.1.1 International Input in Ecological Strategies and Policy Promotion

International institutions such as the UN held the first conferences and concrete steps in finding the right political solution for ecological economy. This represented a big help for the member states in trying to find the right economic strategy and direction towards sustainability. The first steps towards international and national ecological policies under the UN's coordination took place in 1972, with the first world conference on the environment, called *The United Nations Conference on the Human Environment*, which took place in Stockholm. This conference ended with the well-known declaration that proclaims the very big importance of the environment and sets up more principles to enhance the human environment.

According to this document, "man is both creature and molder of his environment" (Declaration of the United Nations Conference on the Human Environment 1972). The question raised by this declaration concerns how "the natural growth of the population continuously presents problems for the preservation of the environment, and adequate policies and measures should be adopted, as appropriate, to face these problems" (Declaration of the United Nations Conference on the Human Environment 1972). Subsequently, the civil society from the developed countries became more aware of the environmental issues of industrialization while the developing countries' leadership could not reach their economic performances and compete with reality.

In order to find a solution to environmental challenges, the *Brundtland Commission* was created by the General Assembly in December 1983 and named after its Chairman, the former Prime Minister of Norway, Harlem Brundtland. This step was taken to prepare a broad report on finding ways, perspectives, and long-term environmental strategies to the year 2000 and beyond (United Nation General Assembly 1983). In comparison with the Declaration of Stockholm (1972), the Brundtland Commission began its work committed to the unity of environment and development. He states that "the environment does not exist as a sphere separate from human actions, ambitions, and needs, and attempts to defend it in isolation from human concerns...but the 'environment' is where we live and 'development' is what we all do in attempting to improve our lot...the two are inseparable" (Robert et al. 2005).

In 1987, the Brundtland Commission produced a famous 383-page report named *Our Common Future*, also known as the Brundtland Report, which for the first time submitted the term "sustainable development," a term that would help the nations' policies in finding the right way of economic development. This report has put the environment and development on the political agenda as one single issue. Sustainable development is defined as "the ability to make development sustainable—to ensure that it meets the needs of the present without compromising the ability of future generations to meet their own needs" (Robert et al. 2005). In fact, this definition is not a radical invention as it makes use of several decades' worth of human awareness. However, it puts together both needs of humankind, consisting in the necessity of goods and development, on one hand, and of environment protection, on the other hand. It really shows what should be the right way to follow in all countries' policies in order to have a better future. As a result, this report presents seven economic policies recommended for the UN member states.

It targets the following aspects and actions: resizing economic growth towards natural resources conservation, changing the process of growing, and satisfying the essential necessities of work, food, energy, water, dwelling, and healthcare for all habitants. Moreover, it aims at providing a sustainable level of population growth, conserving and increasing the resource base, restructuring technologies and control of risks and the integration of decisions regarding economy and environment in a single process (Rusu 2002: 7). As Rusu (2002) states, the main concepts at the core of this report are ecological and sustainable industrial development; sustainable energetics; sustainable water management; and sustainability based on ecological space (2002: 7).

This objective helps us infer that a strategy of sustainable development must contain essential components, such as the stabilization of demographic growth, the reduction of oil dependence, the promotion of renewable energy, soil conservation, the protection of Earth's biological system, material recycling (Rusu 2002: 7), as well as investing in ecological technologies and innovations, and promoting research in this field.

This process in the 1980s laid an important foundation for future collaboration, institutions, and national policies on sustainable development. In this respect, the major Conference on Environment under UN took place in Rio de Janeiro in June 1992, a significant step taken in continuing the process of sustainable development. The main problems addressed at this world event mainly dealt with the pollution by vehicle emissions and toxic components because of production processes, the importance of replacing fossil fuels with alternative energy sources, as well as the water scarcity problem (Rio Declaration on Environment and Development 1992). The results of the conference also consist in raising global awareness regarding the climate change, expressed in a convention that led to the Kyoto Protocol of December 1997, which aimed to stop climate change caused by atmospheric emissions of carbon dioxide. Another product of the Rio de Janeiro Conference was *Agenda 21*, which is an action plan for the international organizations and the governments able to implement ecological policies. This document played a key role in many Eastern European countries, enabling them to elaborate national strategies for sustainable economic development.

The commitment of nations for the new course of development and for ensuring civilization security was confirmed again at the *Global Summit on Sustainable Development* in 2002, which took place in Johannesburg. In this respect, the sustainable development concept became a priority model for most countries of the world (Ursul et al. 2009: 8). Among the main issues discussed at this world event were poverty and social problems, environment degradation and pollution, the negative effects of globalization. In addition, vulnerability to natural hazards, irrational use of natural resources, the political and military instability in multiple regions of the globe, and economic divides and inequalities, within societies and between the rich and the developing countries were approached (Ursul et al. 2009: 15).

To the present day, the concept of sustainable development is still debated among many scientific communities and representatives of civil society, featured in over a million web pages and enmeshed in the aspirations of countless programs, places, and institutions (Robert et al. 2005). To some scholars, this represents the conservation of civilization and of the biosphere, representing a new global concept of the world (Ursul et al. 2009: 23). For others, the goal of sustainable development is to meet the needs, now and in the future, for human, economic, and social development within the boundaries of the planet's life support systems (Robert et al. 2005).

Of highest importance is the fact that sustainable development is a movement accepted by all nations, having even become an essential international value of international relations in the twenty-first century, according to the *United Nations Millennium Declaration* from 2000. The declaration states that "prudence must be shown in the management of all living species and natural resources, in accordance with the precepts of sustainable development" (United Nations Millennium Declaration 2000).

14.2 Regional Input in Enhancing Ecological Policies

The collapse of the Soviet Union also resulted in a multilateral collaboration including in the field of ecological policies and environment protection. This process has had several important steps through conferences and events, resulting in the elaboration of standards and pan-European strategies, as well as national policies for the amelioration of the environment. Together, they constitute the pan-European process called *Environment for Europe* (Capcelea 2003: 11). In fact, the first discussions on the European continent addressing ecological issues took place at the Conference for Security and Cooperation in Helsinki (1975), which drew society's attention to a potential ecological conflict in case of trans-border pollution (Capcelea 2003: 13).

The first European conference dedicated to the environment took place in June 1991 at Dobris, with the participation of 34 Ministers of the Environment from Europe and other states, such as Brazil, Canada, Japan, and the USA, and the Ministers of the Environment from the former Soviet Union states: Belarus, Estonia,

Lithuania, Latvia, The Republic of Moldova, and Ukraine. The conference discussed ways of strengthening cooperation to protect and ameliorate the environment, and of long-term strategies toward an environmental program for Europe (First Ministerial Conference "Environment for Europe" 1991). In the conference's conclusion, it was noted that

> an important cause of environmental degradation is the failure to observe strong pollution control standards… they urged the central and eastern European countries to set a timetable for their applications in the EC and EFTA region and to begin by evaluating the consequences of such a step and technical and financial cooperation (Conclusions of the conference "Environment for Europe" 1991).

The Ministers also stressed the need for information exchange with regard to ecological legislation and program initiatives (Conclusions of the conference "Environment for Europe" 1991).

This process continued with the conference in Lucerne in April 1993, where several documents have been adopted as part of a common action for environment protection. Point 8 from the *Lucerne Declaration* refers to Central and Eastern Europe, stating that

> there will still be areas where pollution affects human health, where ecosystems are at risk of suffering irreversible changes, or where the economic costs of the environment are very high…these priority problems may be addressed in a cost-effective manner, drawing on the experience of past and current programs and offering proposals for reinforcing or reorienting ongoing programs and improving their coordination. It emphasizes the need for international cooperation…including investments and joint ventures, for the facilitation of the transfer of environmentally sound technologies, and for the move towards enforcing international standards, bearing in mind the economic and financial problems as a result of the transition to a market economy (Lucerne Declaration on "Environment for Europe").

From this document, we can observe that, since 1993, the transition of the Eastern European countries to the free market economy also included a transition to a sustainable economy, complicating the requirements for national policies. Because of the financial and economic problems in the 1990s, most of these countries succeeded very little in implementing the principles agreed at the international, regional, and national levels.

The third Ministerial Conference "Environment for Europe" took place in Sofia on October 23–25, 1995, and displayed a higher representation of the European society of Ministers, members of parliaments, representatives of business circles, and NGOs. One of the goals of this event was the review of the *Environmental Action Programme* for Central and Eastern Europe and for further development of this action agenda. The conclusion of the Conference Declaration approaches several key issues such as the implementation of the Environmental Action Programme for Central and Eastern Europe, the financing of the environment programs in Central and Eastern European countries, business and the environment, public participation, environmental conventions, etc. (Ministerial Conference "Environment for Europe" 1995).

The next evaluation of the European environment took place in Aarhus in June 1998, with the participation of 54 member countries of the *United Nations Economic*

Commission for Europe (UNECE). This regional event resulted in the signing and ratifying of the *Aarhus Convention*. The Aarhus Convention is a multilateral environmental agreement that makes provisions for the creation of opportunities for citizens to access information regarding ecological issues and improves transparency for environmental governance (Convention on access to information, public participation in decision-making and access to justice in environmental matters 1998). Another important decision of the Conference in Aarhus is the *Declaration of the Environment Ministers* stressing the importance of the enterprises' involvement in environment protection through efficient ecological management and productivity increase, and by starting a bilateral cooperation between the countries of the region (Capcelea 2003: 43).

Another step forward was the Fifth Ministerial Conference *Environment for Europe*, which took place in Kyiv in May 2003. During the Conference, three Protocols to Conventions of the UNECE were adopted and opened for signing. The Ministers and the Heads of Delegation also endorsed the Guidelines for Strengthening the Compliance with and the Implementation of MEAs in the UNECE region (Fifth Ministerial Conference "Environment for Europe" 2003). On the second day, three important issues were jointly addressed: allowing the market to work for the environment; agriculture as an example of sectorial policy integration; and overcoming institutional weaknesses that prevent integration (Fifth Ministerial Conference "Environment for Europe" 2003).

With the Aarhus Convention (1998) and the declarations at the Kyiv Conference (2003), Belgrade Conference (2007), and Astana Conference (2011), we note that the European process on environment increasingly gains a transdisciplinary approach at the beginning of the twenty-first century. The European community came to the understanding that sustainable development rests not only on the shoulders of the government or of civil society, but also on those of every citizen and enterprise. In turn, local authorities must be as open as possible toward their citizens and economic agents in order to form the necessary functional structures in society and to contribute to the systems' self-organization and the dynamic equilibrium between the society, the decision makers, the enterprises, and NGOs. The improvement of safety and the quality of life, as well as providing a healthy environment and access to healthcare are some of the main catalysts to boost and improve the ecological situation in our countries.

One of the main catalysts and a big attractor for sustainable development in the region of Eastern Europe is the European integration process, which started in the 1990s, in parallel with the Environment for Europe process. By Art.2 of the Maastricht Treaty (1992), one of the objectives of European Union is

> …to promote throughout the Community a harmonious and balanced development of economic activities, sustainable and non-inflationary growth respecting the environment, a high degree of convergence of economic performance, a high level of employment and of social protection, the raising of the standard of living and quality of life, and economic and social cohesion… (The Maastricht Treaty 1992).

In 2001 there were more than 300 official documents on the environment within the EU (Capcelea 2001: 7). The European Union has invested significant resources and good practices in the new member states from Eastern Europe over the last decades, enhancing the standards, strategies, national plans, and implementation at all levels of the sustainable environment development actions through intense multilateral collaboration, financing, and monitoring. The institutions of the European Union play an active and important role in the sectorial economy concerning water, chemical substance production, toxic and dangerous wastes. Its ecological impact is visible in the relations with the European Union's neighbors and the members of the Eastern Partnership. Through its openness to trade in this region (the case of Moldova and Ukraine), it contributes to a change in the imported goods in this economic community and encourages the investment in alternative and green energy, energy efficiency and the reduction of pollution.

Officially, there is also a multilateral collaboration concerning the environment with the Commonwealth of Independent States. This collaboration is expressed by the *Agreement on collaboration in the field of ecology and protection of the natural environment* signed by 10 member states of the Commonwealth in February 1992 (*Tratate internaţionale* 1999). Even though the agreement text provides a set of international norms to help member states in this field of collaboration, the implementation of the agreement was more of a political declaration having no organizational bodies to at least monitor this well-written agreement. Because of the fact that its members are still undergoing a transitional period and are developing countries that face significant financial problems, this agreement remained only an encouragement for the parts towards the elaboration of their national strategies on economic ecology and sustainable development. In most of the member countries, this happened over the next years after the signing of the agreement.

14.3 National Political Inputs in Sustainable Development and Its Challenges

Romania and the Republic of Moldova are part of important international and regional agreements and conventions that help establish national strategies, norms, and policies in enhancing their environment. Both states have undergone transition and invested in democracy and economic development in parallel with the transition to a sustainable economy. In particular, the economic and financial challenges were the biggest in implementing the course for sustainable development.

Romania of the last decades had two strategy documents on environment—the first one was approved at the end of the 1990s and the second in 2008, the latter named the *National Strategy for Sustainable Development in Romania: Horizons 2013–2020–2030* (*Strategia Naţională pentru Dezvoltare Durabilă a României: Orizonturi 2013–2020–2030*, 2008).

The first strategy was difficult to implement taking into consideration the transition period in the 1990s and the context of European integration (Ursul et al. 2009: 182).

The second strategy was also elaborated to create the necessary mechanism in relation to the European Commission regarding the implementation of sustainable development. In other words, this document is approved more for conforming to the European mechanism and standards on environment. A positive aspect of the Romanian strategy on environment consists in the integration of all responsible state bodies and entities for the ecological economic setting up of the current situation, the main objectives and ways of action until 2030, as well as how to implement, monitor, and report the results from local to the national and European Community levels. This strategy contains a set of recommendations based on the EU practice and experience, and specific solutions for Romania with regard to public authorities and the identification of the main direction of action for sustainable development (Ursul et al. 2009: 182).

In the Republic of Moldova, the Supreme Economic Council under the President approved its environment strategy in 2000, with the assistance of UNDP in Moldova, following the international and regional process on this topic. The document is called *National Strategy for Sustainable Development—"Moldova 21."* This includes a long-term program for the socioeconomic development of the country, promoting the following principles and objectives:

- The creation of a free-market social economy
- The establishing of an open civil society, based on democracy and the decentralization of the public sector
- The promotion of the new security concept—economic, social, food, and ecological (Strategia Naţională pentru Dezvoltare Durabilă a Republicii Moldova—"Moldova 21" 2000)

Ursul, Rusandu, and Capcelea state that although the strategy recognizes the importance of the environment for the country's development, it is more focused on the revitalization of the economy and on social aspects, but little attention is given to the environment (Ursul et al. 2009: 182). This strategy was not approved by the Moldovan Government and the Parliament, and lost its legal force.

The Moldovan Environment Ministry played a key role in the promotion of ecological policies. Many sustainable development and ecological policies are stipulated in different sectorial laws that the Moldovan government approved over the last decade. A practical step in the enhancement of sustainable development was taken in 1998 with the creation, by the Moldovan Government, of the *National Ecological Fund*, which supports many projects implemented by local authorities, enterprises, and NGOs from Moldova. In the last 3 years, with the support of the National Ecological Fund, 615 projects were implemented in the Republic of Moldova, aimed to improve the environment and the quality of people's life (Fondul Ecologic Naţional 2014). In addition, in the Republic of Moldova, a system of services was created, aimed to study, control, plan, protect, and improve the environment in order to protect the national patrimony and the rational use of natural resources (Florea 2000: 150).

In the Russian Federation, the *Concept of transition of the Russian Federation to sustainable development* was approved by the President in 1992. This concept has a well-established transdisciplinary approach, stating in its conclusion that

> the advance of humankind towards sustainable development will ultimately lead to the formation of a rational sphere (noosphere), predicted by Vernadsky, when the criteria of national and individual wealth will produce human values and knowledge, which live together in harmony with the environment (КонцепцияпереходаРоссийсКойФедерации К устойчивомуразвитию 1992).

This powerful conclusion was difficult to reach until recently not only by the Russian Federation but by many former Soviet Union republics as well. There is a need for them to develop their *thesaurus* (БрансКий 2000: 115) and find the right connections and functional structures able to produce a healthy environment and economic stability in the region.

This study on the input on all levels of the Eastern European economy made in the last decades leads us to the conclusion that humanity started on an important progress towards sustainable development. However, all actors of the society, to create the necessary functional structures for the new progress of sustainable development, must increasingly integrate all legal norms, policies, and strategies. Our countries must understand that central and local authorities represent the first step moving on the sustainability track and obtaining new achievements for environment protection. The development of democratic institutions and policies on human investment must be one of the main issues on the agenda of the decision makers. The promotion of individual rights, including providing decent life conditions and equal choices for opportunities, is a very important positive feedback for society's contribution to a sustainable development. In addition, the right management of enterprises is an important catalyst in reaching this goal, by providing social responsibility, innovations, new technologies, and efficient risk management.

The transition to the free market economy also involves environment challenges as well as the promotion of sustainable development; the concept was developed in the last 30 years. In other words, the process of sustainable development in many countries of the world began to be implemented at the same time with the collapse of the Soviet Union and when the need of economic growth and transition to the free market economy for many countries was rising. This factor represents another challenge for Eastern Europe, one that needs special attention from the governments of this region on one hand, and international donors or investors on the other hand. However, at the same time, this challenge plays a key role for the socioeconomic effectiveness of these countries in order to stimulate the right industries and the right economic activities to be able to create the right balance between economy and the environment.

A big part of the industry in this region that disappeared after the break down of the Soviet Union can have long-term advantages if we help establish a new market-oriented industry properly set on the sustainable development track. This can be done by implementing the right reforms, supporting the right political mechanisms, and stimulating civil society and the economic agents to contribute to the creation of the functional structures and social connections in achieving this goal.

Our central and local authorities need to create not only legal frameworks to improve communication with civil society and the economic agents, but to enhance the right connections in order to boost this process. This desiderate could be achieved by stimulating e-Governances, consolidating financial autonomy for local authorities (especially in New Independent States from Eastern Europe), promoting more social responsibility for individuals and enterprises, increasing the quantity of project implementation by civil society in the field of the environment, etc. Sustainable development must become a twenty-first century value for individuals, nations, and the international community, contributing to the right mindset able to create the right functional structures to benefit from a fair environment and effective economic development.

References

Acord din 08.02.92 cu privire la colaborarea în domeniul ecologiei şi protecţiei mediului natural ambiant. In *Tratate internaţionale* 16/17, 1999, Acte CSI.

Agriculture officials condemn unnecessary loss and waste of good food. In FAO 2014 [online]. http://www.fao.org/news/story/en/item/219025/icode/. Accessed 28 April 2014.

Capcelea, Arcadie. 2001. *Legislaţia de mediu a UniuniiEuropene (Compedium)*, 102. Chişinău: Centrul Regional de Mediu Moldova.

Capcelea, Arcadie. 2003. *Mediul înconjurător pentru Europa (realizări, probleme, perspective)*, 100. Chişinău: "Mediul Ambiant".

Conclusions of the conference "Environment for Europe" June 1991. In *UNECE* [online]. http://www.unece.org/fileadmin/DAM/env/efe/history%20of%20EfE/Dobris.E.pdf. Accessed April 26 2014.

Convention on access to information, public participation in decision-making and access to justice in environmental matters 1998. In *UNECE* [online]. http://www.unece.org/fileadmin/DAM/env/pp/documents/cep43e.pdf. Accessed April 26 2014.

Declaration of the United Nations Conference on the Human Environment. 1972. In *United Nations Environment Programme* [online]. http://www.unep.org/Documents.Multilingual/Default.asp?documentid=97&articleid=1503. Accessed 25 April 2014.

Fifth Ministerial Conference "Environment For Europe". May 2003. In *UNECE* [online]. http://www.unece.org/env/efe/historyofefe/history.en2011_5.html. Accessed 26 April 2014.

First Ministerial Conference "Environment for Europe". June 1991. In *UNECE* [online]. http://www.unece.org/env/efe/historyofefe/history.en1991_01.html. Accessed 26 April 2014.

Florea, Serafim. 2000. *Factorul ecologic şi dezvoltarea socio-economică teritorială durabilă a Republicii Moldova*, 315. Chişinău: Şearec-com.

Fondul Ecologic Naţional. In *Ministry of the Environment 2014*. http://mediu.gov.md/index.php/en/component/content/article?id=72:fondul-ecologic-national&catid=79:institutii-subordonate. Accessed 26 April 2014.

Johannesburg Declaration on Sustainable Development. In *UN Documents September 2002*. http://www.un-documents.net/jburgdec.htm. Accessed 26 April 2014.

Lucerne Declaration on "Environment for Europe" April 1993. In *UNECE* [online]. http://www.unece.org/fileadmin/DAM/env/efe/history%20of%20EfE/Luzern.E.pdf. Accessed April 26 2014.

Ministerial Conference "Environment for Europe". October 1995. In *UNECE* [online]. http://www.unece.org/fileadmin/DAM/env/documents/1995/sof/conf/bd/sof.conf.bd.1.e.pdf.

Process of Preparation of the Environmental Perspective to the Year 2000 and beyond. In *United Nations General Assembly 19 December, 1983*. http://www.un.org/documents/ga/res/38/a38r161.htm. Accessed 25 April 2014.

Rio Declaration on Environment and Development. June 1992. In *United Nations Environment Program* [online]. http://www.unep.org/Documents.Multilingual/Default.asp?documentid=78&articleid=1163. Accessed 25 April 2014.

Robert, et al. What is sustainable development? goals, indicators, values, and practice. In *Environment April 2005*. http://www.environmentmagazine.org/Editorials/Kates-apr05-full.html. Accessed viewed 25 April 2014.

Rusu, Valeriu. 2002. *Dezvoltarea durabilă—speranţacomunităţilor şi generaţiilor*, 80. Chişinău: Editura PP "Mediul Ambiant".

Strategia Naţională pentru Dezvoltare Durabilă a Republicii Moldova—"Moldova 21." Consiliul Economic Suprem pe lângă Preşedinţia RM. Chişinău, 2000. http://www.undp.md/publications/doc/RAPORT_21.pdf. Accessed 26 April 2014.

The Maastricht Treaty. In *European Treaties 1992* [online]. http://www.eurotreaties.com/maastrichtec.pdf. Accessed 29 April 2014.

United Nations Millennium Declaration. In *United Nations General Assembly, Resolution 55/2, United Nations A/RES/55/2*, 18 September 2000, page x.

Ursul, Arcadie, Ion Rusandu, and Arcadie Capcelea. 2009. *Dezvoltare durabilă: abordări metodologice şi de operaţionalizare*, 251. Chişinău: Ştiinţa.

БрансКий В. 2000. *ТеоретичесКое основание социальной синергетиКе*. In *Вопросы ФилософФии*, vol. 4, 112–129. МосКва: НауКа.

Концепция перехода РоссийсКой Федерации К устойчивому развитию. 1992. In Россия—ЕС. http://russia-eu.ru/node/14. Accessed 26 April 2014.

Chapter 15
Integrity Pacts: A Business Case for Collective Actions

Iuliana Coşpănaru and Victor Alistar

Abstract The purposes of this business case is to show how collective actions can be applied in a country where corruption is present in everyone's minds and where even the cleanest and most transparent entities have to go to great lengths in order to avoid being viewed with suspicion. It is a functional model, proving that collective actions are an effective tool for building integrity and establishing trust and a good reputation. As proven by studies in the field, the Romanian business environment is affected by corruption, despite a dedicated legislative and institutional anticorruption framework. Transparency International Romania proposes that the best way to fight this corruption and build integrity in this environment is through collective integrity commitments. Transparency International Romania has already facilitated the signing of five such Integrity Pacts: two in the business sector, one in the academic sector, one in the healthcare sector, and one in the civil society sector. In order for companies not to engage in corrupt acts, it is necessary to provide incentives and point out the benefits of acting with integrity that outweigh what can be gained through corruption. Companies who wish to build integrity must focus on a series of principles: impact, communication, monitoring, multiplication of sanctions and stimulants, accountability, and assessment. In addition, anticorruption policies in Romania should be focused mainly toward companies that have a great interest in integrity and which can also contribute to raising the capacity of those who lack such a capacity, but have the adequate motivation. Therefore, Transparency International Romania has developed a list of lessons learned and recommendations adapted to the Romanian environment, applicable to and by the Romanian businesses and their relevant stakeholders.

Keywords Business integrity • Transparency • Collective action • Integrity pacts • Stakeholders

I. Coşpănaru (✉) • V. Alistar
Transparency International Romania, Bucureşti, Romania
e-mail: iuliana.cospanaru@transparency.org.ro; victor.alistar@transparency.org.ro

S. Vaduva et al. (eds.), *Business Ethics and Leadership from an Eastern European, Transdisciplinary Context*, DOI 10.1007/978-3-319-45186-2_15

15.1 Building Integrity: A Business Case for Romania

The most recent Corruption Perception Index, launched by Transparency International in December 2014, indicates that three-quarters (75 %) of the 175 countries included here score lower than 50 points in business people's perception.

Romania falls in this last category with 43 points out of 100—which indicates a very clean environment.

On the other hand, the business environment itself is perceived as corrupt by the population at large, according to the Global Corruption Barometer, the 2013 one placing the business environment on the fifth place, after political parties, legislature, the judiciary, and the medical services, with 3.5 points out of 5, where 5 means the most corrupt.

Statistics also indicate that the level of corruption is directly linked with living standard, as the recent economic crisis has fully demonstrated that corruption leads to poverty. Over the last decades, Romania has passed from a problem-analysis era, between 1999 and 2003, to an era of developing the public sector, which led to a new and dedicated legislative and institutional anticorruption framework and to an implementation and impact assessment era—the current one. Yet the impact assessment shows that despite the extremely elaborated framework, little has been achieved in terms of discouraging corruption.

The paradigm Transparency International Romania uses is focused on the vulnerabilities that lead to corruption, which can be determined applying a simple risks and benefits equation. Whenever behaving without integrity will bring many more benefits than the risks are, corruption will flourish. It is similar to a rocking chair with benefits and risks at each of its extremities.

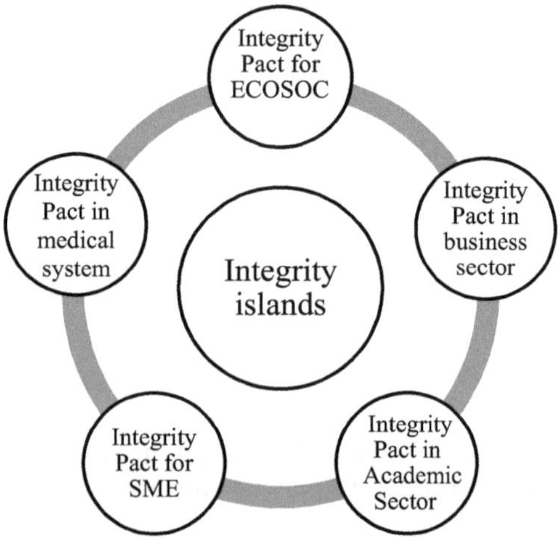

Fig. 15.1 The integrity pacts. *Source*: International conference (Alistar et al. 2013a, b)

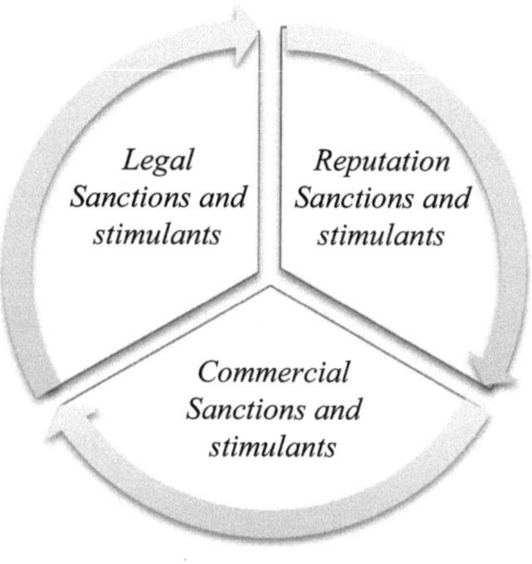

Fig. 15.2 Anticorruption sanctions and stimulants. *Source*: Adapted from Wegner et al. (2013)

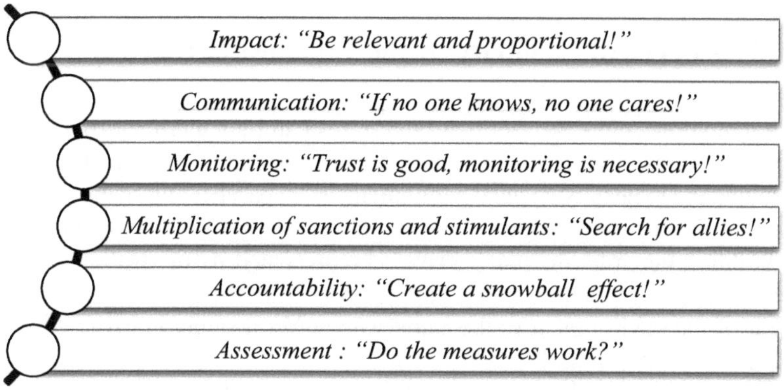

Fig. 15.3 Principles of changing a company's attitude. *Source*: Adapted from Wegner et al. (2013)

What generated the mentioned results? We believe it was the single focus of the Romanian authorities on raising the risks without diminishing the correlative benefits. In Romania, the criminal penalties system seems to perform well, while the recovery of the proceeds of corruption remains limited.

But in order to make it effective, the fight against corruption has to rely not only on the legal sanctions, but also on the social rejection of corrupt behavior. The other side of the coin shows that it is more likely to achieve the expected impact if focusing on building integrity as a win-win approach. In this case, the reputational risk of noncompliance is the best incentive. And because reputation is one of the most important elements of a trademark, where better to start from if not from the business environment itself, whose core mission is to generate profit?

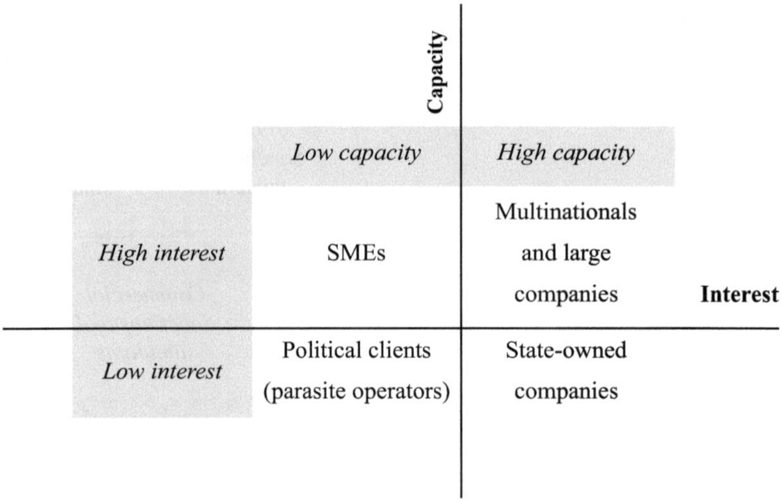

Fig. 15.4 Romanian businesses analysis

15.2 The Faces of Integrity in the Business Sector

Because it acknowledges the fact that businesses can play a crucial role in shaping the way society responds to corruption and can contribute to sustainable economic development and to healthy social development, Transparency International Romania proposed an innovative and integrated model for market integrity. When working toward building integrity, the major driver is represented by motivation. Motivation requires both the alignment of individual behavior with the integrity values, and the alignment of the environment to the same values. Yet a single integrity actor into a vitiated environment will only lead to exclusion.

If it is a corrupt and bureaucratic environment, the business will have to pay additional amounts to enter the market and to survive on it. Your employees will be required to enter into corrupt agreements in order to initiate new business agreements, which opens the door to a multitude of risks, from extortion to criminal sanctions, and the closing of the business.

On the other hand, if there is a clean environment, then integrity requirements will also become applicable to your business, as society and business partners will sanction any breaches and will reject you from the market, by rejecting your goods or services, if not aligned to the policies. The integrity of a business has therefore two sides: the internal integrity—the integrity of your organization: employees, management, finances, operations, and the external integrity—the one of your partners and stakeholders (Wegner et al. 2013). It is therefore crucial to generate change into your close environment and support the multiplication of this change to the close environment of your peers, thus building *Integrity Islands*. And once a critical mass is reached, these islands will incorporate and corruption will become the new islands.

Building integrity in the private sector can benefit from the fact that trust and confidence from the major stakeholders are the endowment for a successful, sustainable, and long-term business. Building such trust and confidence can only be accomplished with the right integrity policies and commitment in place. For example, your customers would no longer only look for the lowest price, but also for the best quality, which also refers to the quality of the company they are doing business with. The public will increasingly encourage companies that disclose their anticorruption and compliance commitments by becoming the customers of companies with the highest integrity commitment. The private sector's commitment to promoting clean businesses is profiled now as a smart and effective solution for either protecting or extending their companies on various markets. Therefore, investment in reputation given by transparent and accountable goods and in services provided to society makes profit sustainable and reinforces the trust of customers and partners.

15.3 Building Collective Actions: Integrity Pacts

The individual efforts of both companies looking for the promotion of a cleaner business environment and of the think tanks proved not to reach the expected impact on public policies, as their actions lacked coordination. This lack of impact makes a strong argument for the pattern that Transparency International Romania suggests to be followed in order to achieve significant improvements—multi-stakeholder collective actions. Moreover, one key instrument for a successful and sustainable position on the market is, no doubt, restoring trust—between people, in institutions, through rules—based on shared values.

Building integrity is therefore not only a challenge for the business itself, but also for its stakeholders. To keep the business accountable for its integrity and transparency, its stakeholders should also be accountable to people for their own integrity and transparency.

With the faith that you can only demand what you can do or are yourself, Transparency International Romania has worked over the last years to catalyze the will of companies, academia, NGOs and social partners, as well as of representatives of the healthcare operators and stakeholders to work together towards a shared vision of integrity.

Five Integrity Pacts have been born from:

- The desire to achieve *a first step towards normality*
- The need to *stop wastefully spending* funds from the system
- The need for *higher ethical standards*
- The need to *unify ethical codes* per sphere of activity
- The need to identify *allies* in supporting the cause of integrity
- The desire to strengthen *an integrity network* that will multiply exponentially

Therefore, in November 2013, a group of companies concerned about the impact that corruption, in all its forms, has on societies, and aware of their duty toward the community generating income for them, decided to build together a platform of action for integrity and for social and economic accountability.

The member companies of the Pact for Integrity and Transparency in Business are taking the mission of contributing to the creation of a culture of transparency and integrity by reordering and consolidating the Romanian society's system of values and principles based on the following foundations: responsibility to society, employees and shareholders, transparency, inclusive development, sustainable development, honesty towards consumers, collective action, proactive attitude, compliance, and complementary credibility. Around the Pact for Integrity and Transparency in Business, four other Integrity Pacts have been signed by representatives of the businesses' stakeholders: NGOs and trade unions, academia, SMEs, and the healthcare system.

The driver is the Pact for Integrity and Transparency in Business, which convenes large multinationals, which have already reached a level of discretion, have a definite market position and have already implemented internal compliance and integrity policies, and are eager to demand the same from their employees, suppliers, distributors, and other business partners. The second pact is dedicated to SMEs, which have a different business profile, with different challenges, needs, and development speeds.

The third Pact engages academia into a social effort to develop and promote innovative and practical ideas and values that can be easily implemented in practice. It also builds on the need to improve the integrity of a fundamental service—education, as so does the fourth pact focused on building integrity in the medical services.

Last but not least, the fifth Pact mobilizes civil society into a self—and external—accountability system, whose role will be to keep the other Pacts accountable, and to empower citizens to do so. The over 60 signatories of the five Integrity Pacts show a critical mass has been achieved and that it is the time for them to join forces to demand integrity and:

- Promote ethical behavior and discourage practices that lack integrity among the signatory institutions of the five pacts.
- Create a climate of good cooperation and mutual trust between the signatory institutions of the five pacts.
- Generate a core of integrity that radiates among other structures that have ties to the signatories of the five pacts.

15.4 Motivating Anticorruption Behavior

15.4.1 Sanctions vs. Stimulants (Adapted from Wegner et al. 2013)

As already stated, motivation is the cornerstone of the anticorruption efforts, and it is proportional to what you gain by complying and what you lose by not complying.

A collective action to build integrity has two major dimensions: promoting the incentives to its members and holding them accountable when they fail to comply.

Mitigating different risks is also part of the motivation to rally towards an integrity-building effort. Such risks include:

- The legal risks, such as the liability of the board members, the criminal liability of the company itself, or even risks of civil compensations for fraud
- The reputation risk, which always depends on the integrity of the dissemination environment—if the dissemination environment is a fair one, than the reputational risk is huge; if the dissemination environment can be used for manipulation, then the reputational risks become only an unfair competition instrument
- The commercial risk: losing market, losing investors, affecting commercial indicators or the management plan

The reverse of these risks are the benefits one can get by having adequate compliance and integrity mechanisms in place. The role of the collective action should be much more focused on encouraging companies to achieve the benefits, rather than just avoiding the risks. Such benefits include:

- Having an integrity and compliance system in place ensures there are lower legal risks, with a direct consequence on the level of insurance premium, which should be much lower.
- Having an integrity and compliance system in place ensures a respectable reputation and a good visibility for the company, which reduces the needs for investing in PR activities.
- Having an integrity and compliance system in place ensures commercial credibility—becoming a predictable partner enables the business to enlarge its market shares and open new business opportunities, while the costs for such operations remains limited.

15.4.2 Instruments to Motivate Anticorruption Behavior (Adapted from Wegner et al. 2013)

A recently launched research carried out at the Humboldt-Viadrina University revealed a series of principles that business leaders should focus on, if they aim to generate an attitudinal change in their companies and to turn to integrity.

Impact: be relevant and proportional—to safeguard a company's integrity it is essential to identify your market and keep within its limits. Extending operations artificially will only increase the vulnerabilities and the risks of corruption, and jeopardize your reputation. On the other hand, it is important that sanctions and stimulants are proportional to the gravity of the breaches and the lack of managerial decisions to limit their effects, as they need to be relevant to the perpetrator. A reputational penalty applied to a company that holds the monopoly on a market will not bring significant attitudinal changes, while a commercial one might seriously impact its operations.

Communication: if no one knows, no one cares—compliant behavior or breaches shall be communicated to the large audience, but mainly to the business clients and partners. If a company holds advanced compliance and integrity programs, but does not speak about them, stimulants in its commercial transactions can't be applied. At the same time, if a partner applies sanctions to a company, it should also allow others to know the breaches or vulnerabilities it faced. Recovering trust is also about communication on the measures taken to repair the breaches.

Monitoring: trust is good, monitoring is necessary—compliance and integrity are not relevant if the company only monitors its internal mechanisms. These mechanisms should exist throughout the supply chain of that company. Noncompliance at the level of one of your suppliers can affect the quality and the whole process in your company, and can further be reflected in the quality of the goods and services you deliver to your customers. But they will not care about who generate the poor quality, they will directly sanction your company. Therefore, it is highly important to request the same standards as for yourself from your suppliers and distributors, as it is important to also monitor their compliance with these standards.

Collective actions: search for allies to multiply sanctions and stimulants—a stakeholder can both apply stimulants and sanctions, as well as galvanize others to do the same, or to apply complementary stimulants or sanctions. This approach safeguards stakeholders from isolation and generates a greater impact of its actions. It also improves the effectiveness of the stakeholder's actions, as it limits the costs and divides the efforts between the others.

Accountability: create a snowball effect—a core group of companies who adhere to the integrity and compliance standards, and who are kept accountable by their stakeholders with regard to their compliance, will require the same standards from their suppliers and distributors in order to avoid a negative impact on their operations. Moreover, they can encourage their business partners to adhere to such standards using commercial stimulants. This approach is also the cornerstone of the Integrity Pacts catalyzed by Transparency International Romania. The Pacts state both the individual and collective commitment of their members to generate a social and economic model based on moral and ethical values as a solution for the sustainable development of Romanian society and the elimination of inequalities, corruption, power abuse, and fraud.

Assessment: do the measures work?—once the collective action is set up, it is important to evaluate whether the actions taken to stimulate or sanction a company's behavior have generated the expected impact with regard to its behavioral changes. Assessment may reveal that the actions taken haven't been adequate to the exact context, in which case they need to be reshaped and adapted, like in any decision cycle. The assessment will also indicate the best practices and the lessons learned that can be multiplied or used to prevent similar future situations.

15.5 Anticorruption Policies in the Romanian Business Climate

To calibrate the anticorruption interventions in the Romanian business environment, Transparency International Romania has assessed the business environment using two arguments: the interest or motivation, and the institutional capacity. The diagram below reveals the four categories of companies operating in the Romanian business environment, followed by an interventions' needs assessment.

Interest	Capacity	
	Low capacity	High capacity
High interest	SMEs	Multinationals and large companies
Low interest	Political clients (parasite operators)	State-owned companies

Multinationals and large companies usually already have compliance systems in place, and are directly interested in building a culture of integrity in order to avoid the extortion phenomenon, mostly generated by the abusive conduct of administrative inspectors. They also hold the adequate capacity to build such programs, as well as generate the collective action and the snowball effect.

The *state-owned companies* usually enjoy good capacity, but have limited interest in promoting corporate integrity, as their activity is regulated by the state, they are hierarchically controlled and operate mostly on the monopoly they hold. Therefore market rules do not necessarily influence their activity, as they are not profit-driven, although adhering to integrity practices might lead to greater performance and to the best use of public money.

The *SMEs*, while not having a large capacity due to their size and operations, are greatly interested in adhering to the standards promoted by the large multinationals with the aim of benefiting from the commercial advantages they might get, once joining this collective action.

Last but not least, *political clients* are usually small businesses, with very limited capacity, but with dedicated operations serving various political interests, without any concerns for the competition or for quality challenges. Therefore they have no interest in supporting the enforcing of integrity standards in their businesses, because their driver is not the profit, nor the market.

Such an analysis indicates that the focus of taking part in integrity programs should be on those businesses who have the greatest interest and who can also contribute to raising the capacity of those who lack such a capacity but have the adequate motivation. Therefore, the needs for mutual support can be clustered in:

- *Multinationals and large companies*
  - To reduce competitive disadvantages produced by high and rigid standards vs. flexible and less compliant actors
  - To define market rules based on their investments in business culture
  - To secure the end product or service based on a safe supplier-chain structure
- *SMEs*
  - To reduce disparities between their level of business cultural development and business climate trends
  - To secure their position as suppliers and enlarge the market share indicators
  - To secure the budgetary costs of developing their compliance instruments
  - To create competitive advantages on the market, fighting with (local and regional) political clients

15.6 Transparency International Romania's Recommendations (Adapted from Kowalczyk-Hoyer et al. 2013, 2014)

Building integrity is not an easy challenge, and is even less easy when the driver is the money that can be easily earned and easily lost if corruption occurs, and the same money that can be hard but sustainably earned, if part of it is correctly invested into developing compliance programs.

Transparency International is working throughout the world to promote business integrity and to evaluate the current level of compliance within companies. In early November 2014, Transparency International has launched the latest report on *Transparency in Corporate Reporting*, which analyzed 124 companies from the Forbes list of the world's biggest publicly traded companies. The companies, whose combined market value is more than US$14 trillion, are ranked based on their reporting of the measures they take to prevent corruption, the information about their subsidiaries and holdings, and the key financial information about their overseas operations. A similar report was launched in 2013, with a focus on the emerging-market multinationals.

Each of these reports provides a series of recommendations to improve the business integrity, building on the experience and results of the assessed companies. Considering that the current market is a globalized one, in which multinationals operate in several countries, including Romania, and on several continents and that the rules and policies at the headquarters of the companies are also applicable to its subsidiaries, Transparency International Romania has learned that, to be effective, such rules need to be adapted to the social, economic, and cultural national contexts.

Therefore it has developed a list of such lessons learned and of recommendations, building on the two reports and adapting them to the Romanian environment to make them applicable to and by the Romanian businesses and their relevant stakeholders.

To companies

- Prohibit facilitation payments.
- Publicly disclose all political donations.
- Publicly disclose exhaustive lists of subsidiaries, affiliates, joint ventures, and other entities.
- Publish financial accounts for each county of operation.
- Strive to lead the way with the most advanced anticorruption and transparency practices and challenge companies operating on the same market regarding their products and services, as well as in all aspects of their business, including their anticorruption behavior.
- Recognize their transparency obligations to stakeholders.
- Raise the level of their anticorruption practice.
- Make their anticorruption programs publicly available.
- Disclose organizational structure in a reasonably accessible manner.
- Unlisted companies and state-owned enterprises should improve their disclosure practices.

To governments and regulatory bodies

- Adequately implement the anti-bribery laws.
- Require companies under Romanian jurisdiction to publish lists of all their subsidiaries, affiliates, joint ventures, and other related entities.
- Require all companies to publish financial accounts on a county-by-county (and, where applicable, on a project-by-project) basis.
- Consider adopting rules for mandatory company reporting on anticorruption measures.
- Accounting standards relating to financial accounting as well as to corporate social responsibility reporting should include corruption-relevant disclosures.

To investors

- Demand that companies report more comprehensively and county-by-county on anticorruption programs, organizational transparency and use this information in investment decisions.
- Demand more comprehensive auditing standards to improve the assessment of company risk exposure.
- Risk-rating agencies as well as corporate responsibility indexes should include transparency measures as an integral part of their evaluation process.

To civil-society organizations

- Demand that companies be more transparent
- Monitor, analyze, and disseminate public corporate information
- Promote the adoption of county-by-county reporting
- Advocate on businesses located or operating in Romania to improve the depth and scope of their commitments to transparency, and in particular to improve their level of anticorruption reporting.

References

Alistar, V. et al. 2013a. Anii de Conformitate—Direcţii de Lucru. *Transparency International Romania*. http://www.businessintegrity.ro/sites/default/files/fileuploads/CibStudiul5.pdf.

Alistar, V., I. Coşpănaru, and C. Slovineanu. 2013b. International conference: Integrity in business—key for sustainable and long-term prosperity, 27–29 November, Bucharest. Transparency International Romania.

Kowalczyk-Hoyer et al. 2013. Transparency in corporate reporting: assessing emerging market multinationals. *Transparency International*. http://www.transparency.org/whatwedo/publication/transparency_in_corporate_reporting_assessing_emerging_market_multinational.

Kowalczyk-Hoyer et al. 2014. Transparency in corporate reporting: assessing the world's largest companies. *Transparency International*. http://www.transparency.org/whatwedo/publication/transparency_in_corporate_reporting_assessing_worlds_largest_companies_2014.

Wegner, S., J. Schöberlein, and S. Biermann. 2013. Motivating business to counter corruption—a practitioner handbook on anti-corruption sanctions and incentives for business. Humboldt-Viadrina School of Governance. http://www.pogar.org/publications/ac/2013/humbolt_practitionerhandbook_incentivessanctions.pdf.

